War Aims
in the
Second World War

War Aims
in the
Second World War

The War Aims of the Major Belligerents, 1939–45

Victor Rothwell

Edinburgh University Press

© Victor Rothwell, 2005

Transferred to digital print 2009

Edinburgh University Press Ltd
22 George Square, Edinburgh

Typeset in Melior by
Hewer Text Ltd, Edinburgh, and
printed and bound in Great Britain by
CPI Antony Rowe, Chippenham and Eastbourne

A CIP record for this book is available from the British Library

ISBN 0 7486 1502 4 (hardback)
ISBN 0 7486 1503 2 (paperback)

The right of Victor Rothwell
to be identified as author of this work
has been asserted in accordance with
the Copyright, Designs and Patents Act 1988.

Contents

German War Aims

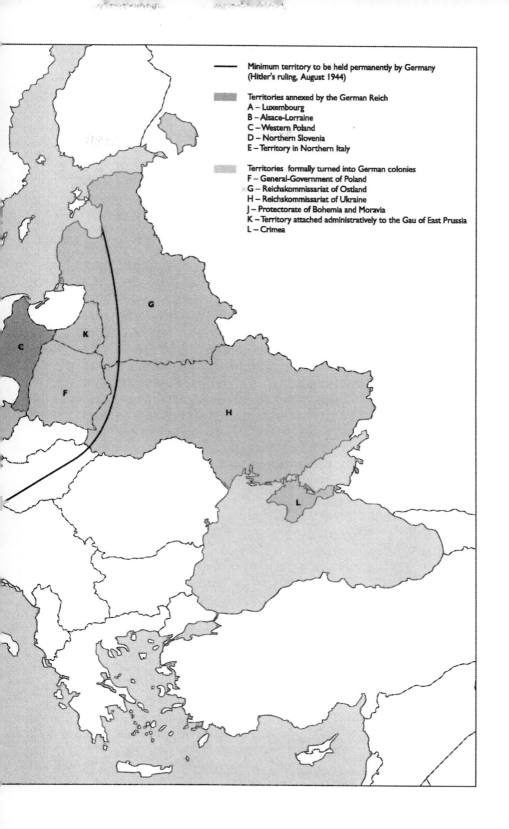

Minimum territory to be held permanently by Germany
(Hitler's ruling, August 1944)

Territories annexed by the German Reich
A – Luxembourg
B – Alsace-Lorraine
C – Western Poland
D – Northern Slovenia
E – Territory in Northern Italy

Territories formally turned into German colonies
F – General-Government of Poland
G – Reichskommissariat of Ostland
H – Reichskommissariat of Ukraine
J – Protectorate of Bohemia and Moravia
K – Territory attached administratively to the Gau of East Prussia
L – Crimea

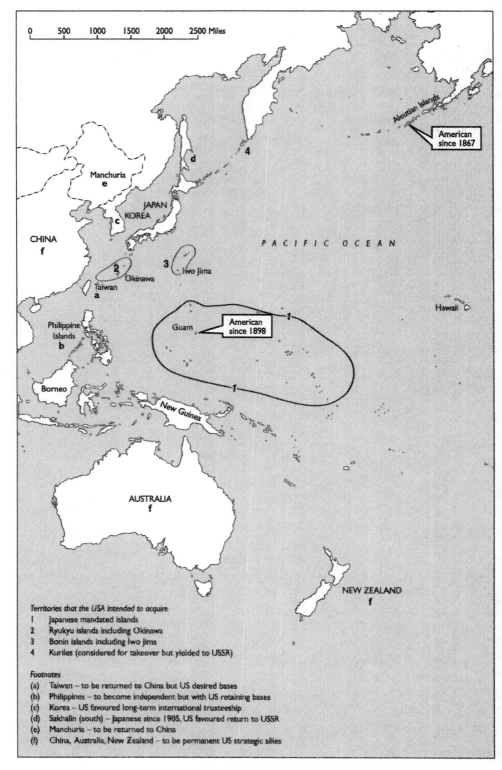

American War Aims

Soviet War Aims

Territory annexed by Soviet Union 1939–40, and re-incorporated in Soviet Union in 1945

Former German and Czechoslovak territory annexed by Soviet Union in 1945

Soviet occupation zones in Austria (evacuated 1955) and Germany

British, French and American occupation zones

German territory gained by Poland in 1945

Area of unfulfilled Soviet ambition in 1940, briefly revived in 1945

Romanian territory awarded by Hitler to Hungary in 1940 and returned to Romania by Stalin in 1945

FINLAND

Leningrad

SWEDEN

Baltic Sea

LATVIA

LITHUANIA

North Sea

Königsberg

EAST PRUSSIA

SOVIET UNION

Bremen

Stettin

Berlin

Warsaw

GERMANY

POLAND

Breslau

SILESIA

GALICIA

Lvov

Prague

CZECHOSLOVAKIA

BESSARABIA

FRANCE

Munich

Vienna

Budapest

AUSTRIA

HUNGARY

SWITZERLAND

ROMANIA

Belgrade

Bucharest

ITALY

YUGOSLAVIA

Adriatic Sea

BULGARIA

Black Sea

ALBANIA

Istanbul

GREECE

Aegean Sea

TURKEY

0   100   200 Miles

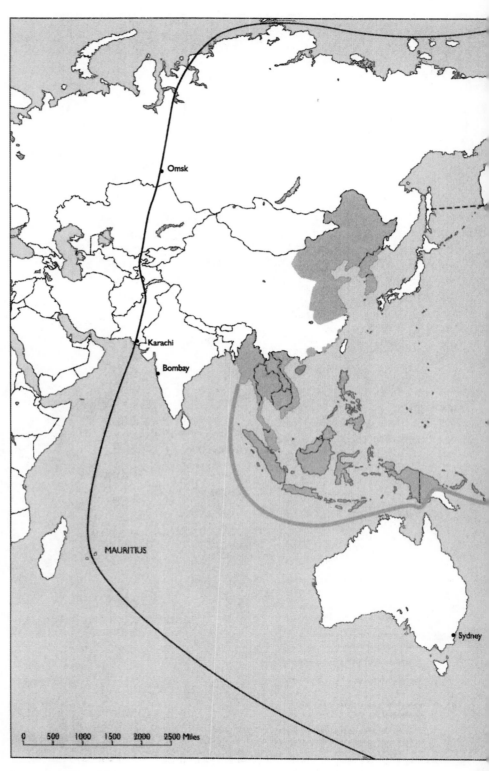

Omsk

Karachi

Bombay

MAURITIUS

Sydney

0   500   1000   1500   2000   2500 Miles

Japanese War Aims

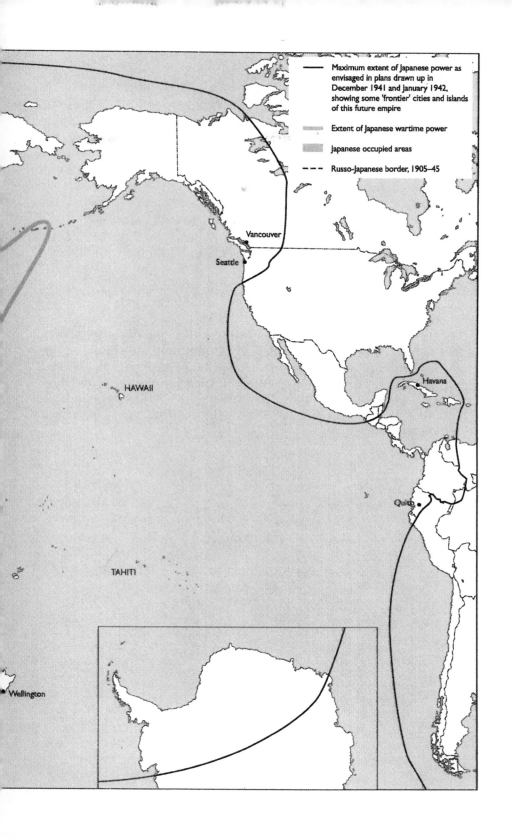

Maximum extent of Japanese power as
envisaged in plans drawn up in
December 1941 and January 1942,
showing some 'frontier' cities and islands
of this future empire

Extent of Japanese wartime power

Japanese occupied areas

Russo-Japanese border, 1905–45

Vancouver

Seattle

HAWAII

Havana

Quito

TAHITI

Wellington

Acknowledgements

This book was born and took shape under the auspices of the Centre for Second World War Studies at Edinburgh University. I am particularly grateful to Jeremy Crang for suggesting the project and for help and encouragement during its journey to completion. I also thank the University for two terms of sabbatical leave in 2002, without which the process of research and writing would have been exceedingly slow.

1

War Aims in Modern History

War aims bearing some resemblance to those that were to feature in the Second World War may be dated back to the sixteenth century when the notion of furthering the interests of the state as an impersonal entity gained in strength, coupled with a conviction that the interests of one's own state were the only ones that needed to be taken into account.[1] This replaced a situation in which royal houses had pursued dynastic ambitions whose realisation, even if it could be achieved, promised few or no benefits to the countries over which aggressive monarchs ruled. The attempts by French kings to conquer Italy between 1494 and the 1550s were a late and unusually prolonged and costly example of this type of warfare. If these wars commanded some popularity in France that was only because of a delusion that they could be of benefit. (A century later Louis XIV worked to give France its 'natural frontiers' on the Rhine, the Alps and the Pyrenees, which was a rational programme in terms of national interest.)

If religious strife may be regarded as the ancestor of the ideological conflicts that were to influence Second World War war aims heavily, then the sixteenth century is again a watershed with the split between Roman Catholicism and Protestantism and the rising power of the Ottoman Empire as an Islamic superstate under the brilliant, if ruthless, leadership of Sultan Suleiman the Magnificent (1520–66). If ideological conflict was important, the willingness to set it aside as in the Grand Alliance of liberal Britain and America with Soviet Russia was also portended four centuries earlier in favour of political or territorial gain. This was evident in the willingness of France to stand by and let the Christian inhabitants of towns and cities be taken into slavery by Muslim raiders as long as they left with their captives and allowed the French to take over the depopulated strongholds. By contrast, the Austrian Emperor Rudolf (1576–1611), unable to save territory for Catholicism from two religious foes, decided to concentrate on the ideologically more threatening, Protestantism in Germany, with the result that the Ottomans were able to retain most of Hungary, which they had conquered earlier in the century.[2]

The evolution of war aims may usefully be elucidated by a degree of concentration on England and its successor, the Kingdom of Great Britain (from 1801 the United Kingdom of Great Britain and Ireland). Dynastic war aims flourished there under Henry VIII (1509–47), who had senseless ambitions to annex territory in France. The last English possession in France, Calais, was lost during the brief reign of his daughter Mary. Her successor, Elizabeth I, was initially obsessed with the ambition to recover that port but, within a few years, gave up that futile ambition, and embarked on a foreign policy which, in the words of historian Susan Doran, had a 'quality of greatness'.[3] She was ready, against her inclinations of monarchical solidarity, to fight wars in support of Protestant rebels in Scotland to prevent it from becoming a French client state on England's northern border, and of Protestant rebels in the Netherlands because England's economic and strategic interest lay in an independent Holland after Spanish rule over Dutch Protestants had become unendurable to them; the only alternative to republican independence would have been French protection and that would have been a disaster for England.

England/Britain was never to revert to war aims that were not substantially based on what was spoken of with reverence as 'the national interest'. The problem lay in defining that interest. The early Stuart monarchs, James I and Charles I, identified it with keeping their realms at peace while warfare engulfed the continent. Their Protestant critics argued for a war in which there would be a happy marriage between spiritual and material aims. Their insistent demand was for a war against Spain in which, by seizing the Spanish treasure ships as they carried silver and other wealth across the Atlantic from Spanish America, England would both enrich itself and save continental Protestantism by impoverishing its enemies' Spanish paymaster. Otherwise, if the Catholics were allowed to destroy Protestantism on the continent, they would then turn their attention to exterminating it in its last bastion of Great Britain.[4] Triumphant by 1649, the Protestant strongman, Oliver Cromwell, adhered to an unrealistic dream of conquering the Spanish colonies in the New

World, converting the native Indians to Protestantism and making England rich.[5]

Under the restored monarchy of Charles II (1660–85) there was a flickering of the old dynastic war aims when the king was ready to aid a much stronger power, France, to cripple or destroy a small country – the United Provinces or the Netherlands entering the picture again – with consequences for Britain that would have been as disastrous as they would have been a century earlier. The national interest as a basis for war aims was to be unchallenged after the revolution of 1688–9, which drove out the Catholic king, James II and VII. Over a subsequent period of 125 years Britain was to be involved in a series of wars in which internal and external war aims co-existed, but with the latter becoming more important until the last and greatest of the wars of that period, the one with revolutionary and Napoleonic France from 1793 to 1815 when domestic-related war aims returned to a foremost place. This was something of a full circle. After 1689 Britain's new Dutch king, William III, fought a war to prevent French hegemony in Europe. Few in England or Scotland cared about that. Protestantism had struck deep roots and the English fought to ensure that the threat which it had faced under James did not recur. Some were also interested in commercial and colonial gains.[6] Securing the Protestant succession remained a central aim of British foreign policy between 1689 and 1720 and of major importance till the 1750s when Jacobitism, the cause of the exiled Catholic Stuarts, was at last perceived as no longer a serious threat.[7] War aims in such conflicts as the Seven Years War (1756–63) became ones of preventing French dominance on the continent of Europe, with the economic and strategic dangers to Britain that that would have posed, and securing overseas commercial or colonial gains, with, despite some grumbling, priority for the former as in the peace settlement of 1763 in which Britain returned some conquered colonies to France and Spain, in part to bring about French surrender of some conquests in Europe.

This was a relatively sophisticated model for war aims for which there was little equivalent on the continent of Europe at that time. The German historian of the European power balance, Ludwig Dehio, saw Britain's role as the guarantor of that balance from the eighteenth to the twentieth centuries as almost a law of nature, so that continental aspirants to European domination, like at times Germany, were doomed to inevitable failure when 'faced with the moral and material resources of the islanders, which she [Germany] could not understand'.[8] More typical was a crude obsession with territorial expansion. This was expressed by King Frederick of Prussia in 1743: 'of all the states from the smallest to the biggest one can safely say that the fundamental rule . . . is the principle of extending their territories'.[9] This was indeed the pattern, even though it can be traced to different roots in different countries. In West Germany in the 1950s, Dehio proposed a thesis, at first resisted but later found persuasive, that the Prussian state had only arisen from minuscule insignificance by adopting war and expansionism as ends in themselves, initiating a process to which it was never possible to call a halt.[10]

In the case of Russia, John P. LeDonne, a historian of geopolitics, has identified an irresistable urge, dictated by geography, to expand. This was an urge that mattered in the European context after Peter the Great had established Russia as a European power in the early eighteenth century. Whether the remark by Catherine II (1762–96) that within two hundred years Russia would rule the whole of Europe is apocryphal or not, it represents the authentic spirit of Russian policy in this view.[11] Other historians detect in the course of Russian history immense but more finite ambitions than that: a readiness to fight wars for economic gains such as guaranteed access to the Baltic, the Black Sea, the Turkish Straits and the Yellow Sea between Korea and China; and religious–ideological aims, notably the unification under Russian rule of all eastern Slavs of Orthodox faith, admittedly without much regard to whether non-Great Russians wanted such unity.[12] This 'moderate' interpretation of Russian grand policy cannot easily be reconciled with its participation in the partitions of Poland between 1772 and 1795, in which Catherine showed herself as eager to rule over Catholic Poles as over Orthodox peoples. She and her fellow rulers in Austria and Prussia plumbed the depths of cynicism in arguing that, by partitioning Poland, they were performing a service for the cause of peace in Europe because the only alternative was a general European war over Poland like the one that had occurred in the 1730s.[13] Though a severe critic of militarism in his native Germany, from which he had to flee, Alfred Vagts singled out Russia as the classic example of a country in which territorial expansion became an end in itself.[14]

Attempting a synthesis, the most recent historian of Russian and other imperialisms, Dominic Lieven, has identified two stages in the imperialist experience of tsarist Russia, of which the second is highly relevant to understanding Soviet policy during the Second World War. In the first stage, the Russian state developed as a partnership between monarch and a warrior–landowning nobility which had territorial expansion to provide both with peasant serfs to exploit as its central driving force. In the second stage, after the support of the nobility ceased to be so important around the middle of the nineteenth century, the tsarist autocracy remained wedded to expansion as essential to its status and prestige, and could see no other way of maintaining them; economic, social and educational advance to reach the levels of Germany and western Europe would have been much more difficult, even if it was judged desirable. There was also a genuine defensive motive to imperial expansion.[15] Another feature of Russian expansionism was in one sense relevant and in another irrelevant to the Second World War experience. This was an unwillingness to give up anything once it had been acquired, which was relevant, and a willingness under tsarism to give the seal of approval to gains made by relatively junior servants of the state acting on their own initiative. Thus in 1851 Tsar Nicholas I refused to discipline a junior officer who had planted the Russian flag at the mouth of the Amur river, staking out a new border with China, on the grounds that, 'Where the Russian flag has been run up, it must not be hauled down.'[16] Any such initiative would not have been tolerated by Stalin.

The greatest power in Europe remained France, which, in the unfolding of its revolution from 1789, brought two new elements into the European war aims panorama. The first was the spreading of a revolutionary ideology which did not shrink from imposing its benefits by force on unwilling recipients. The second related to one man, Napoleon, who transformed the territorial expansionist aims of France from ones that were confined to lands that bordered on France to ones that were European in scope. From 1806 he had no less an aim than to govern the European continent. His opponents – liberal Britain and the conservative monarchies of eastern Europe – had the basic war aim of defeating both prongs of the French danger, though for Britain the threat from revolutionary ideology declined in importance after France under Napoleon became a dictatorship and a police state. Indeed, relatively confident in the domestic stability of his own country, Castlereagh, foreign secretary and chief British negotiator at the congress in Vienna that in 1814–15 followed the French defeat, could aim at a policy of non-interference in other countries' internal affairs once the initial peace arrangements had been made, whereas the other towering figure, the Austrian statesman Metternich, thought that the right of the victorious powers to intervene to forestall upheavals that could threaten their stability was an essential aim. If Castlereagh's objectives seemed insufficient to Metternich, they appeared excessive to most of the former's cabinet colleagues. They remembered that Britain had gone to war with France in 1793 to prevent French control of the Low Countries and took the view in 1814–15 that that alone remained a sufficient British war aim in Europe. Castlereagh had to fight hard for his view to prevail; this was that arrangements for more distant countries, and in this case especially Poland, involved essential British interests. He insisted on being allowed to challenge Russia and demand that it should moderate its claim to almost all the territory of former Poland and, instead, should concede substantial portions to Prussia and Austria. He feared that if those two gained little from what had been Poland they would fight one another for dominance in Germany and create conditions of instability in which there might be another European war from which Britain would not be able to stand aloof. He was able to secure for Prussia in particular gains in former Poland that it regarded as not unreasonable.[17]

The generally peaceful century that followed the Congress of Vienna after 1815 in Europe was interrupted by a series of wars between 1854 and 1878, whose most important consequence was the political unification of Italy and Germany. The war of France and Piedmont against Austria in 1859 was the first planned war of aggression to gain territory in Europe since the time of Napoleon I. Napoleon III agreed to join Piedmont so that it could annex the Lombardo-Venetian kingdom, which was ruled by the Austrian emperor, in return for Piedmont ceding Savoy and Nice to France, though matters were to resolve themselves in a more tortuous and extensive way than the plotters had envisaged.[18] At the opposite extreme to these calculations was the quixotic war aim of courting military defeat. This occurred in 1866 when Prussia and Austria were at war and the latter's military commander, Benedek, informed his sovereign, Emperor Franz Joseph, that the military position was hopeless and that peace should be sought at any price. The Emperor replied that Austria would forfeit its honour if it yielded without a fight and ordered that there should be a battle. The result was the crushing Prussian victory at Königgratz, in which their casualties were 9,000 and Austria's 44,000, and a peace treaty dictated by Bismarck.[19]

An examination of British war aims in the Crimean War of 1854–6, in which Britain and France fought Russia, shows how there could be layers of aims. Most obviously, the aim was to contain Russian power. Thus in 1855 the prime minister, Palmerston, defined 'the main and real object of the war' as being 'to curb the aggressive ambitions of Russia. We went to war not so much to keep the Sultan and his Mussulmans in Turkey as to keep the Russians out of Turkey.' He later felt that this had been largely achieved by the peace settlement in which the Black Sea was neutralised and Russia was removed from all contact with the navigable portion of the Danube and its tributaries, and by making Turkey in effect a protectorate of Europe in the guise, which was theoretically a promotion in its status, of making it a member of the European comity of states.[20] However, 'deeper' and more speculative war aims have been identified, including a widespread desire for adventure among the British bourgeoisie because of boredom with unending peace. Thus *The Times* editorialised: 'This nation is a good deal enervated by a long peace, by easy habits of intercourse, by peace societies, and false economy.'[21] That left the problem of finding an enemy. One historian has argued that attention shifted from France to Russia because the former, the traditional enemy, was too formidable to contemplate as an adversary. With a stronger army than Britain it would have compelled the latter to enter into a costly military arms race. It was also the one country in the world at that time with the capacity to mount a challenge to British naval power. It was better, therefore, to have France as an actual ally.[22] In this context, a basic British aim was to avoid an arms race on land and sea; France was capable of this, Russia was not.

The renewed peace in Europe after 1878 was characterised by the creation of alliances on the continent (Germany, Austria and, uncertainly, Italy aligned against France and Russia), and by the expansion of the practice of military conscription. The hope of liberals that requiring male civilians to perform military service would make war less thinkable as a means to achieve national aims was nullified. All the evidence is that performing military service made populations readier to support war as a means of achieving such objectives. Even the class discriminatory nature of many national conscription systems that enabled the sons of the bourgeoisie to evade service or to perform it for only brief periods and in congenial surroundings fostered a readiness to achieve aims by force. Such young men tended to compensate for the prosaic minimalism or non-existence of their own military contribution by supporting military values and solutions.[23] On the other hand, the growth of democracy and the increasing importance of public opinion did make ruling circles feel compelled to clothe even the most aggressive aims in the rhetoric of righteousness. As two historians of the period have expressed it: 'Most governments claimed at the outset of wars that they were the innocent victims of aggression and urged the people to unite in defence of their fatherland. Governments felt it necessary to conceal their very specific territorial ambitions behind general and idealised value.'[24] Such formulations could also be used to fob off allies, as in September 1914 when Britain and France responded to a detailed list of Russian war aims by stating that what they were interested in was a settlement that would 'ensure for many years the peace of the world'.[25] Europe was on the slippery slope towards the situation in which Goebbels could call Nazi aggression and barbarism in the Second World War 'the German war for freedom'.

The first country, and even before it formally came into existence, to initiate hostilities by asserting that it was only doing so in response to intolerable oppression was the future United States of America in July 1775.[26] The subsequent American tradition was one of avoiding involvement in wars outside the western hemisphere, so that any question of war aims further afield did not arise, and the sense of righteousness that had been expressed in 1775 could continue to flourish. This mindset could not persist undisturbed after the US went to war with Spain in 1898 and, in particular, after it decided to use whatever force was necessary to replace Spanish colonial rule in the distant Philippine islands with American rule. It was one thing for the theorist of naval power Admiral Alfred Mahan to assert that it was an act of humanitarian kindness for an obviously rising power like America to relieve an obviously declining country like Spain of its unsupportable burden of empire. It was another thing for America to keep the Philippines from the rule or even misrule of the Filipinos themselves. At the time of annexation such luminaries as Mark Twain railed against the hypocrisy of claiming to bring the benefits of American civilisation to brown people on the other side of the Pacific while the lynching of black people in the US was reaching epidemic proportions. The annexation of the Philippines was to be a running sore that preyed on the American national conscience during the first forty-five years of the twentieth century. It had the paradoxical effect of fostering revulsion against annexationist war aims by the US or anyone else.[27] Yet the islands had been annexed, and the deep ambivalence in American thinking is reflected in the fact that one of President Woodrow Wilson's reasons for hesitating about taking the country into the war in Europe in early 1917 was that he feared for the effects on 'white' civilisation; if the US conserved its strength as a neutral it could protect the other white nations from the yellow race while they rebuilt their strength after the war.[28]

Another relevant consideration as the world entered the twentieth century was globalisation. In 1900 the US proclaimed the Open Door for all countries to trade with China as an earnest of its interest in the wider Far East besides only the Philippines. Beyond its eastern shore there was a sense of belonging to a community of nations bordering on the north Atlantic that also included Britain, France, Canada and the Low Countries. In February 1917 the young columnist Walter Lippmann coined the term 'the Atlantic world'. This concept was an intermediate stage between a future in which many Americans would think of the country in global terms and a past in which the American world view was largely centred on relations with Britain. There were to be fewer and fewer important Americans who were willing to echo Admiral Mahan when he wrote to President Theodore Roosevelt in 1904 that any blow to the British Empire would also be a blow to the US because 'its strength will be our strength, and its weakening an injury to us'.[29] Preventing this north Atlantic community from unravelling as a result of perceived aggression from an outside quarter might and did become an American war aim.

To return to the European mainstream of the subject, the Congress of Berlin in 1878, with the German chancellor Bismarck presiding, confirmed the achievement by two powers that had been on the brink of war, Britain and Russia, of the essential aims for which they had been willing to go to war, without war being resorted to. Britain gained a free hand to dominate Egypt and the new Suez Canal while Russia secured a position of dominance in the Black Sea. This made it not worth their while to go to war and yet still left so many tensions between them as virtually to rule out any possibility that they would both join with France in an anti-German combination, fulfilling Bismarck's main aim.[30] He, however, had not, in any real sense, engineered this outcome. He had lent a helping hand in a situation in which the rulers of Britain and Russia wished to avoid war. Bismarck's dismissal by the young Kaiser Wilhelm II in 1890 probably marked the real starting point along the road to the outbreak of war in Europe in 1914. Germany joined Russia in being ruled by men who had no concept of an integrating framework for their states except expansion. They had no vision of a peaceful mission for their countries in the world like those that prevailed in Britain and France. They also made their calculations against a background of technical developments, not least in the military sphere, that opened up new possibilities for the achievement of national objectives by force, and of nationalist pressures within their societies that urged them on. Such pressures from within the dominant ethnic group were facilitated rather than impeded by the fact that Russia was not a nation state, with ethnic Russians making up less than half the population, and Germany not a complete one, with large non-German minorities within its borders and the huge ethnic German population in the Austrian Empire outside them.

This was a situation in which war became eminently thinkable and in which the war aims contemplated were grandiose. Thus in the 1892 negotiations that led up to the Franco-Russian alliance in 1894, Tsar Alexander III expressed enthusiasm for war with Germany not only because of the need to deny Berlin the opportunity to destroy an isolated France and then turn against Russia, but also because, 'We must correct the mistakes of the past and destroy Germany at the first possible moment.' Germany would again become a collection of small, weak states, unable to resist Russian demands. It would be misleading not to add that many of the Tsar's advisers thought their master foolish on the grounds that he exaggerated Russian strength, and did not appreciate that Germans would never accept the loss of their hard-won unity, though – the worst of all possible worlds – defeat in war might change the form of government from monarchical conservatism to republican socialism.[31] Restless ambition was to lead Russia into its disastrously unsuccessful war with Japan in 1904–5. That did not cause the death of expansionist ambitions, not even in the Far East, but it did induce a mood of caution in Russian policy-makers, at least until the country became much stronger in military and naval terms. Between 1905 and 1914 Russia was unwilling to fight except to defend vital interests, as in 1913 when it was outraged at Germany's despatch of a mission to reorganise the Turkish army. Foreign minister Sazonov wrote to the Tsar in December: 'To abandon the Straits to a powerful state would be synonymous with subordinating the whole economic development of southern Russia to this state.' The Tsar himself told the British ambassador that if Germany persisted in its evident ambition to establish a protectorate at Constantinople Russia would have no alternative but to go to war.[32]

It was Germany and its junior ally, Austria-Hungary, that were the driving force to war in 1914. The previous year the German chancellor, Theobald von Bethmann Hollweg, had said that if Germany were to go to war it would do so in a spirit of 'aimlessness'.[33] Certainly, Germany was to go to war in August 1914 with Russia, the country on which it had most keenly set its sights, without having formulated any precise war aims. The German policy of Weltpolitik, though not as threatening as the Triple Entente of France, Britain and Russia supposed, had militarised international relations. In July and August 1914 there was a failure of statesmanship in which no leading figure was willing to fight wholeheartedly for peace; the Entente powers because they had become deeply suspicious of Germany, and Germany owing to the temptation to let war come about because that would provide the opportunity to make real its vague ambitions to become the dominant power in Europe and a world power, and, as a possible bonus, to reinforce the domestic political and social status quo by victory in war and consequent huge gains.[34]

Ironically, there was very little desire for war in the one European great power, France, that had a major and specific potential war aim: the recovery of the provinces of Alsace and Lorraine that had been lost to Germany in 1871. This did not produce a war spirit. There were desultory Franco-German discussions on autonomy within the German Empire as an acceptable (to France) conclusion to this matter, and some French policymakers noted with dismay or resignation that in the lost provinces themselves support for a return to being part of France was waning.[35] Germany, in any case, denied France the liberty of deciding for itself whether it wished to go to war to recover the provinces after Germany had decided on war with Russia. Under the extraordinary German mobilisation plans known as the Schlieffen Plan, French neutrality in a German–Russian war was regarded not as a bonus but as a disaster. The plan predicated that first France must be defeated and then Russia only after that. France had, therefore, to be goaded out of any toying with neutrality by facing it with an impossible demand to hand over two fortress towns on its border with Germany or suffer a German declaration of war.

If the major European powers went to war in 1914 with few definite aims, they more than compensated with the amount of attention that they bestowed upon this subject after hostilities had started. Because it touched on a sensitive national nerve Fritz Fischer's account of 1914–18 German war aims, published in 1961, aroused great attention.[36] Besides showing how the German government, within weeks of the outbreak of war, adopted an ambitious programme of political and economic war aims in which outright annexations and the creation of client states were mixed, he dwelt on two further features. These were, first, the tenacity with which the annexationist policy was maintained and even strengthened during the war, and, second, the wide extent to which it commanded support across the social and political spectrum in wartime Germany, to the extent to which it was known to the public. (Aims in the east were fully revealed in the Brest-Litovsk peace treaty that was imposed on Russia in March 1918 under which it lost almost all the non-ethnic

Russian territories of the tsarist empire in Europe.) Argument has, perhaps, still not entirely ceased about whether Fischer's, for all its value, is a somewhat misleading presentation of German policy in the war. Even within the wider ruling elite there was not monolithic unity about war aims. For example, King Ludwig III of Bavaria was an extreme annexationist whereas his son, Crown Prince Rupprecht, held decidedly moderate views on the subject.[37]

Yet victory must rest with Fischer. At the height of the debate that he provoked, another eminent German historian, Klaus Epstein, compared German aims with those of its enemies in a way flattering to the latter. He detected two fundamental differences. First, whereas Britain wanted, and France and even Russia accepted, that a balance of power in Europe had to be restored, Germany was bent on its utter destruction. Second, whereas the allies, for whatever reasons, came increasingly to favour the self-determination of peoples, Germany negated that concept, while sometimes paying formal lip service to it as in the Brest-Litovsk treaty, in which it was stated that the future of the lands of which Russia was being dispossessed would be decided 'in agreement with their populations'; or manipulating it with utter cynicism, for instance by trying to exacerbate tensions between Flemings and Walloons in occupied Belgium.[38] An analysis of allied war aims gives some support to this analysis in Europe, though not further afield. The most important man in British war aims policy during the first half of the war was Edward Grey, foreign secretary since 1905. Before August 1914 he had accepted that there was a liberal party in German ruling circles. He regarded Germany's resort to what he looked upon as aggressive war as proof that that party was ineffectual and that it could only gain ascendancy if the war party was discredited by being made to suffer decisive military defeat.[39] Such defeat was quickly defined as one that would force Germany to restore the full independence of Belgium. This, most assuredly, was not because of any affection for that country, but rather because its strategic position induced a determination to deny its territory to any great power. It is possible that Britain might have declared war on Belgium in August 1914 if it had allowed German troops to cross its territory.[40]

Britain came to accept that the restitution of Alsace-Lorraine to France was almost as important as the Belgian issue, both because that was France's cherished objective once it was at war and because it would reinforce the lesson that aggression did not pay. The break-up of Germany, or stripping it of territory in which ethnic Germans were in the majority, was not favoured, partly because it would have upset the balance of power, making France and Russia too powerful, and partly because it was incompatible with the policy of extending a cordial hand to a Germany that had purged itself of militarism and annexationism. The self-determination of peoples in east and central Europe, portending the break-up of the Austro-Hungarian Dual Monarchy, gradually found more and more favour in British policy-making.[41] Britain developed more self-serving aims of depriving Germany of all its colonies and incorporating most of them into the British Empire, and of denying Germany a navy of any size. These ambitions were rationalised with the notions that Germany did not need a navy or colonies, that their loss would reinforce the lesson that aggression did not pay, and that these losses were morally justifiable because they were trifling compared with the ones that Germany could be expected to inflict on Britain if the former were to win the war. Little economic benefit was anticipated from the German colonies, though there might be a few pickings such as diamonds in South West Africa (modern-day Namibia).[42]

In France the recovery of Alsace-Lorraine became a war aim from which few in the nation deviated throughout the war. It virtually guaranteed that the country would not leave the conflict for any reason short of total military defeat because Germany was determined to retain the provinces, though it did toy in 1917 with making a crassly insulting offer to return some small frontier districts as compensation for the permanent annexation to the Second Reich of the Briey-Longwy basin, the most important industrial area of France, that had been under German occupation since 1914.[43] In addition to Alsace-Lorraine, French wartime leaders spoke about 'necessary guarantees' of future security. Reflecting their country's relative weakness, the definition of these varied not only with fluctuating military fortunes but also with the audience addressed. They chiefly related to German territory west of the Rhine. To the British the French spoke of temporary occupation and permanent demilitarisation (as was actually to be provided for in the treaty of Versailles); to the Russians they spoke of outright annexation to France or at least the creation of buffer states that would be French clients.[44] France joined Britain in seeking extra-European spoils if only because of a conviction that it would be unthinkable to be left out. After Turkey entered the war it became determined to acquire Syria, despite foreign minister Delcassé's view that that region could be of 'no value' to France. If Germany was to lose its colonies, France intended to have a share of the spoils, despite the refusal of French industrialists to issue a statement that such acquisitions would be of benefit to them.[45]

The war aims of the doomed tsarist regime in Russia derive their main interest from any pointers that they might provide to later Soviet war aims. One historian detects a thread in tsarist/Soviet distrust of their allies, though under the last tsar 'to a much smaller degree and for quite different reasons' from those that motivated Stalin.[46] Both regimes had to wrestle with the future of the Polish people, who had lost statehood in large measure through Russian/Soviet actions. In the world wars, the advantages of a bogus autonomy in the first and of a bogus independence in the second suggested themselves to Russian policymakers. In August 1914 Russia offered an unspecified degree of autonomy to 'the Poles' (which implied that the ethnically Polish territories of Germany and Austria would pass into the Russian orbit). Tsarist Russia did not commit itself to the complete break up of the Austro-Hungarian Empire, but it did seek, as a minimum, that it should lose much of its territory with the Romanovs moving in where the Habsburgs were being eased out. Thus there was much favour for the Czech Lands becoming a Russian client state with a Romanov as king in Prague; it is unlikely that democratic Czech politicians like Masaryk and Beneš, who were to found the Czechoslovak republic in 1918, would have been allowed to return.[47]

As to Germany, Russia was resigned to the notion that, unlike possibly Austria-Hungary, it could not cease to exist. Russian thinking about the future of Germany, as presented to Britain and France in September 1914, was that it should lose all territory east of the Vistula to Russia (with East Prussia being directly annexed and West Prussia being assigned to a nominally autonomous Poland), and all territory west of the Rhine to France and Belgium. In addition, Denmark should be extended southwards to receive the Kiel Canal. Germany should lose all its colonies, though Russia wanted none for itself. And the Hohenzollern dynasty should be demoted; it should cease to provide Germany with emperors, though it could retain the throne of Prussia.[48] Grey did not like these aims, which threatened to prolong the war unnecessarily from a British point of view, and which, if they were realised, would make Russia too strong for the health of the European balance. He was also worried about Russian war aims in Iran (then invariably referred to as Persia). Iran had been the main focus of tensions between Britain and Russia for some years before 1914. Britain could not allow complete Russian domination of the country. It was too important strategically on the western approaches to India, and oil had recently been discovered in it. By atrocious bad luck (for British imperialism) that discovery had been made only a year after Britain had signed a convention with Russia in 1907, assigning most of northern Iran to Russia as a sphere of influence, while claiming for itself only a small sphere in the south-east. The oil was in the south-west, which Britain would almost certainly have claimed if its existence had been known. As it was, the area lay exposed to Russian penetration from northern Iran.[49] Oil supplies were certainly a factor in British war aims. Grey's successor but one, Curzon, was to observe that, 'The Allies floated to victory on a wave of oil.'[50]

Grey saw the opportunity to rectify the error of 1907, now that Britain and Russia were allies in war. In March 1915 he negotiated an agreement for the complete partition of Iran between Britain and Russia. The latter could do whatever it wished up to and including annexation of its sphere of influence, while the 1907 neutral zone, including the precious oilfields, was incorporated into the British sphere of influence.[51] Although it was more important to Britain, the deal with Russia on Iran was slipped in with the appearance of an afterthought to the agreement that Russia reached (naturally in secret) the same month with Britain and France, by which the two latter agreed that Constantinople (Istanbul) and the Straits between the Black Sea and the Aegean Sea and the Mediterranean should be annexed to the Russian Empire.[52] By making this agreement Britain and France hoped to keep Russia in the war, to moderate its ambitions in central Europe and, in the case of Britain, to sweeten the way for the simultaneous agreement on Iran. What also stands out is a vision of the exaltation of imperialism as a fundamental war aim. This is reflected in a statement that the British ambassador in Petrograd, Sir George Buchanan, made to the Tsar at an audience in March 1915: 'After the war, Russia and Great Britain would be the two most powerful Empires in the world. With the settlement of the Persian Question the last cause of friction between them would disappear and the world's peace would then be assured.'[53] A curious footnote to this is that British policymakers had decided more than ten years before the outbreak of war that British strategic interests would not be adversely affected by Russian control of the Straits.[54] When Soviet Russia was to revive its Straits ambitions towards the end of the Second World War their successors and their American colleagues were to take a very different view.

The Far East was not overlooked in tsarist war aims. Russia pressed a reluctant Britain to agree to a permanent ban on German trade with China and even a prohibition on German nationals visiting that country. It also attempted to draw closer to Japan; the high point was the visit to Tokyo of a Romanov grand duke in 1916 and the subsequent signing of a convention between the two countries, one of the last of the First World War 'secret treaties'. It stemmed on the Russian side from fear that unless Japan was their ally it might ultimately make common cause with a Germany whose strength, as the policymakers in the ministries in Petrograd were painfully aware, would remain fundamentally unimpaired even if Russia and its allies achieved their maximum war aims. As for Japan, if its wartime readiness to draw closer to Russia was partly the result of a belief, among the dominant section of the oligarchy, that Germany could not offer it anything, it was also in part the product of a conviction that only with Russian support could Japan achieve its prime national goal of expanding its power in China in the face of disapproval from the United States.[55]

That country, certainly after its entry into the war in April 1917, could not have failed to bring about changes in allied war aims. The allies had been concerned with restoring traditional harmony and balance in Europe and with expanding their own imperialisms and crushing the upstart imperialism of Germany. (The latter aim had wobbled when military fortunes were grim; for instance, in 1917 some French leaders pondered whether to offer Germany two of France's largest colonies, Madagascar and Indochina, in return for Alsace-Lorraine.[56]) The 'United States' meant essentially its president, Woodrow Wilson, a towering figure in the history of his country's engagement with the rest of the world.[57] A complex person, Wilson had little difficulty in holding views that many might find ill-matched, including altruism and acquisitiveness. In an essay published shortly before he became president in 1913 he argued that America was 'born to exemplify that devotion to the elements of righteousness which are derived from the revelations of Holy Scripture'. Yet when Europe went to war the following year he was eager to offer American business every assistance to help it to substitute itself for British and German trade in the western hemisphere.[58] This mindset precluded any automatic sentiment of sympathy for Britain and France. In late 1916 he seriously considered entering the war on the German side, and as late as February the next year he told a visitor to the White House that Britain was fighting for commercial supremacy, which he did not wish to assist, and that there was evidence that the peace-loving German people were turning against their Prussian militarist masters.[59]

After America entered the war he continued to regard the gulf between American economic war aims and those of its 'associates' –

the word allies was ruled out – as unbridgeable, and he talked about a doctrine of freedom of the seas which appeared to be directed against British naval power, though he made no effort to give it precise definition during the war or afterwards.[60] He pinned many hopes on a new international body for peace, and publicly advocated American (and German) membership of such a body as early as May 1916. This compelled Britain and France to treat seriously the question of the establishment of such a body as a war aim.[61] This was to become the League of Nations, and the project for it was part of the wider New Diplomacy movement that Wilson championed. This held that the major share in the making of foreign policy ought to be shifted from negotiation among states to the democratic formulation of foreign policy inside states. Public opinion could be relied upon to fix rational and reasonable foreign policy objectives; and, in so far as these clashed with the aims of other states, differences could and would be publicly resolved in the League. In the meantime, Wilson made public statements that were intended to appeal directly to enlightened elements of the population, especially in Britain but also in Germany. This certainly had its effect in the former. By March 1918 the socialist intellectual Beatrice Webb had come to look upon Wilson and the British Labour Party as the only obstacles to 'a cynical peace at the cost of democracy'.[62]

There was a significant change in Wilson's thinking after the US entered the war. He came to accept his associates' thesis about German responsibility for starting the war and the consequent necessity and justification both for inflicting on it military defeat and for the imposition of peace terms that contained a significant punitive element. Like Roosevelt in the next war, wholehearted hostility to the regime in Germany did not mean conversion to regarding America's 'Anglo-Saxon' partner as essentially virtuous. It was the same old Wilson who told a visitor in the summer of 1918 that America was not 'like the English . . . planning to dominate everything'. Yet his partial change of mind had happy consequences for Britain and France for eventual peacemaking, and, more immediately, because it caused him to abandon his initial view after America had entered the war that there was no reason why the US should make a significant military contribution to it.[63] The combination of idealism, American self-interest and willingness to see some merit in some of his associates' war aims was to guide Wilson's hand at the peace conference in Paris in 1919, and was to foretell in many respects US Second World War war aims.

The peace treaties that were signed between 1919 and 1923 failed the test of durability with the exception of the last one, between the west European allies (together with some Balkan states and Japan) and Turkey. This meant that there would be more wars and therefore more war aims. The rest of this book examines the aims of the major powers involved in the conflict of the Second World War with commentary to link their aims with the ones that have been the subject of this introduction.

Notes

1. F. H. Hinsley, *Power and the Pursuit of Peace: Theory and Practice in the Relations between States* (Cambridge: Cambridge University Press, 1963), pp. 14–20.
2. Sir Charles Oman, *A History of the Art of War in the Sixteenth Century* (London: Methuen, 1937), especially pp. 9–11, 769–70.
3. Susan Doran, *England and Europe, 1485–1603* (Harlow: Longman, 1986), p. 83.
4. Marvin Arthur Breslow, *A Mirror of England: English Puritan Views of Foreign Nations, 1618–1640* (Cambridge, MA: Harvard University Press, 1970), especially pp. 50–7.
5. J. R. Jones, *Britain and Europe in the Seventeenth Century* (London: Arnold, 1966), p. 35.
6. John Brewer, *The Sinews of Power: War, Money and the English State, 1688–1783* (London: Unwin Hyman, 1989), p. 140.
7. Paul Langford, *Modern British Foreign Policy: The Eighteenth Century, 1688–1815* (London: Black, 1976), pp. 29–30.
8. Ludwig Dehio, *Germany and World Politics in the Twentieth Century* (London: Chatto, 1959), pp. 15–18, 33. It is faintly embarrassing for a British reader to find a German scholar praising a British leader like Lloyd George 'as an idealist, as the advocate of the island's ethic of justice and of that fair play which is foreign to the nature of the Continental'. Ibid. p. 118.
9. Hinsley, *Power*, p. 177.
10. V. R. Berghahn, *Militarism: The History of an International Debate, 1861–1979* (Leamington Spa: Berg, 1981), pp. 57–9.
11. John P. LeDonne, *The Russian Empire and the World, 1700–1917* (New York: Oxford University Press, 1997), p. xvi.
12. Cyril E. Black, 'The pattern of Russian objectives', in Ivo J. Lederer (ed.), *Russian Foreign Policy: Essays in Historical Perspective* (New Haven: Yale University Press, 1962), pp. 3–38.
13. E. L. Woodward, *War and Peace in Europe 1815–1870 and Other Essays* (London: Cass, 1963), p. 45.
14. Alfred Vagts, *A History of Militarism Civilian and Military* (London: Hollis, 1959), pp. 386–7.
15. Dominic Lieven, *Empire: The Russian Empire and Its Rivals* (London: Murray, 2000), pp. 264–7.
16. G. H. Bolsover, 'Aspects of Russian foreign policy, 1815–1914', in Richard Pares and A. J. P. Taylor (eds), *Essays Presented to Sir Lewis Namier* (London: Macmillan, 1956), p. 322. In June 1940 the Soviet Union forced Romania to cede to it the provinces of Bessarabia and northern Bukovina. The Red Army

also occupied the northernmost corner of the province of Moldavia, including a town and twenty villages. When the Romanian envoy in Moscow asked for their return, the Russian foreign minister refused. 'Molotov did not deny that he might have made a mistake; but he put forward an argument that he considered final: the thing had been done.' Grigore Gafencu, *Prelude to the Russian Campaign* (London: Muller, 1945), p. 195.

17. Henry A. Kissinger, *A World Restored: The Politics of Conservatism in a Revolutionary Age* (New York: Grosset, 1964), pp. 163–5; C. K. Webster, *The Congress of Vienna, 1814–1815* (London: Bell, 1945), p. 119.

18. F. R. Bridge and Roger Bullen, *The Great Powers and the European States System, 1815–1914* (London: Longman, 1980), p. 90.

19. John Gooch, *Armies in Europe* (London: Routledge, 1980), pp. 91–2. Some years earlier Franz Joseph had responded to a suggestion that his empire could only avoid another defeat in war like the one that had been inflicted by France and Piedmont by widening the social base from which the officer corps was recruited by replying that it would be preferable to lose another province. Ibid. pp. 85–6.

20. W. E. Mosse, *The Rise and Fall of the Crimean System, 1855–71* (London: Macmillan, 1963), p. 1; see also René Albrecht-Carrié, *A Diplomatic History of Europe since the Congress of Vienna* (London: Methuen, 1958), p. 93.

21. Vagts, *Militarism*, p. 164.

22. John Clarke, *British Diplomacy and Foreign Policy, 1782–1865: The National Interest* (London: Unwin Hyman, 1989), pp. 246–8.

23. Berghahn, *Militarism*, pp. 15–17.

24. Bridge and Bullen, *Great Powers*, p. 83.

25. C. Jay Smith, Jr, *The Russian Struggle for Power, 1914–17: A Study of Russian Foreign Policy during the First World War* (New York: Philosophical Library, 1956), p. 52.

26. Vagts, *Militarism*, p. 284.

27. David Mayers, *Wars and Peace: The Future Americans Envisioned, 1861–1991* (Basingstoke: Macmillan, 1998), pp. 28, 47.

28. Arthur S. Link, *Wilson: Campaigns for Progressivism and Peace, 1916–17* (Princeton: Princeton University Press, 1965), p. 291.

29. Lionel M. Gelber, *The Rise of Anglo-American Friendship: A Study in World Politics, 1898–1906* (London: Oxford University Press, 1938), p. 134. It is true that, as late as 1939, there was a group of ideologues in the US, including Clarence Streit and George Catlin, who advocated federal union with Britain and, in effect, Anglo-Saxon world hegemony, but they were in a very small minority. See Kees van der Pijl, *The Making of an Atlantic Ruling Class* (London: Verso, 1984), pp. 110–12.

30. Woodward, *War and Peace*, p. 60.

31. George F. Kennan, *The Fateful Alliance: France, Russia, and the Coming of the First World War* (Manchester: Manchester University Press, 1984), pp. 153–4.

32. Henry Kissinger, *Diplomacy* (New York: Simon and Schuster, 1994), p. 198.

33. Fritz Stern, *The Failure of Illiberalism* (New York: Columbia University Press, 1992), p. 93.

34. Hew Strachan, *The First World War: Volume I, To Arms* (Oxford: Oxford University Press, 2001), pp. 34–5, 64–102.

35. John F. V. Keiger, *France and the Origins of the First World War* (Basingstoke: Macmillan, 1983), pp. 69–72; J. F. V. Keiger, *France and the World since 1870* (London: Arnold, 2001), pp. 119–20.

36. Fritz Fischer, *Germany's Aims in the First World War* (London: Chatto, 1967).

37. Hans W. Gatzke, *Germany's Drive to the West: A Study of Germany's Western War Aims during the First World War* (Baltimore: Johns Hopkins Press, 1950), pp. 38–9, 231 n. 166. Gatzke, writing long before Fischer, noted the marriage of the old and new elites, the nobility and the industrialists, in a quest for economic and territorial gains. A *Kriegsziel Bewegung* of industrialists formed a close alliance with the already existing Pan German League. Ibid. pp. 27–8, 65–6, 128–31, 165–6, 187–8, 214, 250–1. However, for a critique of Fischer in particular for exaggerating the unity of the German nation on war aims during the war see Wolfgang J. Mommsen, 'The debate on German war aims', in *Journal of Contemporary History*, vol. 1, no. 3, 1966, pp. 47–72.

38. Klaus Epstein, 'Gerhard Ritter and the First World War', in *Journal of Contemporary History*, vol. 1, no. 3, 1966, pp. 193–210; Gatzke, *Drive*, pp. 158–61.

39. Michael G. Ekstein-Frankl, 'The Development of British War Aims, August 1914–March 1915' (unpublished University of London Ph.D. thesis, 1969), pp. 82–129.

40. Ibid. p. 139. For several years before 1914 Belgian governments had been at least as worried about British as about German possible aggression. See J. E. Helmreich, 'Belgian concern over neutrality and British intentions, 1906–1914', in *Journal of Modern History*, vol. 36, 1964, pp. 416–27. In regard to another small west European country, Britain in 1907 had rejected a proposal for a treaty to guarantee the neutrality of newly independent Norway because the Royal Navy wanted to preserve the freedom to seize a Norwegian port as a naval base in any war with Germany. See Keith Neilson, *Britain and the Last Tsar: British Policy and Russia, 1894–1917* (Oxford: Clarendon, 1995), pp. 292–3.

41. These themes are developed in V. H. Rothwell, *British War Aims and Peace Diplomacy, 1914–1918* (Oxford: Clarendon, 1971), and, regarding British support for a state of the South Slav peoples, in Victor Rothwell, 'British policy on the South Slav question during World War I', in *Yugoslav–British Relations: papers delivered at Kragujevac, 23–25 September 1987* (Belgrade: ISI, 1988), pp. 167–90.

42. Ekstein-Frankl, 'War Aims', pp. 263–72, 288; William Roger Louis, *Great Britain and Germany's Lost Colonies, 1914–1919* (Oxford: Clarendon, 1967).

43. Pierre Renouvin, 'Le gouvernement français et les tentatives de paix en 1917', in *La Revue des Deux Mondes*, 15 October 1964, pp. 507–9.

44. For a short account of French war aims see Pierre Renouvin, 'Les buts de guerre du gouvernement français 1914–1918', in *Revue Historique*, Tome CCXXV, January–March 1966, pp. 1–38. For a more detailed treatment of the most important aspect see David Stevenson, *French War Aims against Germany, 1914–1919* (Oxford: Clarendon, 1982).

45. Christopher M. Andrew and A. S. Kanya-Forstner, *France Overseas: The Great War and the Climax of French Imperial Expansion* (London: Thames and Hudson, 1981), pp. 87, 97–8.

46. Gifford D. Malone, 'War aims towards Germany', in Alexander Dallin et al., *Russian Diplomacy and Eastern Europe, 1914–1917* (New York: King's Crown Press, 1963), p. 134.

47. Alexander Dallin, 'The future of Poland', and Merritt Abrash, 'War aims toward Austria-Hungary: the Czech pivot', in Dallin et al., *Russian Diplomacy*, pp. 1–77, 79–123; Smith, *Russian Struggle*, pp. 117–19.

48. Malone in Dallin et al., *Russian Diplomacy*, pp. 128–32.

49. Olaf Caroe, *Wells of Power: The Oilfields of South-Western Asia* (London: Macmillan, 1951), pp. 68–9.

50. E. H. Davenport and S. R. Cooke, *The Oil Trusts and Anglo-American Relations* (London: Macmillan, 1923), pp. 29–33.

51. Ekstein-Frankl, *British War Aims*, pp. 223–31; LeDonne, *Russian Empire and the World*, p. 148.

52. C. Jay Smith, 'Great Britain and the 1914–15 Straits agreement with Russia and the British promise of November 1914', in *American Historical Review*, vol. LXX, 1965, pp. 1015–34; Smith, *Russian Struggle*, pp. 186–243.

53. Sir George Buchanan, *My Mission to Russia and Other Diplomatic Memories* (London: Cassell, 1923), vol. I, pp. 226–7.

54. Neilson, *Britain and the Last Tsar*, pp. 114–15.

55. Malone in Dallin et al., *Russian Diplomacy*, pp. 149–53, 160–1; Frederick R. Dickinson, *War and National Reinvention: Japan in the Great War, 1914–1919* (Cambridge, MA: Harvard University Press, 1999), pp. 138–51; Morinosuke Kajima, *The Emergence of Japan as a World Power, 1895–1925* (Rutland: Tuttle, 1968), pp. 236–43.

56. Renouvin, 'Les buts', pp. 28–30.

57. Wilson's place in the history of international relations in the twentieth century is discussed in Peter Mangold, *From Tirpitz to Gorbachev: Power Politics in the Twentieth Century* (Basingstoke: Macmillan, 1998).

58. William Diamond, *The Economic Thought of Woodrow Wilson* (Baltimore: Johns Hopkins Press, 1943), pp. 135–7, 151–4. Ernest May confirms that during the first six months of the Great War the US government and American businessmen were at one in their relish for 'the new world to fatten on the follies of the old'. Ernest R. May, *The World War and American Isolation, 1914–1917* (Cambridge, MA: Harvard University Press, 1959), p. 53.

59. May, *World War*, pp. 361–2; Link, *Wilson*, pp. 340–1.

60. Diamond, *Economic Thought*, pp. 184–95; Lawrence E. Gelfand, *The Inquiry: American Preparations for Peace, 1917–1919* (New Haven: Yale University Press, 1963), p. 304.

61. Gelfand, *Inquiry*, pp. 2–3, 120–1; Henry R. Winkler, *The League of Nations Movement in Great Britain, 1914–1919* (New Brunswick: Rutgers University Press, 1952), pp. 53–76, 233–9.

62. Arno J. Mayer, *Political Origins of the New Diplomacy, 1917–1918* (New Haven: Yale University Press, 1959), pp. 53–8, 378; Lawrence W. Martin, *Peace without Victory: Woodrow Wilson and the British Liberals* (New Haven: Yale University Press, 1958), pp. 114–24, 142–6, 178–82; Margaret I. Cole (ed.), *Beatrice Webb's Diaries, 1912–1924* (London: Longmans, 1952), p. 115.

63. May, *World War*, pp. 431–2; Martin, *Peace*, p. 177. For Wilson's transition to a not unfavourable view of many British and French war aims see Sterling J. Kernek, *Distractions of Peace during War: The Lloyd George Government's Reactions to Woodrow Wilson, Dec. 1916–Nov. 1918* (Philadelphia: Transactions of the American Philosophical Society), new series, vol. 65, pt 2, 1975.

2

Germany and Italy

GERMANY

In 1952 Ludwig Dehio, reeling from what had so recently been done in his country's name, wrote that it challenged credulity that a country that had given humanity two of its most important spiritual–intellectual developments – the Protestant Reformation and Marxism – had, in the thirty years between 1914 and 1945, only been able to offer a demonic nationalism from which other peoples could not and should not profit.[1] The former armaments supremo Albert Speer, during interrogation in 1945, observed that Hitler had been hostile to any attempt to export Nazism: 'This, in his opinion, would only result in an undesirable national invigoration of these [other] countries, while democracy would tend to weaken their fighting power.'[2] German war aims in the Second World War were uncompromisingly ethnocentric, and were characterised by immeasurable callousness and cruelty. At a conference on policy in conquered Soviet territory in July 1941 Hitler ruled that: 'Our guiding principle must be that these peoples have but one justification for existence – to be of use to us economically.' Exactly a year later, in July 1942, Martin Bormann drew up a list of 'principles for the government of the Eastern Territories' based on instructions from Hitler. One of these was that 'Slavs' who were not working for Germany should die.[3] Although not all peoples in the German orbit were intended to suffer so drastic a fate, it would be difficult to find statements that express better than these the true spirit of Nazi German war aims. This chapter will also examine Italian war aims and Italy's downward journey from unwanted ally of the Third

Reich to national downfall and becoming itself the object of expansionist German aims.

While Hitler was not the sole progenitor of German war aims, he was of fundamental importance. It is important to note that he did have aims. That meant that he was not wholly typical of the radical right in the Germany of the Weimar Republic. Then, many right wingers criticised German leadership in the recent war for having fought for practical aims and profit instead of playing the 'high serious game of bloodshed', which, in their view, 'at all times had made men what they were'. These nihilists advocated endless war for its own sake, and threw in the idea of a German world empire as little more than a sop to those who were not wholly converted to political irrationalism.[4] The historian Rohan Butler noted the prevalence of 'irrational revolutionary reaction' in much German philosophy of the Weimar period.[5] Hitler was clearly not lacking in that, and yet, even before becoming a politician in 1919, he had had thoughts on war aims that would not have displeased chancellor Bethmann Hollweg, the architect of the celebrated war aims programme of September 1914. In 1943 he reminisced to his military adviser Keitel that he would have lost his motivation to continue fighting on the western front if he had thought that Germany was ever going to leave Belgium.[6] Why Hitler, an Austrian who had served in the west in the Great War, should have become fixated on expansion to the east in search of *Lebensraum*, or living space, for the people of Germany (in which the birth rate fell from 21.3 per 1,000 population in 1923 to 14.7 in 1933, the year of his accession to power) is not immediately clear. It needed some personal experience to draw upon, and this was probably provided by his pre-1914 observation of ethnic conflict between ethnically German Austrians and Slavonic Czechs in the Habsburg Monarchy, in which they were obsessed with race and living space as they competed with one another to become the largest ethnic group in various areas.[7]

More significantly and reverting to the point that Hitler was not all important, it is necessary to examine some of the currents of thought in interwar Germany that influenced him, scarcely an original thinker, and which influenced many to follow him from reasoning and not blind faith. There was widespread belief in German racial superiority, even among many who would have described themselves as liberals, coupled with resentment about a society that was still stratified and in which social mobility was restricted, and fear about an economic situation that was bad and which would very likely become worse unless drastic new policies were adopted from which

Germany would gain and many other European peoples would lose; threatened or actual force would manifestly be necessary to achieve these. Furthermore, there was no reason why they could not be accomplished relatively painlessly. German superiority would allow other countries to be brought into subordination at limited cost, especially if they allowed themselves to be picked off one by one. It is beyond the scope of the present study to investigate in detail the thesis, propounded most recently by the historian MacGregor Knox, that in Nazi Germany and fascist Italy there was a constant dynamic between foreign and internal policy, in which the former was also the latter and vice versa.[8] Thus foreign conquest was the decisive instrument for widely desired social change at home that would sweep away inherited institutions and values, especially ones that derived from the churches and the values associated with the upper middle classes. The historians Götz Aly and Susanne Heim add a persuasive argument: German domination of Europe would create so many opportunities for 'average' Germans that those in the upper social strata need not be stripped of many of their privileges.[9] Germans who were content with the existing state of society could unite with those who were not in a quest for German expansion that was unencumbered by moral constraints or any true understanding of international reality. Hitler himself seems to have had little interest in promoting social mobility. He wanted German society to revert to being rural in focus, and rural societies are usually hierarchical. However, he fostered the tendency already present for Germans to seek simplistic and amoral solutions to their national problems. As Goebbels expressed it: 'National Socialism has simplified the thinking of the German people and led it back to its original primitive formula.'[10]

Given the nature of the Third Reich as a Fuhrer state, it devolved on Hitler to decide on priorities among war aims. He could brush the matter aside as, early in the war, when he remarked that, 'As far as our might extends we can do what we like, and what lies beyond our power we cannot do in any case.'[11] In saying this he belied what he had said on 6 October 1939 when he proclaimed his intention of 'creating a new ethnographic order' in Europe, involving a 'resettlement of nationalities'.[12] In his vision, this was to be primarily in Poland and, above all, the Soviet Union. This brings attention back to why an Austrian corporal who served on the western front and who then wanted Germany to retain Belgium as a colony should have become so fixated on 'the East'. Objectively, he might have been expected to be more focused on France, of which he had first-hand experience and whose highhanded and sometimes wantonly cruel policies towards Germany between 1919 and 1924 had aroused widespread popular Francophobia.[13] The likeliest key to understanding lies in Hitler's mentality as an exceptionally opinionated Philistine who latched on to those popular prejudices around him that he found congenial. The two that he found most to his liking were anti-Semitism and Russophobia-cum-*Lebensraum* 'thinking'; the former was age old and there had been plenty of the latter in the German world since well before 1914. The two fused in the minds of Hitler and his mentor on Russian affairs, Alfred Rosenberg, in the conviction that what had happened in Russia in 1917 and the subsequent civil war was the takeover of that country by the Jews to further their quest for world domination. This created a danger that had to be eliminated as well as creating opportunities for colonisation and exploitation. The only alternatives for Russians and other Slavs, at least in the European parts of the Soviet Union, were to be death or slavery. A Soviet historian remarked justly that Hitler's attitude towards the Russian people was one of 'bestial malice'.[14] What is most remarkable of all is that he reached these views without, quite possibly, having spoken to or set eyes on a Russian in his life. In the case of the Jews, whom he hated so fiercely, he had at least encountered large numbers of them while he was living in Vienna in his youth.

It would be as impossible in a book of this nature to do justice to the Nazis' ghastly aim of exterminating the Jewish people as it would be to ignore it entirely. A few (inevitably inadequate) passages must suffice. The *Lebensraum* slave empire was arrived at long before the aim of Jewish extermination. Hitler had decided by 1925 that the former was his great mission, whereas there is no evidence of Hitler or the Nazis planning Jewish extermination before 1938. The South African leader, Smuts, was right when he said in 1945 that for Hitler Jewish extermination was 'the fundamental of his satanic creed', but it was a development of the previous five years and one which, in its timing, grew out of the invasion of Russia. Around March 1941 Hitler probably gave Himmler a verbal order that all Soviet Jews – supposedly the real rulers of the country – were to be murdered.[15] However, the campaign in Russia was only expected to last for about three months, and probably even Hitler was willing to wait that long before the Jews were killed. While fighting was going on, the mass killing of Jews would not have been possible without the cooperation of the German army and no order issued to the army before the invasion began on 22 June referred to the murder of Jews. The *Einsatzgruppen* death units had been organised, but for the purpose of killing 'Bolsheviks' and anyone who resisted the German forces or was suspected of doing so, though it was expected that Jews would be numerous in both categories. After the Germans advanced deep into Soviet territory and the death squads embarked on their deadly work, the mass killing of Jews rapidly ceased to be almost incidental and became their principal activity, if only because it was easy to do. This radicalised the entire Nazi approach to the Jewish 'problem'. They were also encouraged by another exercise in mass killing that they were carrying out among Soviet prisoners of war. Within six months of the start of the invasion about two million of them died from disease, starvation or shooting. That unwanted human beings could be killed on such a scale with the rest of the world evincing no real interest, even to the extent that it had any knowledge of what was going on, was a powerful indicator of the opportunities that now existed for the 'final solution of the Jewish problem'. Probably in September 1941 Hitler gave a verbal order for the extermination of the European Jews.[16] If the war on the continent had ended in quick victory, Jewish extermination would almost certainly still have taken place, but not as a unique event. It would rather have been the most extreme expression of a manipulation of European populations to achieve a supposedly ascertainable perfect balance between numbers of people and optimum use of economic resources, using racial criteria so that there could be no upper limit on the number of Germans at one extreme and a zero population figure for the Jews at the other.[17] If serious historical work on the Jewish Holocaust is less and less interested in studying it in isolation and more and more interested in studying it within a wider context of German manip-ulation-expansionist aims, then, at the opposite extreme, the subject has, during and since the last third of the twentieth century, received massive attention from mostly American pressure groups with lar-gely non-historical agendas. The result has been to leave a 'tradi-tional' Holocaust historian like Raul Hilberg feeling somewhat redundant.[18]

Expansionist war aims were favoured by many senior figures in the German armed forces, such as the Nazi-minded general, Walter von Reichenau. As early as 1934 he was working on detailed plans for a three-pronged offensive for the 'lightning' conquest of Russia of the type that was to be launched in 1941 with himself in command of the southern prong.[19] Among yet other players, the two most important were the industrialists and the banks (acting in concert) and the SS, all of which had thoughts, sometimes impatient ones, about post-

Hitler arrangements. If the Nazi Reich had survived Hitler, the form of government would probably have changed from Fuhrer state to a partnership between big business and the SS. The former's role remains controversial because of the thesis that, acting in close cooperation with important officials in the economic and foreign ministries and with Nazi 'moderates', it laid down many of the foundations for the postwar economic integration movement in western Europe – the 'tainted source'.[20] Following the German military victories in 1940, there was much support in Belgium, the Netherlands and France for an anti-democratic new order under German leadership.[21] This was promising for German industrialists and banks which had long been convinced that Germany had no tolerable future except in a *Grossraumwirtschaften* (large economic space), and that this should comprise all or almost all of continental Europe. There was much rhetoric, German in its turgidity, about the Reich (Third was officially discarded in 1940 to emphasise the greatness and finality of the Nazi state, though the word 'Reich' implies something of a much higher spiritual order than a mere state) having 'European' aims. In 1944 Karl-Heinz Pfeffer, president of the German Institute for Foreign Affairs, stated that the spirit of the European peoples was good, but that they 'must sublimate it in the Hegelian sense, so that it continues to exist but becomes a living element in a larger unity . . . What we offer is not so much a programme as an idea – the idea of Europe itself.'[22] Hitler himself could declare to his entourage that the 'creation of a united Europe must remain the goal of our struggle', though in a radio broadcast in October 1941 Goebbels's deputy, Hans Fritzsche, almost certainly on the Fuhrer's instructions, warned that brute force would be used against any 'crummy little state' in Europe that requested special consideration. In the spring of 1944 his Luftwaffe adjutant, von Below, wrote: 'His judgments of people, historical personalities and history remained the same. He spoke a great deal about his ideal of the European state in which it would be his objective to fight Jews and Communists and to destroy their influence in the world in every respect. He believed firmly that Providence had given him that task.'[23]

Having said this, the idea that the integration movement in post-war western Europe owed anything positive to Hitler is plainly preposterous. His more 'idealistic' pronouncements of European aims could only be a smokescreen for German nationalist, aggressive ambitions. His instructions to Speer were that integration was for the sole purpose of benefiting Germany and keeping up the German standard of living. An examination of the wartime actions of the German industrialists and bankers and the officials with whom they worked in the state bureaucracy shows that they were much more in tune with Hitler and mainstream Nazism than with the postwar actions of Robert Schuman and Jean Monnet, even if the wartime records of those men are not unblemished. Technically, they based themselves on the central planning of production and commodities which were to be exchanged on the basis of barter. More sinisterly, they were committed to policies which, mercifully, had no postwar future whatever, including the use of racial–biological criteria to restructure the European economy in order to make it competitive, and the use of the defeated Soviet Union as a source of raw materials and slave labour. In addition, a fundamental feature of the German 'European' programme was to provide every assistance in setting up anti-Jewish institutes and organisations outside Germany.

Where, in appearance, German 'European' aims came closest to foreshadowing the future was in seeing the Franco-German relationship as the most important in the Europe of the future, but it was one in which Germany was to be crushingly dominant. The metaphor used most often to describe the future was one in which other European countries were planets which would revolve around the German sun, with France as no more than the most important of those planets. All this, to many Germans, was no more than natural justice. They railed against the balance-of-power policies of their western enemies which (in this version of history) had for centuries denied Germany its rightful place of dominance in Europe. Britain had been the most powerful exponent of such policies in recent times, but the French had started it all. Thus it was that German wartime 'European' theorists ranted against the 1648 treaty of Westphalia as much as against the 1919 treaty of Versailles, which had merely continued what Cardinal Richelieu and Westphalia had begun. France's guilt had been unchanging, and, in early 1941, Friedrich Grimm, the leading Nazi specialist on relations with France, denounced the 'eternal Richelieu, the eternal treaty of Westphalia'. He went on to assure the French that they were not beyond redemption. All they had to do was stand Richelieu's concept on its head and accept that Germany under its Fuhrer was now *la grande nation*.[24]

In February 1940 Hitler defined German economic war aims as a matter of: 'The securing of our own living space, and by this I mean everything that has been cultivated, civilised and economically tapped by the Germans and not the English . . . This Mitteleuropa has been built up through Germany and we want to live in this

German living space. We will not let ourselves be threatened here.' In the summer, following the German victories in the west, the Economics Ministry under Walther Funk, who worked under the overlordship of Hermann Goering, drew up plans in conjunction with German industry. Funk explained to his guests, who were almost a roll call of the men who were to lead West German finance and industry in the 1950s and 1960s, that the most important aim was to place the German economy on a permanent war footing and to make the rest of Europe serve the German war economy. He added that it would make little difference if peace was soon made with Britain because the Reich had to be ready for inevitable future wars. This involved such matters as finding more synthetic substitutes for strategic raw materials that were only to be found outside Europe. These plans further envisaged a customs union with countries to the north and north-west and a close but very different relationship with countries to the south-east because a customs union was only desirable with countries whose living standards were not drastically lower than the German. South-east Europe had much lower ones 'and it was not at all in our interest to confer on that area a similar standard of life to ours'. The south-eastern states were to provide food, raw materials and cheap labour, and were to receive German capital investment but only to boost food and raw material production for Germany; above all, they were not to be industrialised. In practice, the necessities of war obliged Germany to encourage industry in this area, with moderate success in some countries, most notably Hungary; while war conditions produced drastic economic decline in others, including the extreme case of Greece, where non-agricultural output ceased almost completely, and food output by 1944 was only 25 per cent of prewar. Germany's political satellites in the area, Hungary, Romania and Bulgaria, struggled with some success to avoid becoming complete economic satellites.[25]

As the war went on, the Nazi state greatly benefited German industry by enabling it to take what it wanted from the rest of Europe without payment. The German foreign debt rose from 1.7 billion reichsmarks in December 1940 to 31.5 billion by September 1944. Inflation soared in the 'donor' countries as they printed money to pay producers for exports to Germany in the absence of earned foreign exchange. Giant German firms, like IG Farben and Krupp, that, since long before the war started, had wanted an enclosed, self-sufficient German-dominated continent, were enabled to expand massively across Europe, but perhaps the greatest gainers of all were the German banks. They had had little stake in banks outside

Germany before 1939. By 1944 the Deutsche Bank, which maintained a particularly close relationship with IG Farben, was the largest in Europe and the Dresdner Bank the second largest. German industry and finance was thus in a position, if Germany had won the war, to regulate the price of raw materials, production processes and the final marketing of finished goods across Europe. It is manifestly clear that there was little disposition to consider interests other than German in all this. Thus, a historian of the subject concludes that in the wartime activities of German business and the German state there was 'little more than a synonym for German economic hegemony'.[26]

This is a convenient point to discuss two other issues relevant to whether Nazi Germany had 'European' war aims. One concerns propaganda. Until late in the war Goebbels refused to allow 'European' propaganda to be broadcast on the radio or to be introduced into films. He confined it to the printed word in the belief that the mass of Germans did not want to hear about a future that was European but rather one that was exclusively German. The message to them was that since Germany was heroically ridding Europe of its Jewish, Bolshevik and other enemies, it was just that Germany should dictate the terms of the New Order when the time came. Even towards devotees of the written word he was cautious. A directive of 18 March 1940 commanded that: 'Nothing is to appear in the German press about German war aims.'[27] The second relates to the affair of the proposed European Charter which Hitler came under pressure from elements in the Reich and from German allies to adopt in 1943 as the worsening military situation evidently dictated the wisdom of proclaiming war aims that would have a 'European' appeal and which might convince waverers that the enemies of the Axis were the enemies of a reasonable peace. A draft was drawn up in the Foreign Ministry which included the assertion that: 'If Europe has been plagued by wars for centuries it is above all the fault of Britain's policy of playing off one European state against another.' Foreign minister Ribbentrop gave his approval. Italy and Vichy France under the inspiration of Pierre Laval joined to make an appeal to the Fuhrer. Other pleas came from the Norwegian fascist leader, Quisling, and from Hungary (which the Nazis found provocative in view of Hungary's failure to carry out its fundamental European obligation to 'dejudaise' by handing over its Jews to Germany). Hitler's response was negative. He replied that it was better to rely on appeals to heroism and predictions of victory. Thus, even as the war turned for the worse the German dictator was unwilling to nail his colours to a

European mast. He delivered his veto even though Ribbentrop had deleted from the proposals to be put before him for inclusion in the charter an offer to the peoples of Europe of 'the free development of their spiritual, racial and national qualities', which he knew would have aroused his leader's anger.[28]

Turning to the SS under Himmler, while it was inevitably to a large extent the executant of war aims dictated by Hitler, it had aspirations to be an independent actor in two respects. The first, which never amounted to more than anxious pondering, was that of acting against Hitler to preserve as much as possible of what he had gained for Germany in a peace deal with the western powers in the delusion that Britain and the US would be willing to make peace with a Hitlerless Reich and let it keep 'Germanic' areas of north-west Europe and a Lebensraum empire in the east. Himmler kept aloof from active involvement in this and left it to the rising star in the SS, Otto Ohlendorff, who, newly returned from supervising exterminations in the east, discussed the possibilities for doing this with many German industrialists in the winter of 1943–4. Gradually, Himmler realised the futility of this 'peace' project as German intelligence presented him with material about his 'vilification', which he found unfair and incomprehensible in nations that were allied with Stalin, in the Anglo-American media.[29] In 1951 Ohlendorff was to be hanged by the United States, despite hysterical protests in West Germany.

The second area in which Himmler had his own ideas, and a certain amount of power with which to implement them, concerned whether German war aims should be that or 'Germanic', that is including related 'Nordic' peoples, notably the Scandinavians, the Dutch and the Flemings of northern Belgium. Motivated by a narrow interpretation of Nazi racial dogma and by pure German racist egotism, most Nazis, including Hitler, rejected the Germanic concept. Another racial borderland was the French provinces of Alsace and Lorraine, which, de facto, were incorporated into the Reich in 1940. Hitler did not regard them as any great racial prize. He told Albert Speer that their population had become racially 'worthless' during the long periods of French rule.[30] It is remarkable that members of Nazi-type parties in Germanic countries, such as Vidkun Quisling's Nasjonal Samling in Norway, were not allowed to attend even public meetings of the Nazi Party when they visited Germany until after Stalingrad when they were allowed to attend on condition of giving prior notice so that speakers could be forewarned not to make disparaging remarks about Norway, Holland or whatever the country might be. In December 1944 Martin Bormann, who headed the Nazi Party apparatus, made what he thought was the supreme concession of allowing Germanic pro-Nazis who were living in Germany to participate in the work of the party, though they still could not actually become members.[31] In seeking to rescue the Scandinavians, Dutch and Flemings for ultimate full membership with the Germans of one community, Himmler was conscious that he had set himself a Herculean task in which he would have to struggle on two fronts, against the opposition of Hitler and the mass of German Nazis, and to reverse the immersion of these lost brethren for generations in degenerate liberal values. He longed to be able to include Iceland, which was not under German occupation, in this racial rescue mission. While the war went on, these competing visions of the future made little practical difference to German policy. If Germany had won the most likely outcome is that Denmark, Norway, the Netherlands and Belgium would have become SS regencies so that Himmler could attempt germanisation and perhaps convince a sceptical Nazi Party that these other Germanic peoples were worthy of equality with Germans.[32]

It is against this background that German war aims will be considered as the war ran its course. The central figure is, obviously, Hitler, who is not always easy to pin down. At the Nuremberg tribunal Ribbentrop replied to an incredulous American prosecutor who had asked him whether he was asserting that he never knew what German foreign policy was by stating that that was the case because, 'The Fuhrer never revealed his definite aims to anybody.'[33] This echoed Mussolini, who, as early as June 1941, had come to dread the summons from Hitler for them to meet because he knew that it meant having to listen to a monologue that would go on for hours in which his fellow dictator would dwell on recent developments in the war, 'but without an agenda, without examining a problem, without making a decision'.[34] After his first triumph, the victory over Poland, Hitler told his Luftwaffe adjutant that, 'I have no war aims as regards Britain and France', while adding that Britain seemed intent on all-out war against the Germans as a people. Von Below could perceive no war aim in his master's mind other than victory as an end in itself. For a time he hoped to be able to launch a campaign in late October to defeat France, though the real aim was anti-British: 'The war aim was to force Britain to her knees.'[35]

While that goal remained out of reach, it was possible to draw up plans and make progress with conquered territories and, in particular, with their at least partial germanisation. Even in the first Nazi takeover, that of Austria in March 1938, this had been an issue, even though it was a German country and Hitler's own homeland. The Fuhrer had thought it necessary to appoint a Reichskommissar for the reunion of Austria with the German Reich, with a remit to do his job within a year so that the post could then be abolished. In fact, for years Hitler continued to fret that Austria retained some traces of a separate identity. In January 1942 he banned the use of the term Ostmark, which he had himself bestowed on the former country in 1938 because it indicated that the former Austria was still a unit of some sort.[36] Hitler's worries about Austria may well have been excessive even from a Nazi standpoint. There were clearly greater problems when the Czechoslovak state, weakened by the Munich agreement in September 1938, was destroyed by German pressure in March 1939. The resulting arrangements illustrated the scope for two types of war aim that could be pursued by a conquering Germany. German rule and germanisation in the Czech lands, designated the 'protectorate' of Bohemia and Moravia, was one. (There was no real parallel for protectorates in German history; the term was copied from British colonial usage.[37]) The other was the creation of a satellite or client state in Slovakia, where some segments of the population found independence under German overlordship preferable to membership with the Czechs in a multi-ethnic state. To the end of his life Hitler never seems to have doubted that the only ultimate solution to the 'problem' of the Czechs was for all of them to be killed or deported far to the east. While the war went on, he was prepared to follow a more or less rational policy of minimal disruption to the economic life of the Protectorate to maximise its output for the German war economy and to allow a facade of limited self-government with a cabinet of Czechs under the German governor, the 'Protector'. What is most relevant to the theme of this book is the debate – a debate which virtually ignored Hitler – about a rational long-term strategy for the Protectorate. The longer Germans ruled there, the more the prospects for wholesale germanisation looked problematical. A few thousand German peasant settlers were found, but it appeared more and more unlikely that enough of such settlers could ever be discovered to replace the entire Czech population, which, consequently, was examined for unwitting candidates to be germanised. In 1940 a racial inventory, carried out under cover of a health survey, concluded hopefully that as many as 45 per cent of the Czechs had predominantly Nordic characteristics, 40 per cent had some such characteristics, and only 15 per cent were racially wholly alien. The problem, recognised by the Sudeten German deputy 'Protector', Karl Hermann Frank, was that many of these Czech-Nordics, especially in the intelligentsia, would never accept any racial olive branch that was offered to them. These would simply have to be killed. Czech-Nordics who could be won over should preferably be settled in the old, pre-1937 Reich and their places taken by Reich Germans. In that way germanisation could proceed. Of interest was a marriage law of October 1940 by which Czechs who had passed the Aryan racial test could marry Germans, provided that both partners signed an undertaking to bring up any children as Germans, to be educated in German schools. From that time to the end of the occupation the intention remained that the Czechs themselves should make an important contribution to the germanisation of their lands, but that all those who were unsuitable for germanisation or who refused the honour should be killed or removed.[38]

In Slovakia Hitler allowed nationalist politicians to proclaim an independent republic in March 1939, and, after a probationary period in which the conduct of the ruling Slovak politicians proved exemplary, he had decided by October of that year that it should retain client state-type independence permanently. Diplomatic relations were established at legation level, headed by a minister, and the first German minister to the Slovak capital, Bratislava, sent to Berlin, where it was endorsed, the definition of his mission that, 'It is our intention to create, with respect to Slovakia, a classic example of our conception of a protective relationship with a southeastern Slav state.' In practice, in 1939–40, Germany imposed on Slovakia demands for the complete utilisation of its economy for the German war economy and a privileged status for the German minority. The German aim in this small country remained economic exploitation, but not much germanisation until serious revolts against the pro-German government in the late summer of 1944 imbued in Himmler, who was given responsibility for crushing them, the conviction that the Slovaks, who had shown themselves to be nothing but troublesome Slavs after all, must, when the situation allowed, all be exterminated or deported.[39]

The first wartime conquest was, of course, that of the Polish heartland, with that country's eastern regions passing under a horrendously brutal Soviet occupation. Hitler was fairly clear about the two basic aims of economic exploitation and germanisation. The leaders, in the widest sense, of Polish society were to be exterminated and the Polish masses were to serve as unskilled labour in a manner that would be repeated in many other places later. As Reinhard Heydrich elegantly expressed it, the Poles were to be used as 'laboratory rats'. He explained that, 'We want to spare the little people, but nobility, clergy and Jews must be killed.'[40] The point about the clergy in an overwhelmingly Catholic country is significant. The Nazis were determined in the long term to destroy Christianity, and perhaps especially Catholicism. Before his assassination in 1942, Heydrich (again) remarked in a circular to subordinates, 'We should not forget that in the long run the Pope in Rome is a greater enemy of National Socialism than Churchill or Roosevelt.'[41] The Nazis allowed the extermination of the 'nobility', by which Heydrich had meant everyone in the intelligentsia and the professional classes, to ease off somewhat, unlike the relentless drive against the Polish Jews. The Warsaw uprising by the Polish resistance forces in 1944 inspired them with the thought that a renewed annihilatory drive should be embarked upon as soon as possible.[42]

Averse to detail and intent on devoting most of his time to military matters, Hitler entrusted detailed work to Heydrich's chief, Himmler. This was an almost inevitable choice because of the latter's position within the Reich and his passionate interest in germanisation. (The latent conflict between Hitler and Himmler about whether the ultimate racial community should be German or Germanic had no relevance in 'the East'.) In a speech to gauleiters in February 1940 Himmler set out his thoughts on how the victory of the sword in Poland should be followed by a 'victory of the blood'. He noted that it was important to learn from history. The Slavs had never been able to govern themselves. They had sought leaders from German stock – Himmler found it fascinating that the Polish general who had commanded the defence of Warsaw in 1939 had been called Rommel – but those leaders had been racially insufficiently vigilant and had committed the error of interbreeding with Slavs. Even so, some of the population in the east remained chiefly German in blood and should be rescued and completely regermanised. The priority had to be to do this in those Polish areas that had been annexed to the Reich. Two new German *Gaue* had been carved out of western Polish territory, and substantial Polish territories had been added to the existing *Gaue* of East Prussia and Silesia. In the combined population of all four, pure Germans were in the minority, comprising 7.5 million out of a total of 16.5 million. The non-Germans who could not be germanised, who were the vast majority, were to be squeezed into ever smaller and non-contiguous areas, while German areas, starting as racial islands, were to be expanded until they included all the *Gaue*. Germanisation should be accompanied by the highest degree of concern for the environment. For instance, the newly germanised areas should obtain as much as possible of their energy from the

renewable sources of wind and water. Many Poles would be transferred from the annexed lands to the rump of German-occupied
Poland, which had been designated the Government-General, effectively a colony, where their chief purpose would be to provide cheap,
if not slave, labour for the Reich. One million male Polish labourers
were needed there immediately with so much of German manhood in
the armed forces. They were to be denied all social contact with
Germans, and the sole punishment for sexual relations with German
women was to be death. They should be allowed to bring Polish
women with them to satisfy what Himmler acknowledged to be their
rightful needs. Despite the urgency of the matter, it would still be
necessary to be choosy about which Germans from the Old Reich to
admit as colonists; they would have to be convinced National
Socialists and to be willing and able to procreate numerous children:
'We want no false [sic] people settled.' Three months later Himmler
presented Hitler with more detailed ideas on policy in former Poland.
He had drawn up detailed proposals on the selection of children with
Aryan qualities who could be sent to Germany, sometimes with their
parents if they too were of sufficient racial quality and were willing to
be germanised. All other children should receive only the barest
education, which would not include learning to read, and whose
purpose would be to impress on them the need to obey their German
masters. The adult Polish population 'will be available as a leaderless
work-Volk of manual, itinerant labourers', though their standard of
living would be higher than under the Polish state. The Poles had
been hopelessly inefficient, and in future they would make 'trickle
down' gains from German efficiency. Some reality crept into these
musings when lower-level Nazi bureaucrats came to appreciate the
difficulties of implementation. By 1942 those with responsibility for
germanising the annexed Polish territories had concluded that it
could not be done. They did not envisage being able to import more
than 1.5 million Germans from the Old Reich, whereas Himmler had
hoped for 5–6 million. The bulk of the remaining Polish inhabitants
would remain, though they would only be allowed to perform menial
and unskilled labour, providing Germans were in a bare numerical
majority in the annexed territories.[43]

The head of the Government-General, Hans Frank, favoured delay
in the implementation of ideological war aims for pragmatic reasons,
to make the work both of administration and economic exploitation
easier. In the early spring of 1942 Himmler obtained almost complete
effective control over Frank, and insisted on immediate action to
exterminate Jews, which, tragically, was done, and on germanisation,

beginning in Lublin province in south-east Poland. Some vaguely German peasants had been identified in the neighbouring Ukrainian province of Volhynia, and in 1943 Himmler ordered their forcible removal to Lublin province to farms from which Poles had been evicted. Many of the latter turned to guerrilla warfare, and agricultural production in the province almost ceased. Its Nazi governor resigned in despair.[44]

In the two Scandinavian countries that fell to German arms in 1940, Denmark and Norway, Germany did not formulate comprehensive war aims, except for Himmler with his clear vision of a Germanic community of 120 million. (There were, at most, 90 million Germans in Europe.) Perhaps because of its smallness and proximity to the Reich, Hitler favoured the annexation of Denmark as 'a German province', whether its people were the stuff from which Germans could be made or not.[45] In Norway he had two definite aims. The northern port of Trondheim must be annexed as a naval base, a 'German Singapore', with an autobahn connecting it to the Reich; and the country should expand its production of hydro-electric power to supply the whole of northern Europe – again the Nazi concern for the environment. Until almost the end, Germany did not even pretend that Norway might regain its full independence. Then, in late January 1945, the Norwegian fascist leader, Quisling, visited Hitler in Berlin, and returned triumphant to Oslo with a statement from the Fuhrer that he had guaranteed that Norway would be restored to full independence after Germany had won the war.[46]

In the 'Benelux' countries, occupied in May 1940, the easiest item of business was Luxembourg, which was earmarked for annexation and germanisation from the first. In the interests of racial purity Himmler in 1941 approved a proposal that the large Italian minority in the former grand duchy was to be repatriated as soon as the war ended. The Netherlands was the 'Germanic' country that many Nazis were most ready to acknowledge as nearest to being actually German. The evil treaty of Westphalia had cut it adrift, and its degenerate ruling class had been seduced by overseas commerce and English and French culture. However, the resentment of most Dutch against German occupation was manifest, and the Dutch Nazis under Anton Mussert were nationalists who wanted a Greater Netherlands including Belgian Flanders and some French territory in a very loose association with Germany. The Germans concentrated on economic exploitation and suppressing resistance, while Himmler brooded on the wholesale postwar transfer of the Dutch population to the east as the best means of germanising them.[47] With his doubts about the

Germanic concept, Hitler felt no instinctive preference for one of the two component peoples of Belgium, the Germanic inhabitants of Flanders, over the other, the Francophone Walloons. He chose pragmatists, and not Nazi ideologues, to head both the military and civilian administrations in Belgium. However, by May 1942 he had decided that Belgium, the Netherlands and much of northern France must be annexed to the Reich and somehow 'reclaimed' racially for Germany. Pragmatism crept in as the war worsened. In 1943 Hitler and Himmler gave their permission for the quite large numbers of Walloons who had volunteered to join the SS to be allowed to do so. The latter expressed his pleasure at being able to witness 'the renaissance movement of a basically Germanic people'.[48]

In France, after its defeat, German aims were clearest in Alsace-Lorraine and in the 'closed' or 'forbidden' part of the occupied half of the country from the Pas-de-Calais in the north-west to Besançon in the south-east. Alsace-Lorraine was incorporated into Germany in 1940 (though not formally annexed), while it was intended that the rest should also be fully incorporated. It was recognised that most of the population in the closed zone, who were referred to in Nazi documents as 'trash', and many in Alsace-Lorraine would have to be expelled because they lacked any German chromosomes. The rest were to be divided into those with doubtful racial credentials, who were to be resettled in former Polish or Soviet territory, and those with more certain credentials who could remain. Massive numbers of Germans from the Old Reich would have to be brought in, leading to an eventual population ratio of sixty Reich Germans to forty *Volk* or local Germans.[49] As far as the rest of France was concerned, Hitler dismissed it as an irrelevance with the exception of some Atlantic ports that he intended to annex as naval bases. In September 1941 he told Otto Abetz, the German ambassador to France, that after the Soviet Union had been crushed he would need very little from the rump French state: 'Germany would gain so much territory and so many raw materials in the east that she would not need France at all.'[50]

The high tide of German victories in the west in 1940 is a convenient point at which to consider a series of German war aims that were to be largely or completely unrealised. If Hitler could not trouble himself to formulate war aims for the greater part of France when he could essentially do what he liked with that country, it is not surprising that he lacked comprehensive aims for a Britain that was undefeated. With a continental empire achieved or within Germany's grasp, there was some hope that Britain would tire of a hopeless war.

From 1940 Goebbels developed the obviously not new theme of Britain's utter detachment from the continent of Europe, which it would never understand and which it must abandon its malign wish to dominate.[51] In general, it would simply be misleading to argue that Germany or Hitler had intentions towards Britain so definite that they can be termed war aims. A rare example of a definite aim against Britain is the exception that proves the rule because it referred to occupied territory, the Channel Islands. They were to be annexed to the Reich and their population deported. They would serve as a naval base and as a resort for Germans on holiday.[52]

On colonial war aims, Hitler yet again found it difficult to rouse himself to take an interest. He could not ignore the fervent desire for a colonial empire in some sections of the Nazi Party, the Foreign Ministry and, especially difficult to ignore, the navy. He himself accepted that Germany would need a colonial empire to be fully rounded as a world power, but his chief colonial interest was in balancing the competing claims of France, Spain and Italy to gain or keep their support. (It may be presumed that Hitler was unaware of Ribbentrop's demand to Spain in September 1940 that it should cede Spanish Guinea, its small colony in the Gulf of Guinea, to the Reich to round off a proposed German colony in equatorial Africa.[53] Hitler would have regarded endangering negotiations for Spain's entry into the war over this derelict and indefensible mainland enclave and offshore island as pure madness.) In March 1941 he did authorise the setting up of a de facto colonial ministry. The calculation was that, after the speedy defeat of the Soviet Union, France, Spain and Turkey could be dragooned into the war with Britain. If Britain quickly made peace it need only lose a few colonies. According to the testimony of one of the generals at his court, Franz Halder, Hitler felt no enthusiasm for the break up of the British Empire because the main beneficiaries would include America, Japan and others more than Germany.[54] Even so, if Britain did fight on after Russia had fallen, it would lose a great many of its colonies, of which Germany would keep some, while, as noted, giving some to Italy, Spain and perhaps Vichy France, apart from whatever America and Japan might seize. One reason for being lukewarm about colonies for Germany was racial and sexual. The thought of German troops in tropical colonies having sexual relations with native women was loathsome. Hitler did not trust his Germans to follow what he admired as the British practice in India of staying socially and sexually aloof from the native masses.[55]

Essentially, Hitler, in the second half of 1940, far from being drunk with success, was in a defensive frame of mind in relation to the west. He wanted to consolidate what he had gained there, and did not want more expansion except for certain steps to safeguard the gains that had been made. He spoke, probably with some sincerity, to Spanish foreign minister Serrano Suner about the need for a 'European Monroe Doctrine' to protect the old world from the new. To Soviet foreign minister Molotov (of all people) he expatiated about the need to prepare Europe for defence against an 'Anglo-Saxon power which had a more solid foundation, by far, than England . . . It was not a question of the immediate future; not in 1945 but in 1970 or 1980 at the earliest, would the freedom [sic] of other nations be seriously endangered by this Anglo-Saxon power.' But it was necessary now to take action against Anglo-Saxon 'attempts to acquire dangerous bases'.[56] What Hitler feared was a powerful US, aided by a Britain that was somehow motivated both by Jewish machinations and by a sense of Anglo-Saxon racial solidarity, attacking 'his' Europe, probably long after he had died. To counter this, he sought from Spain the outright cession of one of the Canary Islands for Germany to establish a naval base on it, and for Spain to agree that, in the peace settlement with France, it should moderate its demand for the whole of French Morocco to allow Germany to acquire the great port of Casablanca, which it would also need for a naval base. In the meantime Spain should allow Germany to station two motorised divisions in Spanish Morocco, so that French Morocco and Algeria could be occupied with lightning speed if Vichy or its proconsuls in North Africa showed signs of going over to the 'Anglo-Saxons'. The entire aim was one of defensive consolidation in western Europe, and not one of seeking a springboard for more expansion into the western hemisphere or Africa. Spain's refusal in December 1940 to enter the war or to accede to any of Hitler's requests left the south-western flank of the new German western empire simply undefended for the time being. This was a fact of which President Franklin Roosevelt took careful note and great advantage after America entered the war. Hitler, for his part, intended to occupy Gibraltar and, almost certainly, French Morocco as soon as the campaign in European Russia was successfully concluded.[57]

The entry of Italy into the war in 1940 and the fond belief that Germany would soon be in control of the Transcaucasus region of the Soviet Union compelled it to consider its aims in the Middle East. It had at least to pretend that it recognised Italy's claims to hegemony in this area, and a Foreign Ministry memorandum in August 1940 defined Germany's interests as restricted to a share in oil resources, air routes and 'archaeological activities'.[58] As on the south-west flank, Germany's main concern was with defensive arrangements to safeguard a largely European Nazi empire. The Italian military performance inspired little confidence that it could fulfil the role that Germany had initially been willing to assign to it. The Germans thought that taking over Britain's position in Egypt and the Anglo-Egyptian Sudan would stretch Italian capacities to their limit. They inclined more and more to favour Turkey as the regional hegemon with 'important and honourable duties' in guarding the south-west flank of the new Europe. In return, Turkey could recover whatever territory it wanted from the former Ottoman domains in Syria and Iraq, could share power with Germany in the Caucasus, and could gorge at the expense of Greece, annexing the eastern Aegean islands that Mustafa Kemal would have liked to include in his republic. Palestine, Lebanon and the rumps of Syria and Iraq could become independent Arab states. However, the Nazis were clear in their minds that the Arabs were racially inferior, and there would, there-fore, be no pleasure to be had from helping them in anything except for the extermination of Jews in their region. Germany would almost certainly have accepted with alacrity any British peace offer that required it to recognise the pre-eminence that Britain had gained in the Arab Middle East as a result of the First World War.[59] The last episode in German involvement in this area was the occupation of Tunisia in November 1942, following the Anglo-American landings in north-west Africa and the British victory at El-Alamein. Germany had no political ambitions in this French protectorate except to seek to keep a balance between the competing claims of the Vichy regime, Italy and Tunisian nationalists. Even so, Hitler intended the occupa-tion to be long term and to serve as a springboard for the occupation of much of the rest of North Africa. The aim of defending the German position in Europe was again paramount.[60]

If the Nazis could not easily sympathise with Arab nationalism, neither could they, especially Hitler, with Indian. He regarded British rule in India, as he understood it, as, in many ways, a model for the raj that he planned in Russia, though German rule there would be much more ruthless – a word of the highest praise in the Nazi lexicon – than the British had ever been in India.[61] German propaganda criticisms of British imperialism decreased from 1941 as the Nazi empire took shape, with little pretence that its methods would be squeamish. Early in 1942 Hitler rejected a Japanese proposal, supported by Ribbentrop, that the two countries should proclaim the independence of India as a joint war aim. Much of the impetus for this came from

Subhas Chandra Bose, an important politician in India, who had sought refuge in Germany. Hitler's rebuff of Bose, whom he was happy to send by U-boat to Japan, was partly because he still hoped for peace with the British if he could convince them that he did not wish to deprive them of their empire and as they gradually came to realise that the outcome of their alliance with the US would be one of their empire 'gradually becoming a colony of the American Jews'. Partly it was because he found the idea of supporting a brown people's struggle repellent. The German propaganda machine did eventually start to make noises in favour of Indian independence, but Hitler could still express praise for British rule in the subcontinent as late as March 1945.[62]

Hitler's reference to Jewish rule in the US provides a convenient point at which to discuss his war aims towards that country. Little in German war aims is more difficult to pin down. Certainly there was a transition from regarding the US in the late 1930s as a racially mixed and therefore unpleasant country, but one which, presided over by a leader who was a harmless windbag, could be largely ignored, to a growing fear of America after war started in September 1939. Hitler regarded a showdown as ultimately inevitable but not likely before 1970 or 1980, by which time he would be dead and Britain would probably have broken with the US after it had committed such enormities as annexing Canada. Such was his view in the autumn of 1940. A year later, he had become convinced that the US, with Jewish influences in the ascendant, was going to attack his European order within months or even weeks.[63] The deluded and repulsive nature of Hitler's opinions about the US being controlled by Jews must not be allowed to obscure the fact that, on all the evidence, the German dictator actually believed this to be the case. Thus, on 11 December 1941 Hitler and Mussolini simultaneously made speeches at the same time as their envoys in Washington were handing in war declarations at the State Department. Mussolini, speaking from his accustomed balcony, made a speech whose content was relatively rational, stressing the value of Japan to the common cause. Hitler, speaking for hours to the Reichstag, made only a few references to Japan, and placed 'Jewry' at the forefront of his reasons for declaring war on America. Not content with creating Bolshevism and the Soviet Union, 'Jewry' had, asserted Hitler, taken over full control of the US since Roosevelt had become president, and was aiming at an 'un-limited, world-governing dictatorship'. It would have been necessary to go to war with this menace 'even if we were not allied with Japan'. The impression of irrationality is reinforced by the fact that when

Hitler conferred with the Japanese ambassador, Oshima, on 3 January 1942 he outlined some ideas on how the two countries might defeat Britain, but admitted that he had no idea how to defeat the US, on which he had so recently declared war.[64]

In one respect Hitler had been realistic. In encouraging Japan to make war on America for months before Pearl Harbor, he did not, aware of the Japanese lack of interest in anti-Semitism, mention the Jews. He had dwelt more generally to Oshima in June 1941 on the mortal threat that their countries faced from the US 'in its new imperialistic spirit'.[65] Yet an awareness that, in taking on America, he might bring on ruin would seem to be reflected in his statement in January 1942 that the only alternatives for Germany were victory or ruin, implying that the latter was possible: 'If the German nation is not ready to engage itself for its self-preservation, very well, then let it disappear.'[66] The key to understanding is that Hitler thought that 'Jewry' had left him with no alternative but to declare war. The only conclusion that can be reached is that Hitler, with his deluded mindset, had no war aims towards the United States except for defence against what he imagined to be Jewish-instigated American aggression against Germany.

In the early spring of 1941 Germany carried out a hastily improvised but brilliantly successful campaign of conquest in Yugoslavia and Greece. War aims had to be improvised, and ranged from ones that arose almost without consideration to others in areas where there was no obvious goal to aim at either in Nazi ideology or German national interest. In the former category, it was almost a reflex action to incorporate former Habsburg territories in the extreme north of Yugoslavia into the Reich, though, like Alsace-Lorraine in the west, they were not formally annexed. Actual germanisation was recognised as a challenge. The Nazi authorities counted only 27,000 'full' Germans in a population of 550,000 in the incorporated territory, and, as the war went on, they constantly revised upwards their estimates of the number of Slavs who could be germanised and therefore allowed to remain.[67] Italy was recognised as the dominant power in mid-former Yugoslavia (Croatia and Bosnia-Herzegovina) and in most of Greece, though Germany occupied and would probably have permanently kept the great port of Salonika, south-east Europe's outlet to the Aegean. There was no obvious place in Nazi schemes for Serbia, though Germany might have permanently retained Belgrade as a strong point on the lower Danube.[68]

For Germany these were distractions as the country prepared to achieve its supreme aim of an empire in the Soviet Union, in which the key words were to be *Lebensraum* and *Untermensch*. Public discussion of the former was taboo in Germany from 1933 until it was allowed to reappear as a theme in regime propaganda in late 1938, partially camouflaged as 'class struggle among nations'.[69] The 'theory' of the Russians and many of the other Soviet peoples as subhuman *Untermenschen*, who were fit only to be slaves, naturally had to await the initiation of the Soviet–German war before it was publicly broadcast, but it had permeated Gernan society since long before that and provided a kind of 'moral' basis for the war aims against Soviet Russia that were being drawn up. Besides racial 'science', history was also invoked from the very ancient (proto-Germans had supposedly lived in southern Russia in pre-Christian times and so Germany would merely be reclaiming what rightfully belonged to it) to the more modern (the Russians had placed themselves beyond the pale when their invading army massacred East Prussian civilians in August 1914 and when they fomented the Bolshevik–Spartacist upheavals in Germany in 1918–19).[70] Perhaps most bizarre of all was the argument whose starting point was that southern Russia had been Europe's granary between 1900 and 1913, including the production of large quantities of animal feedstuffs whose importation had enabled German farmers to produce the meat and bacon for which Germans craved. The Bolshevik withdrawal of Russia from the European economy had made it impossible for this state of affairs to be resumed except at the cost of mass starvation in Russia, for which Judaeo-Bolshevism, and not National Socialism, would ultimately be to blame. Germans were as entitled to meat and bacon in the future as they had been before 1914. So were other west Europeans, except that they, unlike the Germans, would have to pay for it. At a conference of senior officials, presided over by Goering in November 1941, it was decided that southern Russian food surplus to German requirements should be sold at a great profit to other European countries: 'This will also open up a source of income for the Reich that will enable us to repay in a few years a substantial proportion of the debt incurred to finance the war, while sparing the German taxpayer as far as possible.'[71]

Setting aside the historical absurdity and cynical greed of this last point, there was an element of faint stirrings of conscience in some Germans who were involved in this enterprise about war aims that the world had been spared since the time of Genghis Khan and his Mongol hordes. These can also be detected in Hitler's nominee as Minister for the Occupied Eastern Territories, Alfred Rosenberg, who remarked to the staff of his fledgling ministry on the eve of the invasion that, although harsh times faced Russia, which he referred to as 'Muscovy', it could find salvation if it were to 'turn its face to the East again' – to the 'Siberian outback'. For the voice of Nazism unencumbered by conscience or a compulsion to resort to double think, attention may turn to Himmler, who, a few days earlier than Rosenberg spoke, had told a conference of top SS commanders at his castle at Wewelsburg that the forthcoming invasion would determine for all time whether Germany would become a great world power – actually a correct statement – and that it would open the way for the end of the Jewish presence in Europe and for the Soviet Slav population to be reduced by 20–30 million.[72]

What made the war aims brew being concocted for Russia so potent was that it was a German, and not only a Nazi, preparation. If Hitler and Nazi ideologues were fixated on settling millions of Germans as peasants in the 'East' (and were undeterred by security service 'situation reports' and other evidence that almost no Germans wanted to become farmers there), there were many more in Germany who craved for the 'spatial unassailability' that an empire in the east would supposedly provide, both in the east itself, where enemies could be held at bay thousands of kilometres from the Reich, and in the west because eastern raw materials would nullify any attempted maritime blockade of Germany. German historians have shown that German big business wanted possession of the east from 1933, that is from as soon as there was a government that might give it to them. In 1940–1 many firms participated in planning for the invasion with a view to the earliest possible obtaining of resources in which they were particularly interested, and were generally delighted to learn that ruthlessness would be employed in securing it. Oil was a particular magnet. Russia had it in the Caucasus, and it was intolerable that Stalin could cut off supplies from this source at any time. German generals and admirals also needed oil and listened to Hitler's arguments that the conquest of Russia would force Britain to yield (which they found persuasive), and that if Germany did not attack the Jewish–Bolshevik regime in Russia first it would sooner or later attack Germany (which they regarded as self-evidently true).[73]

The food situation in Germany in the winter of 1940–1 was extremely difficult.[74] However, the manner in which the economic departments of the German state bureaucracy (acting wholly independently of Hitler apart from the very general point that they knew that the Fuhrer favoured ruthlessness) proposed to solve it for the next winter beggars belief. Very briefly, the food surplus areas of the Soviet Union would send all their output to Germany except for the barest minimum needed to keep the peasants alive. Towns and cities in these areas would be denied food and their populations would perish unless they could find work on the land. Denied food supplies, the population in the food-deficient areas would perish unless they fled out of European Russia. After depopulation and after they had pillaged these areas and destroyed any assets that could not be removed, the Germans would leave them. The planners recognised that Germany did not have the manpower to occupy the whole of even European Russia, in which, in any case, many areas were not worth occupying. The problem of what to do with them would be solved by turning them into an uninhabited wilderness. A planning document produced in Goering's Four Year Plan office a few weeks before the invasion and entitled the 'Green File' noted matter of factly that: 'Many tens of millions of people in the industrial areas [of Russia] will become redundant and will either die or emigrate to Siberia.'[75]

In the areas that were to be permanently occupied, the existing rural population would remain as peasant serfs except in vast areas to be colonised by Germans in the form of ribbons of settlement along autobahns that would extend through the Ukraine and eastwards as far as the Urals and the lower Volga. Some colonisation projects would have priority, most notably the Crimean peninsula, whose germanisation was one of Hitler's obsessions. Although most colonisation would be in the fertile south, there would also be a northern colony, to be known as Ingermanland, to the south of Leningrad, which city was to be completely erased. This area was highly food deficient, and would presumably have served as one of the racial 'walls' to which Himmler, the germanisation supremo, was addicted. An idea of the demographic devastation that the Ingermanland project would have entailed may be gleaned from the fact that, whereas the colony was projected to have a German population of 200,000, the population of the city of Leningrad alone had been 3.2 million in the Soviet 1939 census. Many non-Slavic and non-Asiatic Soviet minorities were to be offered a tolerable place in Nazi aims. The Nazis being the Nazis, there had to be a strong element of absurdity in this. By early 1942 German eastern 'experts' were working hard in looking for long-submerged non-Slav ethnic groups in occupied territory. These were to be revived, if they had ever really existed in the first place, in a policy of ethnogenesis. Among minority nationalities that did exist, the most favoured were probably the Estonians who were considered to be suitable for wholesale germanisation because of the infusion into them over the centuries of much good Swedish blood. However, ethnic or *Volk* Germans living in conquered Soviet territory were not considered suitable to serve as a nucleus for germanisation. They were to be resettled in the Reich and settlement in the east was to be done with Reich Germans, untouched by any Soviet experience.[76]

As an exasperated as well as horrified German historian has pointed out, the economic exploitation aim as formulated before the invasion started made no sense even in its own terms. Large-scale food production for export can only work within a wider, modern infrastructure (to manufacture and service tractors and combine harvesters, to take one obvious example).[77] Even so, the complete seriousness of the aim cannot be doubted. Early in the invasion, when it appeared to be going well, Field Marshal von Bock, the commander of the army group driving towards Moscow, was startled to receive a visit at his command headquarters by two high Nazi Party officials who told him that forty million 'surplus' Russians were to be starved to death and that all who remained were to become slaves.[78] Apart from the Jews, the category of Soviets who bore the brunt of this intention were the 3.9 million Soviet prisoners of war who were captured during the first six months of the war, of whom, according to a Soviet estimate of February 1942, only 1.1 million survived by that date.[79] There would have been genuine problems in feeding such numbers, and therefore they were an obvious starting point for the aim of starving 'surplus' population to death, besides large numbers who were shot for racial or political reasons after a crude screening process. In September 1941, not content with a mortality rate from starvation and disease of 1 per cent per day in some of the camps for Soviet prisoners, the chief administrator of German POW camps, Lieutenant General Hermann Reinecke, a Nazi careerist, issued a directive for guards in the camps to look for opportunities to shoot prisoners on the slightest pretext, and threatening any guards who showed indulgence to prisoners with punishment.[80] It might be added that the Soviet regime, which regarded prisoners as traitors, lent a helping hand by sending the Red air force to bomb the vast concentrations of prisoners behind German lines.[81]

The failure of the Barbarossa plan to achieve anything resembling its objective – the conquest of most of European Russia within three months – left little alternative but to reconsider the original war aims in the Soviet Union. Not surprisingly, Hitler was loath to admit the need for modification. In September 1941, when appointing the gauleiter of East Prussia, the coarse even by Nazi standards Erich Koch, to be his Reichskommissar in the Ukraine, he told him that one of his first duties, which was mercifully not actually to be carried out, must be to destroy the cities and industries of his new dominion; 'hardly anything will be left standing in Kiev', according to the notes of an aide at Fuhrer headquarters.[82] Yet even Hitler had to do some rethinking after the failure of the offensive to capture Moscow in December 1941. Plans for wiping out the population in whole areas were shelved in a situation in which the Reich needed as many live Soviets as it could find for use as slave labour. The attractions of using Soviet industrial plants for the German war effort were also irresistible. Yet it was only a transition from an aim of extermination to one of more widespread slavery than had originally been envisaged. A meeting of Eastern Ministry officials in February 1942 was fascinated by the analogy of ancient Sparta, with its rigid hierarchy: 'The Germans will be the Spartans, the middle class, consisting of Letts, Estonians, etc., will be the *perioikoi*, while the Russians will be the helots [slaves].'[83]

Plans for a great summer offensive in southern Russia in the summer of 1942, with the Caucasus oilfields as the biggest prize, were accompanied by discussion about the type of regime to be set up in the areas that were soon to be conquered. Client states, not outright colonies, were accepted as a possibility in some of the lands that lay outside the zones of intended German colonisation, and, during their brief occupation of the Northern Caucasus and the Volga steppes, the Germans were to display a superficial benevolence to the Muslim and Buddhist nationalities in those areas that was to cost those peoples dear after Soviet power had returned. The military crisis for the Germans of the winter of 1942–3, culminating in the surrender of the remnants of the Sixth Army at Stalingrad, led to a determined effort by some senior military commanders on the eastern front and some sympathetic officials in the German government to press for a proclamation to all the inhabitants in occupied Soviet territory, signed by Hitler himself, promising reforms, including the end of the collective farms, which the Germans had retained as the best way of exploiting the peasants, proper schools and education, and political independence. Hitler may have wavered after Stalingrad, but the stabilisation of the front by March confirmed his intuition that a defeat inflicted on Europe's highest race by one of its most inferior could only be a freak that would not be repeated.[84] He refused and continued to refuse into the spring and summer, even after it was suggested to him that such a declaration need be nothing but a pack of lies, to be dishonoured after Germany was back on the path to victory. He asserted that the announcement of liberal aims would confuse the German soldier about what he was fighting for,

would win less support from the racially degenerate occupied populations than the continued application of the whip, and might set
in motion a process of abandoning the original aims that even he, the
Fuhrer, might find it difficult to reverse.[85] In November 1943, with
German forces ejected from most Soviet territory, Hitler rejected a
proposal to make an insincere offer of independence to the racially
not unsound peoples of Estonia and Latvia, among whom there was
burning hatred of the Soviet regime that could be utilised. He ruled
that these lands were to become part of the Reich, and that there must
not be even the temporary pretence of anything else.[86]

What lay behind this was an ineradicable desire in the supreme
Nazi leadership to commit murder, enslavement, deportations and
resettlement of entire populations in the 'East' in the conviction that
only thus could Germany be great or even survive. On 23 November
1942, the day that the encirclement of the Sixth Army was completed,
Himmler proclaimed that the East would be 'today a colony, tomorrow a settlement area, the day after tomorrow part of the Reich'. This
would lead to a 'Gothic-Franconian-Carolingian Reich' that would
stretch from the Atlantic to the Urals.[87] Hitler, speaking about war
aims with, for the first time, full candour to senior generals on the eve
of the battle at the Kursk salient in July 1943, which was intended to
reverse Germany's fortunes on the eastern front, told them that the
morale of the common soldier required 'positive war aims' and that
those remained what they had been when Barbarossa was launched:
'We need Lebensraum. This must be made clear: the fight, gentlemen,
is a fight for Lebensraum. Without this Lebensraum the German
Reich and the German nation cannot endure.'[88]

Defeat at Kursk and the westward advance of the Red Army did
not produce any change in Hitler's war aims. During the later part of
the war, he combined a fair degree of realism about the immediate
situation with wholly unrealistic dreams about ultimate victory. He
had a surprising ability to infect his entourage with his delusions.[89]
Members of this inner circle noted in March and April 1944 that their
Fuhrer was aching to reconquer Russia. He told them that, after the
Anglo-American threat in the west had been defeated, he would
switch forces from France to the east, step up armaments production
(especially of tanks), and carry out in 1945 the full conquest of Russia
that had eluded him in 1941. In the meantime, those western Soviet
border territories still in German hands must be retained.[90] The
victories of Anglo-American forces in France from June still did not
produce a change. The day after the failure of the 20 July bomb plot to
kill Hitler, Himmler issued a message to officers under his command,

restating the fundamental aim of resisting the 'Asiatic' onslaught against European civilisation, and of 'the expansion of our settlement space. In the course of the next few years we will at least recover what we have lost in Russia. Defensive borders will be created, the east will become a troop-training area where every division will be able to engage in keen exercises against [partisan] bands at least once a year or at least twice yearly.'[91] Himmler, Hitler and a substantial portion of the German nation pinned their hopes on splits in the enemy alliance, miracle weapons and the still potent myth of German racial superiority, according to which the country could not ultimately fail to achieve aims upon which it had set its heart.[92] In late August Hitler told some close associates that the irreducible boundaries of the Reich and surrounding colonial dependencies were, until the time came for reconquest in the east, to be the Somme to the west, the Alps to the south, southern Norway to the north and in the east along the front between the Baltic and the Carpathian mountains, including western Hungary.[93]

A kind of realism in German war aims occurred in the summer of 1944 when Himmler decided to extend his patronage to A. A. Vlasov, a Red Army general who had been seeking German support to form an anti-Soviet Russian army since his capture in 1942. Germany had had vast numbers of Soviet captives and defectors working for it since that date but mostly not on the war fronts and with no political recognition. In September 1944 Himmler authorised Vlasov to set up a Russian Liberation Army (RLA), which the SS would arm and equip. In Prague in November it issued its manifesto. This called for 'an honourable peace with Germany', denounced Anglo-American 'plutocrats', and set out a programme of self-determination for the different nationalities of the Soviet Union, and 'the setting up of a new, free democratic order without Bolsheviks and without exploiters'. On 28 January 1945 Hitler, no doubt through gritted teeth, appointed Vlasov officially as commander-in-chief of the RLA, and it fought ferociously against the Red Army for the next two months before giving up the struggle and seeking refuge from Soviet vengeance (in vain except for a few who found it in the principality of Liechtenstein). An instructive sidelight on the RLA is provided by the Vlasov air force. The Germans decided that the RLA would be incomplete without an air arm, and an order for the setting up of one was signed on 19 December 1944 by Goering in his capacity as commander of the Luftwaffe. About eighty Russian air force pilots responded to appeals to defect, and many of them were back in action on the German side towards the end of the war. These pilots included two, Antilevsky and Bychkov, who had been awarded the highest Soviet decoration for valour, the title of Hero of the Soviet Union. Theoretically, this was equivalent in British terms to two airmen who had been awarded the Victoria Cross defecting to Nazi Germany and then returning to the skies to fight their former comrades in the Royal Air Force. It illustrates the reservoirs of hatred for Stalin's tyrannical regime that existed to be tapped by a Germany that was willing even to pretend to offer the Soviet population liberation from communist oppression and a political and social system of their choice. By 1945 it was too late, even if the offer had been sincere.[94]

Hitler pinned much greater hopes on striking a devastating military blow against the western allies through the Ardennes hills, 'the Battle of the Bulge', which would supposedly cause them to perceive that the cost of defeating Germany was too high. Britain, as the weaker of the two allies, was the ultimate target, even though it was American troops who were to be subject to actual attack. The strategic aim of the offensive was to cut off and 'destroy' between twenty-five and thirty British divisions north of the corridor to the sea at Antwerp that the German onslaught would create. This would supposedly result in irresistible pressures in Britain to conclude an immediate compromise peace with Germany. Hitler explained this thinking to one of his favourites, SS Colonel Skorzeny, in late October 1944, adding that once the westerners had dropped out: 'Then he would concentrate all our forces in the east and in a few months remove the threat from that quarter for ever. Germany's historic destiny was to hold the fort against Asia.'[95]

The Ardennes offensive ended in inevitable failure in January. This caused the Nazi leadership to go into denial not only about the days of their regime being numbered but also about whether expansionist war aims needed to be completely abandoned. On 19 January, three days after cancelling further operations in the Ardennes, Hitler approved a plan drawn up by Ribbentrop and the Foreign Ministry for a peace move directed at the western allies under which Germany would retain not only Austria and the Czech Sudeten territories annexed in 1938, but also the western Polish provinces that it had annexed to the Reich in 1939. National Socialist rule in Germany was not negotiable, but Germany would be willing to rejoin the League of Nations. Senior German diplomats were sent to the capital cities of European neutrals with the hopeless mission of making contact with British and American representatives to discuss this important offer.[96] In the meantime, the westerners were to be made to continue to pay the fearsome cost of fighting Germans. This was done.

Contrary to legend, there was no faltering in the German military effort against the western allies' armies until almost the very end. Nazi war aims in the last phase of the Reich's existence would have been risible if they had not contributed to the prolongation of the war and cost thousands of lives.

ITALY

In September 1943 Hitler remarked that, 'Italy never was a power, is no power today and will not be a power in the future.'[97] There was an often unrecognised, medium-power defensive element in the aims that impelled Italy to enter the war in Europe on 10 June 1940. This centred on preserving the country as a fully independent state and, as a secondary aim, one under the continuing rule of the Fascist Party. Mussolini put a brave face on the *Anschluss* of March 1938 between Germany and Austria, but he and other Italians, many of them with unconcealed dismay,[98] realised that it had nullified Italy's most important gain from the Great War, the absence of a great power on the northern borders. After the signing of the Pact of Steel with Germany in May 1939 the Duce had told the army's assistant chief of staff that he feared that Germany might invade Italy. This fear of German aggression led him, in early 1940, to order the spending of one billion lire on fortifying the border with the Reich; 600 million were to be spent on the border with France. Mussolini feared attack from either a Germany that had achieved victory over Britain and France or from the democracies if they won the war and, having destroyed Nazism in Germany, regarded Fascism in Italy as an intolerable anachronism. Such an outcome appeared inconceivable in June 1940, but not several months earlier when Mussolini had decided to take Italy into the war.[99] Whether or not Mussolini was really 'Hitler's secret enemy', he undoubtedly distrusted 'the German world' whenever he contemplated the historical record of relations between Germans and Italians.[100]

Even so, there were also manifestly sources of ideological and geopolitical affinity between Italy and the Third Reich. The former's aspirations to make gains at the expense of Britain and France and in Africa and the Middle East did not clash with the eastwards thrust of German expansionist thinking. Where there was a clash, as in the Balkans, Italy could retreat to an extent and concentrate on making gains elsewhere. This applied particularly to Yugoslavia. The destruction of that country was, for Mussolini, an obsession, and he envisaged Italian power arising on its ruins, especially in Croatia. To aid this, he encouraged and financed 'promiscuous terrorism', especially by Croat fanatics like the ones who assassinated King Alexander in 1934.[101] But when Germany increased its influence in Yugoslavia in the late 1930s Mussolini could only watch with impotence, and console himself with completing the Italian grip on Albania and determining that Italy should have Greece.[102] Besides the evident availability of many other gains to the south, the northwest and even the north (in November 1938 Mussolini anticipated the annexation of the Ticino when Switzerland suffered the inevitable fate of small states in the modern world and was 'demolished'), there was also the ideological bond which the Duce acknowledged to an envoy of Hitler's in January 1936 when he spoke of a 'community of destiny' between the two regimes.[103] Even leaving aside the much studied subject of the regime's treatment of Jews, there was a very strong racist basis to Mussolini's version of Italian imperialism, which did not differ enormously from Nazi racist theorising and practice, at least about non-white peoples.[104]

Mussolini was heir to an Italian nationalist tradition, whose exponents included the nineteenth-century ideologue Guiseppe Mazzini, which held that Italy was naturally entitled to at least the status attained by the Roman Empire. Soon after the start of his time in office in 1922 he pondered whether Italy could aid a nationalist revolt against British rule in India as a means of weakening Britain generally so that it could be driven out of the Mediterranean, without which, he asserted, 'It is impossible for Italy to be prosperous and powerful.' The year 1929 found him wondering whether an alliance with (Weimar!) Germany could be used to prise France out of Corsica and Tunisia.[105] By the winter of 1938–9, in his addresses to the Fascist Grand Council, he was becoming ever more insistent on the need to acquire those French territories and the British Mediterranean colonies of Malta and Cyprus.[106] However, this could not be an end in itself but only the preliminary to making Italy an oceanic power, the Mediterranean being a mere sea. As early as 1926 or 1927 he had told a group of senior military figures that: 'A nation that has no free access to the sea cannot be considered a great power. Italy must become a great power.' In 1936 he told a Nazi visitor, Hans Frank, that British enslavement of Italy had to end: 'England is our jailer; it wants to hold us shackled in the Mediterranean.' By June 1940 the time had come to solve 'the problem of our maritime frontiers' and to 'break the military and territorial chains that suffocate us in our sea'. When King Victor Emmanuel had earlier advised caution, the Duce had replied that it was intolerable for Italy to be 'de facto a British colony'.[107]

It is small wonder that these ill-concealed Italian ambitions produced a real and lasting antagonism towards Italy in imperial-minded British politicians like Anthony Eden and senior diplomats like Maurice Peterson. The latter was sent on a mission to Rome in late 1933 to negotiate a precise border between Libya and the Anglo-Egyptian Sudan. He found Italy 'in the grip of an extreme nationalism', and its negotiators made such extreme demands that Peterson felt compelled to break off talks with the quip that it was generous of the Italians to allow Britain to retain Khartoum.[108] Peterson would not have been wrong if he had supposed that Mussolini actually wanted the Sudanese capital. In March 1935 he told the industrialist Alberto Pirelli that the impending conquest of Ethiopia would be only a first step, to be followed by driving Britain out of Egypt and Sudan and 'an empire that stretched from the Mediterranean to the Indian Ocean'.[109]

Finally, it is important to note two considerations. The first is that these 'blindly and dogmatically geopolitical' aims were to Mussolini not only valid in themselves but were also essential as a means of upturning Italian society, destroying the 'decadent' upper classes and the influence of the Catholic Church, and generally decivilising the Italian people and turning them into a master race of warrior brutes. In 1937 foreign minister Count Galeazzo Ciano recorded remarks of Mussolini's about his mission to remake 'the character of the Italians through combat'.[110] Second, and leaving aside all argument about whether the civilised and easygoing characteristics of the Italian people were intractable, Italy was grotesquely unprepared to realise either of the fundamental sets of war aims which have been described in the condition that it was in during the Second World War. Preserving real independence from Germany and not declining into a satellite could not be easy when the country had been impoverished by the costs of the Ethiopian war and Italian intervention in the Spanish Civil War between 1936 and 1939, which had left little money to modernise and build up the armed forces in preparation for another war. In a more general economic sense Italy's condition had become dire. It had had a gross national product half that of Germany's in 1933, but by 1939 that had fallen to only 18 per cent of German national income.[111] This military and economic weakness made it questionable whether expansionist war aims could be realised.

The difficulty in believing that Mussolini was really unaware in

1940 that Italy was, in almost every respect, dysfunctional for war has led to arguments about what he had in mind when he declared it on Britain and France on 10 June. The view that Mussolini entered a war that he thought to be almost over in order to make gains in the peace settlement after making little or no military effort has been championed by the late Mussolini biographer Renzo De Felice. The historian MacGregor Knox has argued powerfully for a very different interpretation in which a Mussolini who was unwilling or unable to comprehend the state's weakness was planning campaigns of conquest in loose alliance with Germany before that country achieved its victories in western Europe. In April 1940 he told a confidant that 'he' would fight great battles at sea and in the Balkans. By June, he did not want Britain to follow France in suing for an armistice. On the contrary, he wanted time to conquer Egypt from Britain, and informed Germany that no help from it would be needed except for some aerial support for the assault on Alexandria. He stressed to the military commander in Libya, Marshal Rodolfo Graziani: 'I repeat that at the peace table we shall take home with us only what we conquer militarily.'[112] Perhaps the last word belongs with the historian Denis Mack Smith, to whom Mussolini was guilty of 'unpardonable ignorance'; he deluded himself about what the Italian forces could do.[113] Before, however, their prosaic incapacity became painfully obvious even to the Duce, Italy had some bruising encounters with its new German comrades-in-arms.

Mussolini's letter to Hitler informing him that Italy would enter the war within days surprised the ambassador in Berlin, who had to deliver it, in that: 'Strange to relate, the message contained no expression of solidarity and no reference to the inevitability of a common victory . . . It ended with a simple and cordial declaration of comradeship.'[114] The implication that Italy would be proudly independent soon ran up against evidence that Germany expected it to be a compliant junior ally. In his first meeting with a senior Italian (ambassador Alfieri) now that Italy was at war, the Fuhrer's remarks were encouraging: the satisfaction of Italy's claims against France would be 'a matter of honour and an essential prerequisite for the establishment of peace between France and Germany'.[115] By the time Mussolini and Ciano met Hitler and Ribbentrop in Munich a few days later the line had changed. Hitler stated that the armistice terms for France would not be made harsher to realise immediately Italian territorial war aims. Ribbentrop warned Ciano that neither would Germany commit itself to supporting the acquisition of Egypt and Sudan by Italy, which might prolong the war with Britain for a purpose of no interest to Germany, and Hitler himself spoke about the desirability of preserving the British Empire. The only colony about whose loss to France Hitler did speculate was one in which Italy was not interested; Madagascar might become a Jewish state. Ciano urged on a perhaps bemused Ribbentrop that Germany should not make peace with Britain unless it agreed to the return of all the pre-1914 German colonies and that the Reich should consider annexing the Belgian Congo. No doubt the Italian thought that if Germany demanded major colonial gains for itself it would have to insist on others for Italy, whose acquisitions, if any, would therefore be a byproduct of German success.[116]

Further humiliation followed in July when Hitler rejected Mussolini's plea for Italian troops to be allowed to participate in the invasion of England – 'a desperate expedient to deny Hitler a purely bilateral settlement with Britain' – and in early October when Germany unilaterally moved troops into Romania to protect the oilfields from British air attack or a Russian incursion by land. It was this latter that caused Mussolini to order something that he had admittedly been contemplating for some time, an invasion of Greece, to be launched before the end of that month.[117] This was to coincide with a mighty offensive from Libya to drive the British out of Egypt. The Greek project was a natural move in terms of Mussolini's concept of Italian imperialist expansion, but, in its timing and in that of the offensive in North Africa, it was an Italian declaration of independence from Germany, as some Italian anti-fascist exiles noted. In a letter explaining the Greek move to Hitler, Mussolini demanded that France should not be allowed to re-enter the war on the Axis side, of which there were rumours, and that entry by Spain should be delayed. Mussolini knew that Franco was interested in acquiring French Morocco and at least part of Algeria, territories that he wanted for Italy, and he anticipated that after Italy had covered itself in military glory Germany would have to force France to hand over to it Nice, Corsica, Tunisia and French Somaliland as the first instalment of Italian war aims demands against that country.[118]

Catastrophic Italian failure in both Greece and North Africa, with the Greeks pressing into Albania and the British deep into Libya, ended Mussolini's hopes of real independence from, or equality with, Germany. He had to accept this, even though for him it was 'like a millstone round his neck'.[119] Italy had to scavenge for gains from German victories. Following the German conquest of Yugoslavia and Greece in the early spring of 1941 the Reich dictated partition arrangements for the former that, on paper, were favourable to Italy, which received the greater part of the overthrown state, including overlordship of the new and large state of Croatia, in which Bosnia was included. However, in practice Germany retained throughout former Yugoslavia whatever it thought that it needed for security, and looted or retained for itself whatever resources that it wanted. Italy's most tangible gain was that it directly annexed much of the Dalmatian coast, the main criterion for annexation being whether an area had belonged to the old Venetian republic.[120] There was a similar situation in occupied Greece: nominal Italian authority over the greater part of the country, actual German dominance over most of it. Meanwhile, there were plenty of other sources of humiliation. The embassy in Berlin was flooded with complaints from Italians who had volunteered to work in Germany that Nazi officials were warning them in direct terms that they were not allowed to have social or sexual relations with German women because Italians were racially inferior and any offspring would be degenerates.[121]

None of this nor the fact that Hitler had not informed him about the imminent German invasion of Russia at their meeting on 2 June deterred Mussolini from responding to that attack with an immediate Italian declaration of war on the Soviet Union. Like the Finns in the far north, this southern European had no conception of the annihilatory nature of German aims against Russia. Replying to Hitler's letter informing him of the invasion, he assumed that a Russian state would continue to exist, referring to 'a renewed Russia reduced in size' which could be brought 'into a circle of economic cooperation with the rest of Europe'. Privately, Mussolini hoped that the Soviets would fight the Germans to a standstill as the best means for Italy to recover real independence. For his part, Hitler told associates before Operation Barbarossa started that not the least of the benefits that it would confer would be that it would enable him to have minimal regard for Italian ambitions; the Italians had failed miserably and deserved little.[122] In November 1942 German troops moved into the unoccupied zone of France following the Anglo-American landings in French North Africa. Italy was at last allowed to occupy Corsica, and the King was no doubt not alone among Italians in rejoicing that his realm had at last acquired an island without which 'Italy would remain incomplete.'[123] Yet this was manifestly war aims reduced to a pathetic absurdity.

This is not the place to examine Italy's botched attempt to exit from the war in the summer of 1943 except to note that, while it was going on, the country's enemies, old and new, were closing in. The British foreign secretary Eden ('porco Eden' as some Italians called him, to his amusement) demanded extreme caution in dealings with Italy, even with Mussolini overthrown, because any Italian government would demand territorial integrity within the borders established in 1919 and the early 1920s, which, in his view, would be neither possible nor desirable.[124] The German response to Italian 'treachery' included the separation from it of some of its northern territories in which neither the Fascist Party nor Mussolini's Italian Social Republic, itself a puppet regime, was allowed to operate. The lands south of the Austrian Tyrol – the region of Trentino-Alto Adige in modern-day Italy – which it had gained from the former Habsburg Empire in the 1919 peace settlement became, together with the addition of the province of Belluno, the *Alpenvorland*, with the gauleiter of the part of Tyrol that Austria had been allowed to retain as high commissioner. Although, as with Alsace-Lorraine, there was no formal annexation to the Reich there could be little room for doubt that that would happen if Germany emerged victorious. Hitler himself remarked that Italian treachery had at least enabled the Reich to recover 'two beautiful German provinces'. Many of the ethnic German majority in the northern part of the region, the Upper Adige or South Tyrol, struck poses of racial superiority over the ethnic Italian population in a way that guaranteed that intercommunal relations after the war, when these provinces were returned to Italy, were certain to be tense.[125]

Further east, the obsessive Italian fear that Germany coveted Trieste became reality in October 1943 when the Julian region, including Trieste, was combined with formerly Yugoslav coastal territory in Slovenia and Dalmatia to form the dependency of *Adriatisches Küstenland* under the supervision of the gauleiter of the neighbouring German province of Carinthia. It was intended that at least part of the *Küstenland*, definitely including Trieste, should ultimately be annexed to the Reich.[126] During the later part of the Second World War, with a German client regime in the non-annexed north and a government that functioned under Anglo-American tutelage in the liberated south and centre, Italy reverted from statehood and dreams of empire to being the mere 'geographical expression' that that arch opponent of its national aspirations, the Austrian chancellor Metternich, had called it more than a century earlier.

Notes

1. Ludwig Dehio, *Germany and World Politics in the Twentieth Century* (London: Chatto, 1959), p. 37.

2. Richard Overy, *Interrogations: The Nazi Elite in Allied Hands, 1945* (London: Allen Lane/Penguin, 2001), p. 327.
3. Norman Rich, *Hitler's War Aims: The Establishment of the New Order* (London: Deutsch, 1974), p. 330; Gerald Reitlinger, *The House Built on Sand: The Conflicts of German Policy in Russia, 1939–45* (London: Weidenfeld, 1960), p. 200.
4. Research Institute for Military History (various contributors), *Germany and the Second World War: Volume I, The Build-up of German Aggression* (Oxford: Clarendon, 1990), pp. 35–7. Henceforward volumes in this invaluable series are referred to as *GSWW*.
5. Rohan D'O. Butler, *The Roots of National Socialism, 1783–1933* (London: Faber, 1941), p. 244.
6. Reitlinger, *House Built on Sand*, pp. 341–2. On the 1914 war aims programme see Fritz Fischer, *Germany's Aims in the First World War* (London: Chatto, 1967), pp. 98–119.
7. Z. A. B. Zeman, *Pursued by a Bear: The Making of Eastern Europe* (London: Chatto, 1989), p. 107.
8. MacGregor Knox, *Common Destiny: Dictatorship, Foreign Policy, and War in Fascist Italy and Nazi Germany* (Cambridge: Cambridge University Press, 2000).
9. Götz Aly and Susanne Heim, *Architects of Annihilation: Auschwitz and the Logic of Destruction* (London: Weidenfeld, 2002), p. 101.
10. Rich, *Hitler's Aims*, p. 15.
11. Clifton J. Child, 'The concept of the New Order', in Arnold and Veronica Toynbee (eds), *Hitler's Europe* (London: Oxford University Press, 1954), p. 61.
12. Aly and Heim, *Architects*, p. 73.
13. Gerwin Strobl, *The Germanic Isle: Nazi Perceptions of Britain* (Cambridge; Cambridge University Press, 2000), pp. 9–10, 16–18.
14. Grigory Deborin, *Thirty Years of Victory* (Moscow: Progress Publishers, 1975), p. 115. Walter Laqueur, *Russia and Germany: A Century of Conflict* (London: Weidenfeld, 1965), pp. 148–50, is illuminating. There is an older account of Hitler's early foreign policy thinking in Geoffrey Stoakes, *Hitler and the Quest for World Dominion: Nazi Ideology and Foreign Policy in the 1920s* (Leamington Spa: Berg, 1986), pp. 110–39, and a more recent one in Knox, *Common Destiny*, pp. 63–6, 72–8.
15. Peter Padfield, *Himmler: Reichsführer SS* (London: Cassell reprint, 2001), pp. 323–4.
16. Christian Streit, 'The German Army and the policies of genocide', in Gerhard Hirschfeld (ed.), *The Policies of Genocide: Jews and Soviet Prisoners of War in Nazi Germany* (London: Allen and Unwin, 1986), pp. 1–14. See also the account in Philippe Burrin, *Hitler and the Jews: The Genesis of the Holocaust* (London: Arnold, 1994).
17. This is developed in Aly and Heim, *Architects*.
18. Tim Cole, *Images of the Holocaust: The Myth of the 'Shoah' Business* (London: Duckworth, 1999), p. 170.
19. F. W. Winterbotham, *Secret and Personal* (London: Kimber, 1969), pp. 56–9. Sadly for von Reichenau, his long years sitting behind a desk planning invasion ill-prepared him for the rigours of campaigning in the Russian winter. In January 1942 he died in southern Russia from a stroke.
20. John Laughland, *The Tainted Source: The Undemocratic Origins of the European Idea* (London: Warner, 1998).
21. Mark Mazower, 'Hitler's New Order, 1939–45', *Diplomacy and Statecraft*, vol. 7, no. 1, 1996, pp. 29–30.

22. Laughland, *Tainted Source*, p. 15.
23. Mazower, 'New Order', p. 34; Anthony McElligott, 'Reforging Mitteleuropa in the crucible of war', in Peter Stirk (ed.), *Mitteleuropa: History and Prospects* (Edinburgh: Edinburgh University Press, 1994), p. 151; Nicolaus von Below, *At Hitler's Side: The Memoirs of Hitler's Luftwaffe Adjutant, 1937–1945* (London: Greenhill Books, 2001), p. 200.
24. Laughland, *Tainted Source*, pp. 128–32; Robert Edwin Herzstein, *When Nazi Dreams Come True: The Third Reich's Internal Struggle over the Future of Europe after a German Victory* (London: Abacus, 1982), p. 195.
25. Peter M. R. Stirk, 'The Idea of Mitteleuropa', and McElligott, 'Reforging Mitteleuropa', in Stirk (ed.), *Mitteleuropa*, pp. 18, 132–44; Herzstein, *Nazi Dreams*, pp. 105–7.
26. McElligott, 'Reforging Mitteleuropa', in Stirk (ed.), *Mitteleuropa*, pp. 144–50; Padfield, *Himmler*, pp. 206–8.
27. Herzstein, *Nazi Dreams*, pp. 131–6, 153.
28. Ibid. pp. 200–11, 225–47; Laughland, *Tainted Source*, pp. 32–9, 128–9.
29. Herzstein, *Nazi Dreams*, ch. 3; Padfield, *Himmler*, pp. 478, 481.
30. Overy, *Interrogations*, p. 325.
31. Herzstein, *Nazi Dreams*, pp. 74–80, 177–8.
32. Ibid. pp. 81–2, 87–8.
33. Ibid. p. 215.
34. Santi Corvaja, *Hitler and Mussolini: The Secret Meetings* (New York: Enigma Books, 2001), p. 218.
35. Von Below, *At Hitler's Side*, pp. 37, 41.
36. Rich, *Hitler's Aims*, pp. 14–20.
37. Strobl, *Germanic Isle*, pp. 62–3.
38. Rich, *Hitler's Aims*, pp. 29–48, 55.
39. Ibid. pp. 55–67.
40. Knox, *Common Destiny*, p. 106.
41. Anthony Rhodes, *The Vatican in the Age of the Dictators, 1922–1945* (London: Hodder, 1973), p. 309.
42. Padfield, *Himmler*, pp. 573–4.
43. Ibid. pp. 289–93, 301–2; Rich, *Hitler's Aims*, p. 77; Aly and Heim, *Architects*, p. 261.
44. Rich, *Hitler's Aims*, pp. 89–100.
45. Ibid. p. 112.
46. Ibid. pp. 131–40; Norman J. W. Goda, *Tomorrow the World: Hitler, Northwest Africa, and the Path toward America* (College Station: Texas A. & M. University Press, 1998), p. 27; Rowland Kenney, *The Northern Tangle: Scandinavia and the Post-War World* (London: Dent, 1946), p. 230.
47. Rich, *Hitler's Aims*, pp. 142–60.
48. Ibid. pp. 172–94.
49. Ibid. pp. 197–9, 210–11, 231–8.
50. Ibid. p. 222.
51. Strobl, *Germanic Isle*, pp. 209–14.
52. Rich, *Hitler's Aims*, pp. 398–9.
53. Goda, *Tomorrow the World*, pp. 74–5, 87–8.
54. V. Trukhanovsky, *British Foreign Policy during World War II, 1939–1945* (Moscow: Progress Publishers, 1970), p. 104.
55. Rich, *Hitler's Aims*, pp. 411–12; Herzstein, *Nazi Dreams*, pp. 23–5; Strobl, *Germanic Isle*, pp. 89–92. It is worth noting that the gap between this thinking and some in a liberal democracy like Britain was not unbridgeable. In the

fateful year 1933 a professor of history at the University of Oxford published a book in which he attributed the decline of Portugal in part 'to reckless intermarriage among the lower classes with the Congo nigger'. Sir Charles Oman, *Things I Have Seen* (London: Methuen, 1933), p. 167.

56. Goda, *Tomorrow the World*, pp. 88, 112.
57. Ibid. pp. 30–1, 66–7, 74–5, 78, 85–8, 92, 99, 122–31, 142–55, 175–81.
58. Rich, *Hitler's Aims*, p. 413.
59. Lukasz Hirszowicz, *The Third Reich and the Arab East* (London: Routledge, 1966), pp. 38–9, 214–16, 314–15.
60. Ibid. ch. XIV.
61. Strobl, *Germanic Isle*, pp. 59–64, 76, 89–92.
62. Ibid. pp. 173–6, 214–15; Herzstein, *Nazi Dreams*, pp. 220–5; Research Institute for Military History, *GSWW: Volume VI, The Global War* (Oxford: Clarendon, 2001), pp. 125, 132, 1207–8.
63. Victor Rothwell, *The Origins of the Second World War* (Manchester: Manchester University Press, 2001), ch. 13 attempts to summarise the evidence.
64. *GSWW: Vol. VI*, pp. 144–5, 175–6.
65. Research Institute for Military History, *GSWW: Volume IV, The Attack on the Soviet Union* (Oxford: Clarendon, 1998), p. 1046.
66. *GSWW: Vol. VI*, p. 130.
67. Rich, *Hitler's Aims*, pp. 268–73.
68. Ibid. pp. 289–94, 311–16.
69. *GSWW: Vol. I*, p. 116.
70. Alexander Dallin, *German Rule in Russia, 1941–1945: A Study in Occupation Policies*, 2nd edn (Basingstoke: Macmillan, 1981), p. 68; *GSWW: Vol. IV*, pp. 502–3.
71. Aly and Heim, *Architects*, pp. 235–41.
72. Ibid. p. 242; Richard Breitman, *Official Secrets: What the Nazis Planned, What the British and Americans Knew* (London: Penguin Books, 2000), p. 40.
73. *GSWW: Vol. IV*, pp. 32–4, 119, 161–3, 170, 320, 379–80, 518–21. Hitler endorsed the 'spatial unassailability' concept, though evidently as something of an afterthought. Ibid. p. 1235.
74. Ibid. pp. 187–9.
75. Reitlinger, *House Built on Sand*, p. 62.
76. The principal source for the account of these plans here is *GSWW: Vol. IV*, Chapters III and VII for the planning of these aims, and Chapters, VI and VII for the attempt to implement them. See also Dallin, *German Rule*: Rich, *Hitler's Aims*, ch. 11; and Michael Burleigh, *Germany Turns Eastwards: A Study of Ostforschung in the Third Reich* (London: Pan, 2002), pp. 202–4.
77. Rolf-Dieter Müller in *GSWW: Vol. IV*, p. 181.
78. Wilfried Strik-Strikfeldt, *Against Stalin and Hitler: Memoirs of the Russian Liberation Movement, 1941–1945* (London: Macmillan, 1970), pp. 39–40.
79. Reitlinger, *House Built on Sand*, p. 120.
80. Ibid. p. 109.
81. See 'Voinov', *The Autobiography of a Soviet Waif* (London: Harvill, 1955), pp. 216–17, for an account by one on the receiving end of the bombs.
82. Timothy Patrick Mulligan, *The Politics of Illusion and Empire: German Occupation Policy in the Soviet Union, 1942–1943* (New York: Praeger, 1988), p. 11.
83. Aly and Heim, *Architects*, p. 262.
84. David Irving, *Goebbels: Mastermind of the Third Reich* (London: Focal Point, 1996), pp. 418–19.
85. Mulligan, *Politics of Illusion*, pp. 49–52, 173–4; Dallin, *German Rule*, pp. 153–64.

86. Rich, *Hitler's Aims*, pp. 361–4.
87. *GSWW: Vol. VI*, p. 1208.
88. Mulligan, *Politics of Illusion*, p. 175.
89. *GSWW: Vol. VI*, pp. 134–8.
90. David Irving, *Hitler's War* (London: Hodder, 1977), p. 618.
91. Padfield, *Himmler*, p. 517.
92. Gerhard L. Weinberg, 'German plans for victory, 1944–1945', in his *Germany, Hitler and World War II: Essays in Modern German and World History* (Cambridge: Cambridge University Press, 1995), pp. 274–86. On the expected splits, see Field Marshal Keitel's testimony during Soviet interrogation in 1945 in Herman Rozanov, *Behind the Scenes of Third Reich Diplomacy* (Moscow: Progress Publishers, 1984), p. 25.
93. Heinrich Schwendemann, ' "Drastic measures to defend the Reich at the Oder and the Rhine . . .": a forgotten memorandum of Albert Speer of 18 March 1945', *Journal of Contemporary History*, vol. 38, 2003, p. 611.
94. Leonid Mlechin, 'Vlasov and Vlasovites', *New Times*, 44, 30 October–5 November 1990, pp. 36–40. The Prague manifesto is reproduced in Strik-Strikfeldt, *Against Stalin and Hitler*, pp. 258–63. In a speech to Gauleiters in October 1943 Himmler had told them that he had rejected overtures from 'that Russian swine Herr General Vlasov'. Padfield, *Himmler*, p. 467.
95. Otto Skorzeny, *Special Mission* (London: Futura, 1974), p. 145; see also Rozanov, *Behind the Scenes*, p. 30.
96. Rozanov, *Behind the Scenes*, pp. 49–59; Paul Schmidt, *Hitler's Interpreter* (London: Heinemann, 1951), p. 270.
97. R. J. B. Bosworth, *Italy and the Wider World, 1860–1960* (London: Routledge, 1996), p. 53.
98. Elizabeth Monroe, *The Mediterranean in Politics* (Oxford: Oxford University Press, 1938), pp. 239–40.
99. Luigi Villari, *Italian Foreign Policy under Mussolini* (New York: Devin-Adair, 1956), pp. 244, 248, 255–6, 266. Villari was a diplomat under the fascist regime; his book combines apologia with much of interest. On Mussolini's fears before June 1940 of a German attack see Dino Alfieri, *Dictators Face to Face* (London: Elek, 1954), p. 35. On his fears of attack by the democracies, especially Britain, see for the immediate prewar period Maxwell H. H. Macartney and Paul Cremona, *Italy's Foreign and Colonial Policy, 1914–1937* (London: Oxford University Press, 1938), pp. 325–9, and Brian R. Sullivan, 'More than meets the eye: the Ethiopian War and the origins of the Second World War', in Gordon Martel (ed.), *The Origins of the Second World War Reconsidered*, 2nd edn (London: Routledge, 1999), pp. 190–8.
100. Richard Owen, summarising a book by Fabio Andriola on *Mussolini: Hitler's Secret Enemy*, *Daily Telegraph*, 29 August 1997.
101. Esmonde M. Robertson, *Mussolini as Empire-Builder: Europe and Africa, 1932–36* (London: Macmillan, 1977), p. 24; Knox, *Common Destiny*, p. 123.
102. Sullivan in Martel (ed.), *Origins*, pp. 185–6.
103. Knox, *Common Destiny*, pp. 109, 142–3.
104. Luigi Preti, 'Fascist imperialism and racism', in Roland Sarti (ed.), *The Ax Within: Italian Fascism in Action* (New York: New Viewpoints, 1974), pp. 187–97.
105. Sullivan in Martel (ed.), *Origins*, p. 196; Knox, *Common Destiny*, pp. 21, 131.
106. MacGregor Knox, *Mussolini Unleashed, 1939–1941: Politics and Strategy in Fascist Italy's Last War* (Cambridge: Cambridge University Press, 1982), pp. 38–40.

107. Knox, *Common Destiny*, pp. 120, 142–5; Knox, *Unleashed*, pp. 96–7.

108. Sir Maurice Peterson, *Both Sides of the Curtain*, (London: Constable, 1950), pp. 97–8.

109. Knox, *Common Destiny*, p. 140; see also Knox, *Unleashed*, pp. 18–19.

110. Knox, *Common Destiny*, pp. 95–7, 146.

111. Sullivan in Martel (ed.), *Origins*, pp. 187–9.

112. MacGregor Knox, reviewing one of De Felice's volumes, in *Times Literary Supplement*, 26 February 1999; MacGregor Knox, 'The fascist regime, its foreign policy and its wars: an "anti-fascist" orthodoxy?', in Patrick Finney (ed.), *The Origins of the Second World War* (London: Arnold, 1997), p. 164; Knox, *Unleashed*, pp. 67–9, 200–2, 251–2.

113. Denis Mack Smith, *Italy and Its Monarchy* (New Haven: Yale University Press, 1989), pp. 289–91.

114. Alfieri, *Dictators*, pp. 38–9.

115. Ibid. p. 58.

116. Knox, *Unleashed*, pp. 126–33; Villari, *Foreign Policy*, p. 269; Schmidt, *Hitler's Interpreter*, pp. 177–8.

117. Knox, *Unleashed*, pp. 135, 140–3; Ray Moseley, *Mussolini's Shadow: The Double Life of Count Galeazzo Ciano* (New Haven: Yale University Press, 1999), pp. 113, 116.

118. Knox, *Unleashed*, pp. 197–203, 211, 222–3; 'Pentad', *The Remaking of Italy* (Harmondsworth: Penguin, 1941), p. 256.

119. Alfieri, *Dictators*, p. 97.

120. Elizabeth Wiskemann, *The Rome-Berlin Axis* (London: Collins/Fontana, 1966), pp. 318–26.

121. Alfieri, *Dictators*, p. 115.

122. Corvaja, *Hitler and Mussolini*, pp. 217, 223, 227, 245; Knox, *Unleashed*, p. 289.

123. Mack Smith, *Italy and Its Monarchy*, p. 297.

124. Richard Lamb, *Mussolini and the British* (London: Murray, 1997), pp. 305–7; for 'porco Eden' see *The Memoirs of Sir Anthony Eden: Full Circle* (London: Cassell, 1960), p. 184.

125. Antony Evelyn Alcock, *The History of the South Tyrol Question* (London: Joseph, 1970), pp. 60–77.

126. Bogdan C. Novak, *Trieste, 1941–1954: The Ethnic, Political, and Ideological Struggle* (Chicago: Chicago University Press, 1970), pp. 70–4.

3

Britain and France

This chapter will deal primarily with British war aims towards the country with which it went to war in 1939, Germany. It will conclude with a discussion of British and American aims – war aims would be a misnomer – towards France, and of the war aims of France itself in the various forms that that country took between 1939 and 1945 (independent state, Vichy regime, Free French movement). British aims in relation to the Soviet Union will figure in both this chapter and in Chapter 5 on Soviet war aims. British aims in relation to the United States will mostly be dealt with in the chapter on that country, though the point may be made at the outset that when Britain went to war its rulers did not expect, and in many cases did not want, that there would be a significant American dimension to the war or to peace terms. The assertion in a recent academic study that all the major participants in the Second World War other than Britain itself shared one war aim – 'They all wanted to dismantle the British Commonwealth'[1] – does not withstand examination except in the case of the US. The preceding chapter questioned whether it could apply to the war aims of Nazi Germany, and a later chapter will question its validity for the Soviet Union. Neville Chamberlain, prime minister until May 1940, desired only benevolent neutrality from the US, and even that more in appearance than in reality to keep Japan out of the war. He worried that the US would demand bases in British colonies in the western hemisphere and trade concessions to weaken the Empire as an economic unit, and even feared that America might offer in return only the cancellation of debts owed to it by Britain from the Great War, not aid in the new conflict.[2] Underlying this was the cumulative disillusionment of the British political elite with the

US between the two wars, which, in the view of Donald Cameron Watt, had, by 1939, reached such a pitch that occasional expressions of the need to court American goodwill had become 'a pointless concession to amiable post-prandial rhetoric'.[3] Besides such 'concessions', there were also deep fears, for example a report from the embassy in Washington in October 1939 that the US was trying to extinguish British influence in Australia and even New Zealand.[4]

Involved in a war that they had so recently been trying to avoid by the policy of appeasement, it is hardly surprising that early indications of war aims from the government should have been vague and, if a meaning could be distilled, it was one of the need for spiritual, rather than territorial, change. In November 1939, foreign secretary Halifax proclaimed that Britain was fighting for peace, freedom, security and the sanctity of treaties. In a speech on the 26th of the same month the Prime Minister himself said that: 'Our desire . . . would be to establish a new Europe; not new in the sense of tearing up all the old frontier posts and redrawing the map according to the ideas of the victors, but a Europe with a new spirit in which the nations which inhabit it will approach their difficulties with goodwill and mutual tolerance.'[5] After Churchill became prime minister, public statements on war aims became unfashionable. In one speech in September 1941 he said that he preferred to dwell on war principles in which it was to be understood that war aims were included.[6] This was partly because the pressure was for war aims promises that would relate at least as much to the domestic realm as to the external, with the promise of a better life for the ordinary man and woman, about which he did not wish to make promises. Internal war aims, divorced from any direct connection with the international situation, are a vast subject that would require a separate book. It must suffice to state that they existed in all belligerent countries. In the British case, the testimony of an official American visitor, Isaiah Bowman, after a visit to London in the spring of 1944 is eloquent: 'He had been impressed in England by the overpowering fact . . . that at every dinner-table and in every conversation the British talked about their economic situation at the end of the war. This question was a perfect nightmare to them.'[7] Except when the war was at its most critical, most of the British population were, as this observation indicates, primarily concerned with expanding welfare services, improving housing and, above all, with preventing the return of the mass unemployment of the early 1930s. Even full employment after the end of the war was not, for a long time, to banish this spectre. In 1947 Oliver Franks noted of the undergraduates whom he was teaching at

Oxford University that: 'Almost all of them are deeply worried about securing employment. They take no encouragement from the almost universal shortage of workers in all walks of life . . . The world to which they look forward seems insecure, impoverished and uncertain.'[8]

Churchill's dislike of public debate of war aims had a counterpart in his dealings with the Foreign Office. When, in March 1943, it sought permission to follow up signs from Moscow that the Soviet government was ready to discuss war aims, the Prime Minister's response, in the words of a senior official, Christopher Warner, was 'a series of most vicious screams' and orders 'that the whole subject of postwar matters should be dropped at once like the hottest of hot bricks'.[9] Officials could not, however, be prevented from thinking out loud among themselves. In October 1939 another senior figure, William Strang, wrote: 'We are fighting to preserve our position in the world against the German challenge, to establish peace and freedom in Europe and to safeguard Western civilisation. It is less dangerous in the immediate future for western Europe that Russia should displace Germany in eastern Europe than that Germany should maintain herself.' He added, 'the real danger to be avoided is a turnover of Germany to Bolshevism'.[10] Strang provided a foretaste of British policy in Europe once the Cold War got into its postwar stride: the readiness to yield eastern Europe to communism while resisting Soviet domination in western Europe and at least the greater part of Germany. The war years may be seen, in a sense, as a detour from this. In 1940–1 British policymakers veered more and more to the conviction that Germany would probably never cease to be an enemy. In a speech three weeks before the German invasion of Russia, foreign secretary Anthony Eden declared: 'Our political and military plans for peace will be designed to prevent a repetition of Germany's misdeeds.'[11] This predisposed Britain to look for evidence that long-term cooperation with the Soviet Union might be possible on the basis of resisting German bids for revenge in the future, always assuming – and this was for a long time in doubt – that the Soviets could survive the German onslaught and then recover the lost ground. The extensive discussions, especially in the Foreign Office, on the nature of Soviet aims in the months after June 1941 produced a consensus that they were much more concerned with security than with ideology, but no clear view on how the Soviet leadership, which was seen as collective and not one in which Stalin was all-powerful, defined security. It could be anything from seeking almost nothing west of the June 1941 borders to imposing communism on Germany.

Britain should treat them with sensitivity and as absolutely equal partners in the hope that that would be an inducement to pursue moderate aims.[12]

The cautious confidence that Britain and the Soviet Union might be able to agree on long-term objectives coincided with the hardening of attitudes towards Germany, to which some reference has already been made. Shortly before he returned to the office of foreign secretary in December 1940, Eden expressed the opinion that, 'Hitler is not a phenomenon but a symptom, the expression of a great part of the German nation.'[13] (This, as well as the fact that his personal security was very tight, helps to explain the British lack of interest in assassinating Hitler. There were great doubts about whether anything would be solved by the elimination of this 'symptom'.[14]) Churchill appears to have caught up with this mood by the spring of 1941. A little earlier he had spoken to a number of listeners, including Roosevelt's envoy, Harry Hopkins, of Germany as 'part of the family of Europe' from which it could not be expelled. It should be disarmed but not suffer reparations or other economic penalties. By the spring he was advocating ferocious economic servitudes and was gloating over German war casualties. Even so, in November 1941 he could still tell the War Cabinet that he refused to rule out the possibility of negotiations with a military regime that had overthrown Hitler. He quarrelled about this with Eden before the latter's visit to Moscow, and the Foreign Secretary was obliged to present Churchill's views as his own to Stalin, to the latter's alarm about British intentions.[15] Yet the hardening of political hostility never seriously eroded the widespread belief in British ruling circles, stemming from the writings of Keynes and Europe's dismal economic experiences in the interwar period, that impoverishment in Germany and prosperity in the rest of Europe were incompatible. Eden, both in public and private, was a typical adherent of this doctrine, which helps to account for the swift and even contemptuous rejection of the Morgenthau Plan for the 'pastoralisation' of Germany in late 1944. The Armistice and Post-War Committee of the War Cabinet, discussed below and dominated by those who took a stern view of the German problem, agreed that the 'plan' 'would not be the solution to the problem of preventing future German aggression'. However, Churchill resisted formal repudiation of the plan while the war went on out of fear that that might have a dampening effect on the fighting spirit of allied troops.[16]

There was actually remarkably little consideration of the future of Germany at War Cabinet level, with only three desultory and indecisive discussions taking place in 1943–4.[17] The Cabinet Committee on Armistice and Post-War Matters, which was set up under the chairmanship of the deputy prime minister, Clement Attlee, in 1943 (and which at first functioned under a different name), was the forum for some discussion of long-term issues, but, as the order of words in its title implied, considerations relevant to the immediate termination of the war came first.[18] This left much scope for discussion, and for the possibility of initiating policies which the political leaders might have difficulty in reversing, to departments, especially the Foreign Office, and to interdepartmental committees, most notably the Post-Hostilities Sub-Committee of the Chiefs of Staff, which was set up under a Foreign Office chairman, Gladwyn Jebb, in August 1943.[19] It is remarkable how closely the Whitehall experts on Germany shared the hostile and pessimistic, though not completely hopeless, views on Germany as a permanent or semi-permanent threat to British security that opinion polls revealed as prevailing among the British public. This extended to Hitler's domestic opponents, who, at least in regard to foreign policy and German expansion, were seen as differing from him only on tactics.[20] Lord Vansittart's *Black Record*, based on radio broadcasts and published as a cheap pamphlet in January 1941, was regarded as broadly portraying the truth about the Germans, even if it made awful propaganda (and came as a godsend to Goebbels).[21] The actual propaganda line from late 1941 was to warn the Germans that the longer they allowed the war to go on, the harsher would be their fate, without spelling out details. In January 1944 Churchill endorsed the President's Unconditional Surrender doctrine, which is discussed in the next chapter, as admirable for that purpose.[22] All this helps to explain Churchill and Eden's savage dismissal of the bomb plotters who tried to assassinate Hitler in July 1944. This was savage both in public (notably a House of Commons debate on 2 August) and in private, where hopes were expressed that all the plotters – including the particularly plausible Adam von Trott – would be executed. Otherwise the 'military tradition' in Germany would continue to thrive under cover of a smokescreen that would blind all too many in democratic countries to the fact that they would be 'preparing for a Third World War' in the words of a memorandum drawn up in the Political Warfare Executive. Only after the war ended was Churchill to revise his view of the bomb plotters of July 1944.[23] Despite such dismissal, Frank Roberts of the Foreign Office thought that the plot's failure and the subsequent purge, which, as the months went by, was seen as having taken on the dimensions of an attempt by the Nazis to exterminate all 'saner elements' in

Germany, might make it necessary to deprive it permanently of its main industrial asset, the Ruhr coalfields.[24]

In the face of such attitudes, the British sympathisers with non-Nazi Germans in the churches and parts of the Labour Party were uninfluential. Besides not reflecting public or official opinion, their pro-Germanism was grounded in unreality in the sense that it stemmed from preconceptions and often from nothing more precise than an optimistic view of human nature; the serpent of knowledge about German history and society, especially as it had developed under the Nazis, was rarely allowed to intrude.[25] This was grasped at the time by the Foreign Office, whose impatience with and contempt for the pro-Germans was typically expressed by Strang when, in the summer of 1943, their most celebrated figure, Bishop Bell of Chichester, suggested that since Stalin was apparently recruiting Germans for postwar purposes – a reference to the National Committee for a Free Germany, which is discussed in Chapter 5 – Britain should recruit liberal Germans as a counterweight to these presumably pro-communist ones. Strang wrote that Bell was trying to play the card of the 'communist bogey' and added, 'He and his like will lead us into a new war in half a generation if they are given their way.'[26] The official conceptual framework for consideration of the future of Germany was, therefore, one of an entire people wedded to power politics of the most aggressive kind. Characteristic of the nearest approach to optimism was the statement at the first meeting of Attlee's postwar committee that if the Germans were subjected to democratic propaganda for fifty years after the war some of them might successfully be re-educated.[27] Also symptomatic was the abortive proposal at the end of the war to transfer the Berchtesgaden area to Austria to prevent Hitler's retreat from becoming a Nazi shrine. It was thought that an Austrian government would not allow such a development but that an independent German government probably would.[28]

Having established a framework, British war aims towards Germany will be examined in their two aspects: first, what was wished to happen if there had been no constraints resulting from membership of the Grand Alliance and relations with other European countries; and, second, the German factor within the workings of the alliance and British thinking about its future relations with other democratic European states. While Germans could not be killed in cold blood as the Nazis were doing to others on a vast scale, it was deemed desirable that German war casualties should be very high, thus reducing the country's military manpower capacity. The casualties from civilian bombings, as in Dresden in 1945, fitted well into this concept. Churchill's horror at Stalin's proposal in 1943 to execute 50,000 captured German officers is discussed in the chapter on the Soviet Union. It was qualified by the hope that a very large part of the officer corps would die in battle. When he repeated to Stalin his warning against committing such an atrocity nearly a year later, he again made a qualification, which was that he would have no objection to captured German officers being purged of their arrogance by being made to perform menial labour. He also once advocated the enforced postwar separation of millions of German men from their womenfolk to produce a hiatus in the German birth rate. The encouragement in Germany by every possible means of contraception was strongly favoured in the German Department of the Foreign Office, which was set up in October 1943.[29] Yet, apart from wanting fewer German babies to be born, Britain did not adopt policies for the savage treatment of Germany after victory; leniency went well beyond rejection of the Morgenthau Plan. At first, Britain was inclined to favour the infliction of no territorial losses on Germany and to allow it to keep Austria and parts of its Sudetenland gains from Czechoslovakia Expert opinion, particularly within the Foreign Office, was even more opposed to the dismemberment of Germany into two or more states than it was to large territorial amputations. However, on this the diplomats were confronted with a lack of support from above. Eden and Attlee were undecided about dismemberment, while Churchill was clear that he would prefer Germany to become two states, a northern based on Prussia, and a southern, preferably to be united with Austria and possibly Hungary, and, best of all, to be a monarchy under the Habsburgs or the former Bavarian royal house of the Wittelsbachs.[30] At his conference with Stalin in October 1944, Churchill advocated three German states, the third to be formed from the Ruhr and adjacent industrial areas of western Germany. He may consciously or subconsciously have been trying to salvage something from the Morgenthau plan with its call for the deindustrialisation of the Ruhr combined with vagueness about what should be done in the rest of Germany.[31]

If dismemberment was to be prevented, Attlee's agnosticism about it was unfortunate; whereas Eden stood in awe of Churchill and was unwilling to challenge him,[32] Attlee was always ready to do so, and always with some chance of success. He apparently found it difficult to focus his mind on the purely political and territorial aspects of the German problem as opposed to those rooted in the German economic and social structure. About the latter, his views are described by his biographer as 'fundamentalist'. Certainly Attlee thought that it would be 'just retribution' for the Germans, and a matter of indifference to the British, if Russia used millions of German prisoners as slave labour. And in the summer of 1944 he duelled with Eden against what he saw as a tendency in planning to be 'unduly generous' to the Germans, and to let them 'get away with it', 'it' being lack of 'realisation of German enormities'. Eden rejoined that the Deputy Prime Minister's thinking might lead to chaos in Germany, and a pro-German reaction by the British public and occupation forces, the latter moved by their 'English hearts'.[33] Yet even Attlee favoured harsh and drastic treatment only so that the economic and social restructuring of Germany could be accomplished quickly and Britain be allowed to withdraw from German affairs soon after the war ended. His doubts grew about whether dismemberment could be imposed by force.[34]

The experts' argument was that dismemberment would be un-workable because the peoples of the western democracies would not for long be prepared to use force to maintain it, and because the Germans would never accept it. In addition there was a feeling that breaking up a large country 'was a retrograde step which ran counter to modern ideas'. It would be to 'impose on Germany something contrary to the general trend in the rest of the world'.[35] The Foreign Office was willing to encourage separatist tendencies in what was regarded as the unlikely event of their arising, but not to impose them. In July 1944 the permanent under-secretary, Cadogan, defined that as 'our accepted policy'.[36] The Foreign Office was able to block firm British adoption of a policy of breaking up Germany as an aim to be pursued in dealings with the partners in the Grand Alliance except in one intriguing case. This was that of Austria. During 1943 Britain, reversing its previous inclination, took the lead within the alliance in pressing for a commitment that the reconstitution of Austria should become a common war aim. This led to a decision at the Moscow conference of foreign ministers and the subsequent summit meeting at Tehran that year that Austria should indeed be restored. Most British experts regarded Austria's separation from the Reich as the one practicable step in dismemberment that could be taken, and made to endure. That they did seek for it to be taken shows a single-minded preoccupation with reducing German power; their reading of the available evidence was that most Austrians favoured continuance of the 1938 *Anschluss*, and, even apart from that, the interwar Austrian republic had shown itself to be of doubtful political or economic viability. If Britain had thoughts in

1943 or 1944 about Germany as an eventual anti-Soviet partner it would not have pressed for anything so hazardous, it believed, as the revival of a separate Austria, though there was the greatest difficulty, as Attlee noted in November 1944, in deciding whether to regard the reconstituted Austria as friend or a defeated foe.[37]

In a sense, the question just referred to about Austria was not of the first importance. The war aims towards Germany proper that were taking shape in British planning circles in the later stages of the war were generous ones so that, unless the Germans really were inherently and irremediably aggressive, reconciliation was to be offered; Germany was, in effect, to be given another chance. Its territorial losses were to be small, its national unity was to be preserved, and its economic life was to be unhindered except for the prohibition of arms production with no pretence that that was anything but enforced unilateral disarmament. Even in that matter, restrictions on German heavy industry to reduce its military potential were to be minimal, and what a later age would call 'sunrise' industries like electronics were not to be banned, even though it was appreciated that they might be the basis for the war industries of the future. There was even reluctance to ban the manufacture of synthetic rubber.[38] Although Britain not only accepted but supported the doctrine of Unconditional Surrender, it favoured a detailed surrender document which would have had some of the features of a contract between the Germans and their conquerors; both the United States and the Soviet Union were to reject this in favour of a simple instrument of surrender.[39] British policy desired a fairly rapid advance to renewed German independence, possibly with an apolitical 'government of experts' to smooth the path to that goal.[40] This emphasis on speed must be seen within two contexts: a wish not to lavish scarce manpower and material resources on a prolonged occupation regime; and the thorough-going consensus within the British political establishment that the country's future lay essentially with the Commonwealth rather than with Europe. In mid-1943 the War Cabinet was full of doubts about whether Britain should take on major commitments in all or a large part of Germany, though the pressures to do so proved irresistible.[41] The British were indifferent to whether the resulting Germany would be a liberal democracy. They would have been content if it had become the sort of country which postwar Japan was to become: an efficient industrial giant, wholly concerned with paying for its way with ever expanding exports. (An Anglo-American peace settlement imposed on Germany would almost certainly have borne a close resemblance to the one that the US largely alone was to impose on Japan.) One official mentioned a 'super-Sweden',[42] though that seems an affront to the democratic traditions of the Swedes. Another pronounced, with an air of finality, that a democratic regime 'showed itself obviously unsuited to the German temperament before the Nazi rise to power'.[43]

British policymakers always understood that the final package of aims to be imposed on Germany would be a balance between their preference for reconciliation and re-education and the military and diplomatic facts of life at the end of the war.[44] In developments that are discussed in some detail in the chapter on Soviet war aims, Britain took an increasingly expansive view of how much German territory Poland should receive, though it remained wholly unreconciled to a border as far west as the Oder–Neisse one that Stalin gave to Poland. It was, however, almost powerless over this, as it was also over Stalin's decision on the total reversal of the Munich agreement imposed on Czechoslovakia, something that President Beneš himself had not dared to hope for.[45] Individuals came to an understanding of how important the Soviet Union would be in deciding peace terms for Germany and for east and central Europe at different speeds. In his memoirs Churchill was to remark sourly that 'for more than a year' after Hitler invaded it Russia was a burden, not a help in the war.[46] His more liberal-minded foreign secretary would not have agreed, and was motivated by a vision of long-term Anglo-Soviet partnership based on common fear of Germany when he visited Stalin in December 1941. In one of their meetings he said to Stalin, 'I can assure you that we are entirely realistic in our determination to stop the Germans from repeating their aggression, and I very much hope that you fully understand that.' The following month, Geoffrey Harrison of the Foreign Office was writing: 'Whatever our own contribution [to military victory], it is likely that it will be the Russian army which will break the back of German resistance, and we must therefore now take very serious account of M. Stalin's views.'[47]

It is convenient at this point to digress from the main thread of British aims towards Germany to discuss the way in which Soviet military survival and then success led to the shrinkage of British aims in east-central Europe. In 1942 it was hoped that Soviet power could be largely excluded from all this area in return for British and American recognition of the territorial gains that the Soviet Union had made in 1939–40. As late as November ambassador Clark Kerr reported from Moscow that restoration of the 1941 borders was the main Soviet aim, and that, although they wished to 'claim a sort of undefined protectorate over the other Slav peoples of Europe', the need for postwar reconstruction meant that they would 'probably be prepared to take things quietly for a considerable period of time'.[48] The officials were most worried about an east European country that was not Slavic, Romania. British policy in 1942–3 was to encourage a federation of central European states, of which the most important would be Poland, to form a bulwark against both German and Russian power. Romanian membership would be desirable. In March the head of the Southern Department in the Foreign Office, Pierson Dixon, wrote that: 'The object of this [federation idea] would be to ensure the emergence after the war of an independent Romania in regard to which country Soviet designs are dubious.' The difficulty was that, as was noted in June by an even more senior official, Orme Sargent, the federation was intended in part to exclude Russian power and yet could not be formed in the face of Soviet opposition.[49] Soon the Foreign Office was in receipt of (correct) indications that the Soviet Union was intent on special ties, which it interpreted as meaning de facto annexation, with Romania and Finland. Finally, during 1942, it should be noted that the three great allies united formally in December to announce that it was their common aim that Albania, annexed by Italy in 1939, should be reconstituted after the war as an independent state, though no commitment was given on restoring its old borders, and Britain thought that Greece had a strong case for being allowed to annex part of southern pre-1939 Albania.[50]

The new year brought with it the Soviet victory at Stalingrad, and, with it, a reassessment of what Britain could realistically aim at in eastern Europe. There was still hope of holding Russian power at bay from Romania's two neighbours, Hungary and Bulgaria, which were also aligned with Germany. Romania was written off. The supreme British leadership made this very clear indeed more than a year later in the spring of 1944 when Eden gave the Soviets an undertaking that the Special Operations Executive would send no more agents into Romania – some had been sent against Foreign Office wishes – and when Churchill sent Molotov a message in which he said that, 'We regard you as our leaders in Romanian affairs.'[51] On the much written-about subject of British dealings with wartime Yugoslavia, there was also a process of retreat, though in that case because of the successes of the communist Partisans under Josip Broz Tito. In April 1943 Eden minuted that 'a communist Jugoslavia would be a cause of unsettlement to all its neighbours'. It became clearer and clearer that there was going to be such a Yugoslavia whatever Britain wanted, and that many of those neighbours would themselves be communist, including Albania, where, it was noted in late 1944, the few non-communist guerrillas had been exterminated by the communists under Enver Hoxha.[52] The British efforts to salvage something for Poland in the north of the region and to exclude communism completely from Greece are dealt with in the chapter on Soviet aims. Here it only remains to take note of Churchill putting a brave face on the shrinkage of aims when, in a paean of praise to pragmatism, he remarked to the House of Commons in May 1944 that 'in one place we support a king, in another a communist', referring to George II of Greece and Tito.[53] His celebrated percentages deal with Stalin in October on a share out of influence in the countries of south-east Europe was an attempt to deny what he himself had admitted in May. It is only fair to Churchill to note that he was not alone in the British elite in his illusions. It was not his proposal in August 1944 to send a token force of 1,200 troops to Hungary to 'show the flag' as if that could have achieved anything, even if it could have been done.[54]

To return to the mainstream of discussion, during 1942 the Economic and Reconstruction Department of the Foreign Office produced the Four-Power Plan for the permanent direction of world affairs by the three members of the Grand Alliance (with China included as a nominal member, and leaving open the possibility that France might eventually be admitted as a genuine partner). Its principal author, Gladwyn Jebb, was to claim in his memoirs that the ideas embodied in it became 'the basis for all forward thinking on both sides of the Atlantic' about the postwar political future.[55] It would be truer to say that, if it was influential, that was because the thinking in it coincided with Roosevelt's Four Policemen concept, which is discussed in the next chapter, and that both merged into one another in planning for the United Nations organisation. Yet for all its emphasis on the containment of Germany and Japan as the cement which would keep the alliance together, the plan declared the unity of Germany, though undesirable, to be probably unavoidable, and even stated that if the Soviet Union went its own antagonistic way, Britain would inevitably be driven to seek collaboration with Germany, especially if the US had reverted to isolationism.

British policy could, then, touch on the possibility that Germany might have a choice between a British and a Soviet alignment. This could dictate leniency towards Germany. In May 1943 Jebb wrote that the many good reasons for not dismembering Germany were reinforced by 'the reason that if Russia should break with us and America after the war we should not then altogether have burnt our boats so far as the Germans were concerned'. Five months later the War Cabinet, in one of its rare and always indecisive debates on the future of Germany, produced an echo of this: 'One view advanced in discussion was that the increasing power of Russia might make it inexpedient to carry too far a policy of breaking up the unity of Germany.' The person expressing this 'one view' appears to have been Churchill himself.[56] Yet such thoughts were usually stilled by what were perceived as favourable trends in Soviet policy and by consideration of German national character and history. Though the British were not without hope that the Germans would draw the appropriate lesson from suffering total defeat twice in less than thirty years,[57] they thought it much more likely that they would seek a comeback into power politics by turning in defeat to communism, to a Bismarckian alliance with Russia without ideological synchronisation, or simply to playing off east against west from some ostensible middle ground, thus becoming 'the arbiter of the situation' as Eden warned in March 1944.[58] In April 1944 deputy foreign secretary Richard Law expressed the typical fear that if there were ineffective or unpopular regimes in the Balkans after the war Germany might seek to reimpose its domination there.[59] Defeat, thought Foreign Office experts, might convince the Germans that episodes like the 1941 'Barbarossa' invasion represented 'only a yearning to be received into the bosom of the Eurasian heartland – a development which would serve us ill'. Then again, the Germans' 'innate reverence for ruthless power' might make them look upon Stalin with the same eyes now gazing in admiration at Hitler.[60] They either did not consider the German reaction to the brutality with which the Russians would be likely to treat their conquered enemies or thought that the Germans would accept it uncomplainingly. It was left to the war secretary, Sir James Grigg, to suggest 'that, on the long view, it would be no bad thing if Germany should suffer so greatly from very rough Russian treatment that a purged Germany might turn towards association with Western Europe rather than eastwards'. (However, Grigg disliked and distrusted the United States as much as Soviet Russia; he was convinced that both wished to reduce Britain to third-rate status, and, by the end of 1944, that 'they no longer take any pains to conceal their intentions'.)[61]

The tendency in Soviet policy in favour of the long-term continuance of the Grand Alliance was not regarded as irrevocable. As Clark Kerr was to warn from Moscow in 1944, it was exceptionally difficult to make predictions about the course of future national policy in a state like the Soviet one in which none of the constraints that existed in a liberal society applied: public opinion counted for nothing and ideological considerations were whatever the rulers declared them to be. The only safe point that could be made about their capacity for about-turns was that they would think twice before challenging a foreign power that was 'tenaciously abiding by its objective'.[62] Policymakers in London agreed with this analysis, but also feared that tenacity would be of no avail if Stalin could find a bigger fish to fry in the form of Germany. The senior Foreign Office official Orme Sargent assumed early in 1942 that his maximum objective was 'to create a series of autonomous Soviet Socialist Republics in different parts of Germany', and that only military developments and calculations of self-interest would cause him to moderate that aim.[63] The setting up in Moscow in the summer of 1943 of a National Committee for a Free Germany and a League of German Officers, which are discussed in Chapter 5 below, was viewed in London as moves towards a Russo-German alignment and not, their true nature, as bids for a compromise peace between equals by a Soviet regime that despaired of being able to win complete victory or of receiving really significant Anglo-American aid in its struggle.

Whatever the Soviets were doing, Britain rejected any idea of making a bid of its own for German favour. As Churchill said to Stalin at the Tehran conference, the three powers should 'keep a close personal friendship and supervise Germany in their mutual interest'. The Prime Minister was well embarked by this time, as one of his personal aides put it, in 'trying hard to march in step with Russia towards the broad and sunlit uplands'.[64] Long after the war, Strang of the Foreign Office still supposed that at Tehran Stalin regarded security from Germany as his primary aim and added: 'We contemplated an equal place in the containment of Germany for the Soviet Union.'[65] By 1943 Britain's aims in Germany had been reduced into seeking a legally guaranteed position in post-surrender Germany, while conceding to many Soviet demands over the country that British experts regarded as detrimental if liberal forces were to stand much chance of asserting themselves. The former policy centred on the negotiations for the division of Germany into occupation zones which were started, on British initiative, after the Moscow conference of foreign ministers in October agreed to Eden's proposal to set up a European Advisory Commission in London as a clearinghouse for political business. Britain struggled hard (against the US, not Russia) for its occupation zone to be the industrial north-west, not the more pastoral and difficult-of-access south. The prolonged discussions about the zonal division of Germany during the first nine months of 1944 provide an insight into British thinking about its aims in postwar Europe, particularly if east–west relations developed favourably. The best of all worlds would be a virtual return to the 1830s when Palmerston and Nicholas I – a liberal British foreign secretary and an ultra-reactionary Russian tsar – had worked together to order the affairs of Europe and, in particular, to solve problems caused by the troublesome July Monarchy in France – the Germany of the time, as it were. The United States would be admitted to the new club but only as a junior member. Thus, whereas the British were so much in awe of the Red Army that they worried that Stalin might reject their offer of 40 per cent of the territory of Germany within its 1937 borders as insufficient, they were adamant in rejecting the US wish for the American zone to be the north-west of Germany. Because of its economic assets this was the most important part. Geographically, it neighboured the Netherlands, Denmark and Norway, over which Britain expected to exercise some postwar leadership. (When the Belgian exile government in London learned that Britain was 'assigning' its country to the US, it protested indignantly that it wished to be under Britain's wing; Britain relented and agreed.) Finally, harking back to the supreme manifestation of past greatness, Britain wanted the German navy's major bases so that it would be in command of naval disarmament, though it was prepared to allow the US a subsidiary role in that because otherwise, feared Admiral Sir Andrew Cunningham, 'We might find ourselves similarly excluded in the Pacific at the end of the Japanese war.' Thus Britain and Russia agreed in principle on zones in February, whereas Anglo-American agreement (on British terms, though the US was given enclaves with two ports) was not reached until Churchill and Roosevelt met in Quebec in September. And yet, there was a dark side to British thinking about zones. They did not ignore a worst-case situation in which relations with the Soviets collapsed into hostility and America withdrew into isolation. Britain would simply lack the manpower to occupy the former American zone, and would not be able to prevent the Red Army from moving in. It would, however, remain in occupation of the part of Germany most important to its security. Whatever the course of Anglo-Soviet relations, the British had to bear in mind Roosevelt's warnings that it had been a far from automatic step for him to agree to an American occupation zone, and that he expected all US troops to be out of Europe within two years of the war ending.[66]

Wracked with such doubts about American intentions, the British braced themselves to make many concessions to the Soviets about policies in postwar Germany. There could be no rebuilding of the German economy without regard to Soviet demands on reparations and levels of output, no matter how unwise these might be considered to be. The re-education effort that was envisaged would have to be a tripartite affair, to deny credence to incessant Nazi propaganda that there were fundamental conflicts between the western powers and Russia.[67] The German Social Democrats were to be kept at arm's length, which was continued even after a Labour government was elected in 1945. This was, at first, partly because of a belief that the SPD would have little support in postwar Germany. However, even after the opening months of the occupation regime had revealed the falsity of this assumption, Strang could still recommend at the end of 1945 that Britain should remain 'equivocal' towards that party, whose outlook was conceded to be 'most nearly in accord with the general feelings in western Europe' of any party in the German political spectrum, because any favouritism to democratic socialists, whom the Soviets notoriously regarded as their worst enemies, might damage Anglo-Soviet relations.[68] On the thorniest problem of all, dismemberment, the Foreign Office was steeling itself by early 1945 to accept what was imagined as an iron Soviet resolve to carry it out. This expectation appeared to be borne out by the Soviet stance in February at the Yalta conference, at which Eden noted that, 'Molotov wished to tie us hand and foot to dismemberment before enquiry was made.' As Vojtech Mastny notes, this may have stemmed from a Soviet wish to present the Germans with an impossible demand so that they would not try to surrender to the western powers alone. The conference agreed that Germany should be dismembered if the three powers 'deemed [it] requisite for future peace and security', and clearly implied that they did so deem by setting up a committee, to meet in London, to 'study the procedure' for dismemberment. The Foreign Office could resist pressures from other British quarters but not from the Soviets. In its rearguard action against dismemberment it had at least been able to persuade the Attlee committee to 'suspend judgment' the previous year. Now, after Yalta, Eden presented the same committee with a memorandum which was stated to be written 'on the assumption that it will be decided to proceed with dismemberment', and which declared that the time had come to consider such matters as the reparations obligations of the individual states into which Germany was to be divided. Then, in late March, the Soviet embassy in London amazed and delighted the British Germany experts by stating that the Soviet government was now definitely against the break-up of Germany. Roosevelt's death on 12 April intervened too soon to allow a response to this change in Russian policy from the one man in the supreme trio who was singlemindedly in favour of dismemberment. The issue of responsibility for preventing an agreed break-up of Germany is, therefore, not clear-cut. What can be asserted is that by 1945 the British accepted that the decision did not lie with them, and would probably finally be made in Moscow even more than in Washington.[69]

If Britain, in the later stages of the war, scaled down its aims in Germany and even more so in eastern Europe (excluding Greece, which it regarded as an extension of its informal empire, which it was determined to preserve, in the Middle East[70]), it could not do the same in western Europe. Before the war ended the Foreign Office was heavily involved in contingency planning for a western group of democratic states. This would function in the event of the dissolution of the Grand Alliance, with the US reverting to isolationism and Russia building up its own bloc in eastern Europe. The British thought this an endurable prospect if both blocs were directed against Germany. If they were antagonistic to one another, then the question of Germany, or part of it, as an ally would come on to the agenda. The Chiefs of Staff warned that a western group threatened by Russia would stand no chance unless western Germany was included. This bristled with difficulties. Even if a British government and the British public could find their way to accepting Germany in such a role, it was doubtful whether countries such as France, which had undergone the pain and humiliation of actual German occupation, would also do so.[71] Furthermore, the communist parties of western Europe would clearly have been mobilised against a western security group with anti-Soviet overtones, and Britain's leaders of the late war period had no confidence in the ability of the continental masses to resist the blandishments of communist utopian propaganda. In the War Cabinet in November 1944 Churchill denounced as folly a proposal by Attlee to make the removal of the Franco regime in Spain a war aim. He argued that that would amount to fostering communism in Spain, with the 'infection' then spreading to France and Italy. He contended that 'every country that is liberated or converted [sic] by our victories is seething with communism', and 'only our influence with Russia prevents their actually stimulating this movement'.[72] Such 'influence' was clearly something to be retained if at all possible.

In these circumstances, in the summer of 1944, Eden, besides adopting a new line of argument that its moral stature would be an important element in preserving Britain's great-power status in the postwar world, preached the doctrine that at all costs Britain must not entertain 'the idea at the back of our minds that the

Germans may serve as part of an anti-Soviet bloc'. Any western group must be exclusively against Germany, and should complement, not replace, the Anglo-Soviet alliance, which was 'the arch of our policy with close association with western Europe the western buttress'. If there was any hope of keeping the US in western European affairs that would also be the only way to do it.[73] At the end of August, Eden reaffirmed to the Attlee committee that all planning about Germany should be based on the need to continue to contain and restrain Germany's power'.[74] Soon afterwards, the Foreign Office fought a largely successful duel with the Chiefs of Staff against contingency planning for possible war with the Soviet Union. The evidence supports the claim of the Official Historian of the Foreign Office during the war that, as German collapse neared, British policy became 'more anxious' to secure collaboration with Russia.[75]

In this way, British wartime aims towards Germany became ones of choosing the lesser of two evils. The greater evil would have been to adopt aims towards Germany that entailed a break with Russia. That country was the strongest in Europe as the war ended; Cadogan, head of the Foreign Office, joked to himself in his diary in August 1945 about the 'Big 3 (or 2½!)'.[76] It was also a country which, in the British official estimation, had travelled a long distance during the war towards becoming a 'normal' nation state, with limited national aims, with which cooperation should continue to be possible.[77] In any case, as the great planner Gladwyn Jebb was to remark, it would have been politically impossible during the war to adopt war aims that could in any way have been construed as anti-Russian or anti-Soviet. Any government doing so would have been swept from office by the force of public opinion.[78] The lesser evil therefore prevailed, that of adopting war aims towards Germany that were illiberal compared with those which would ideally have been preferred. The dangers inherent in this were expressed by Orme Sargent, who was soon to become head official at the Foreign Office, in a survey that he wrote of the European scene after VE Day, in which he observed that: 'It is not overstating the position to say that if Germany is won over to totalitarianism this may well decide the fate of liberalism throughout the world.'[79] This echoed many wartime expressions about the future of Germany. In September 1943 Eden had written in a cabinet paper that: 'The only policy holding out any real hope for the future is one which, while taking all necessary safeguards, aims ultimately at the re-admittance of a reformed Germany into the life of Europe.'[80] The following February J. M. Troutbeck, head of the German Department in the Foreign Office, warned that too much ruthlessness towards

Germany would 'run the danger of evoking a wave of sentimental pro-Germanism in this country and America precisely as happened last time'.[81] In all probability, he was both making a genuine point and rationalising his own attitude to a country which was still seen as essentially a part of western European civilisation. The liberal faith was also reflected in a Foreign Office memorandum for the War Cabinet in November 1944, which, in discussing Germany's future, argued: 'But their eventual constitutional settlement must be of their making, not of ours. Otherwise nothing that we can do will prevent its collapse.'[82]

What makes this liberal preference the more remarkable is the intense pessimism about the Germans in most British quarters. An official report in September 1944 confidently predicted that a secret Nazi organisation was to be expected after the war which would, in the long term, 'present the allies with a formidable problem'. Likewise, 'There will be an attempt to maintain a secret association of aircraft personnel which will hope, when the time is ripe, to lay the foundation of the German Air Force of the future.'[83] The anti-German mood reached its peak as the war drew to its close with the discovery of the death camps. In March 1945, the most right-wing member of the Cabinet, Grigg, warned Field Marshal Montgomery, the designated governor of the British occupation zone, that it was essential that his troops should obey the order against fraternisation with the German population, who, only recently, 'were boasting what they as the Master Race would do to you as their slaves, who were applauding the utter disregard by their leaders of any form of decency or of honourable dealings'. He continued that if the Germans under occupation pretended good will, its purpose would be 'to make fools of you again and to escape the loathing which their actions deserve'; and he concluded that a hard time lay before the German nation 'to re-educate it and bring it back into the society of decent humanity'.[84] He would clearly not have dissented from the majority verdict when an opinion poll in April 1945 indicated, in the wake of the publicity about the Belsen concentration camp, that only 7 per cent of the British public thought that Germany could be educated into a new outlook.[85] Barely a week after VE Day, the Chancellor of the Exchequer, Sir John Anderson, another arch-conservative, remarked that the real problem in ensuring security against Germany would begin to arise in ten years, by which time, he presumably meant, Germany would have had long enough to recover its strength.[86] With such thoughts in their minds, the British ruling elite did not, as the war in Europe ended, feel reduced to complete despair by the prospect that continued cooperation with the Soviets would entail the adoption of some harshness in the treatment of Germany.

FRANCE (INCLUDING BRITISH AND AMERICAN AIMS TOWARDS FRANCE)

Although there were serious tensions before the military catastrophe of the spring of 1940 in British relations with its initial major ally, France, there was also a sense of a community of interests between two great powers that were past their peak and that wished only to retain what they already had. This was reflected in the Anglo-French joint declaration of 28 March 1940 against a separate peace by either of them with Germany: 'They undertake not to discuss peace terms before reaching complete agreement on the conditions necessary to ensure each of them an effective and lasting guarantee of their security.'[87] Less than three months later, and shortly after rejecting the British offer of a union between the two countries, France signed an armistice with Germany in which, besides having to consent to German occupation of more than half its territory, it had to agree to an article that formally subordinated it to German power. According to article 10: 'France agrees not to develop in the future any hostile action against the German Reich with its remaining armed forces or in any way.'[88] Although one senior official could write to the foreign secretary, Lord Halifax, after this that, 'We shall have to envisage a new orientation after the war . . . some time may elapse before we can fit in France,' the reality was that the reconstitution of France as a great power and an essential ally for Britain in world, and especially European, affairs was, without any real period of interruption, regarded as a necessity.[89]

The question, until late 1942, was whether this could be done by enticing the government at Vichy to return to the war, as Churchill desired after overcoming his initial indignation about the armistice, or whether the purpose could only be served by a purified France blooming from the nucleus of the Free French movement under the leadership of Charles de Gaulle. His longstanding obsession with French independence and great-power status had, prior to 1940, been based largely on hostility to the Third Republic's acceptance of British leadership in the 1930s, which, in his view, had been obnoxious in principle and disastrous for France in practice.[90] Whether government or, as he would have preferred, movement was to be backed, Eden rousingly announced the fundamental aim towards

France in a Bastille Day radio broadcast in July 1942: 'For us the full restoration of France as a Great Power is not only a declared war aim and the fulfilment of a pledge made to a sister nation, but also a practical necessity, if post-war reconstruction is to be undertaken within the framework of that traditional civilization which is our common heritage.'[91] De Gaulle would need much convincing that these were not mere words; for him, the restoration of the full independence of France was insufficient and even degrading as a supreme war aim. He anticipated a general mood that was to take hold in the country after liberation that the country must be restored to full greatness with no overtones or undertones of again being attached to the apron strings of the 'English governess'.[92] In the ungreat (for France) circumstances of 1942 the Foreign Office saw a moral dimension in British aims towards it, with morality and practical objectives being inextricably linked. This aspect was brought to the fore when the US decided to facilitate its takeover of Algeria and Morocco in November 1942 by using the services of the opportunistic Vichyite, Admiral Darlan, regarded as a supporter of collaboration with Germany until the fortunes of war had changed. The Foreign Office combined pure moral indignation (Darlan was 'the antithesis' of 'international decency') with political concern that, as Eden wrote to Churchill, 'We shall be committing a political error which may have grave consequences not only for our good name in Europe but for the resistance of the oppressed people for whom we are fighting.'[93]

After the providential assassination of Darlan by a French monarchist on Christmas Eve 1942 and the earlier German military occupation of the part of France that had been left unoccupied in 1940, the government at Vichy became a pure nullity in British eyes. From then onwards, the British aim of securing a strong France allied with Britain to resist renewed German aggression had to be pursued with or despite the towering (in every sense) figure of de Gaulle, whose stormy relations with the British have been extensively chronicled.[94] To a British statesman like Anthony Eden, there was no alternative to courting France and, therefore, de Gaulle. In the last week of 1943 he wrote to Churchill that the idea of Britain and Russia standing alone in postwar Europe did not appeal. He pleaded with him to help to avert that: 'You can do more with them than anyone else [referring to the French], and we have just got to build up a France somehow; though the Bear's manners are steadily improving, I still have no ambition to share the cage alone with him.' For Eden, this went hand-in-hand with doubts about whether there was any great future for the

Anglo-American relationship. He was rather unimpressed by Roosevelt, at least initially, and he had no friends in the State Department. He was irritated by the American tendency to moralise, as he put it 'at least where non-American interests are concerned'.[95] The problem was that de Gaulle found it unbearably patronising when he came across indications like the one in a 1944 official report on postwar aims that Britain had embarked on a quest 'to restore the greatness of France' that had even higher priority than Anglo-American relations.[96] He proclaimed as early as 1942 that Europe after the war should be regulated by a Franco-Soviet entente to the exclusion of the 'Anglo-Saxons'. In a speech in March 1944 he spoke of a west European grouping of states from which, by implication, Britain would be excluded.[97]

In their quest for what the historian John C. Cairns called 'a suitable France', the British had to contend not only with de Gaulle's prickliness, but also with the United States, whose vision of such a France could hardly have been more different from Britain's. This provides a convenient opportunity for a preliminary discussion of American war aims before they become the subject of a full chapter. President Franklin D. Roosevelt was in no doubt that Britain would remain a world power after the war. In November 1942 he paid Britain a backhanded compliment by remarking that: 'We will have more trouble with Great Britain after the war than we are having with Germany now.'[98] By contrast, he wanted France to disappear permanently from the front rank of states, and was attracted to the idea of the Vichy regime remaining in power after the war, partly because he patronisingly doubted whether France could function except under a semi-authoritarian form of government, but chiefly because such a regime would presumably be as ready to yield to American power as to Nazi German when that had been in the ascendant. In particular, his 'suitable France' would be ready to give up its colonies as the starting point for an American aim of using the war to initiate a general dismantling of European colonial empires. In this view the President misjudged Vichy, which was determined to retain the French empire. Between 1940 and 1942 it stoutly resisted German demands to be allowed U-boat bases or even simple consular representation in French West Africa. (This sheds an interesting light on the Rooseveltian war aim that consisted of pure American aggrandisement at the expense of France. This was the takeover by the US of Dakar, the administrative centre of French West Africa, which the President considered to be essential to enable the US to defend the western hemisphere.) In August 1941 France signalled its intention to retain Indochina by signing a formal protectorate treaty with the Laotian kingdom of Luang Prabang in place of 'provisional' arrangements that had been in force for fifty years. (The new 'permanent' arrangement lasted for less than four years.)[99] The absolute necessity of retaining the empire was the one issue on which Vichy and all Free French were united. Jacques Soustelle, one of the latter, took the view in 1943 that French Africa 'should be for France what the Far West was for the United States'. From early 1944, before and after it became the government of the state, the Free French authority worked on plans to hold on to the empire by modernising it so that it would become a French Union in which most of the colonies would become overseas territories with their own elected deputies in the National Assembly in Paris. All French people would have been reduced to apoplexy if they had overheard Roosevelt's favourable comments at the Tehran conference in 1943 about a German report drawn up in 1940 about the revival of medieval Burgundy by joining the French provinces of Alsace and Lorraine with Belgium and Luxembourg.[100]

The readiness to employ Darlan was the most graphic illustration of the sort of France that Roosevelt wanted, though he misjudged Darlan, who had brought a 'Greeks conquering Romans' mindset to his collaboration with Germany, which aimed at making France eventually not merely the equal but the superior of Germany in Europe; in late 1942 he probably thought that the 'naive' Americans would be easier to manipulate than the Germans.[101] In any case, although Roosevelt virtually disavowed Darlan even before he was killed, that was chiefly in response to protests from liberal opinion in America and to embarrassment at the support that the deal with Darlan had attracted from some American right wingers. It betokened no real change in policy to France. American overtures to Vichy figures, including even the widely reviled Pierre Laval, continued to almost the eve of D-Day, though whether they emanated from Roosevelt himself or from figures in his entourage like the former ambassador to Vichy, Admiral Leahy, is unclear.[102]

Roosevelt's desire to reduce France to a lowly status had a sting in it for Britain in that the latter wanted a strong France as an essential component of its age-old balance of power policy in Europe, and the President had no time for the balance of power. At the Yalta conference in February 1945 he castigated Churchill for wanting to turn the eastern border of France into Britain's furthest line of defence, even though, as Henry Kissinger wrote, 'At that time, this happened to be the only conceivable means of opposing Soviet expansionism.'[103] Earlier, in the middle war years, the British became aware that they might have to confront the US about the French colonial empire, whose retention, minus only Syria and Lebanon, they regarded as an essential feature of great-power status for France.[104] Indochina appeared likely to be the focal point of Franco-American confrontation. In January 1944 Roosevelt told the British ambassador that Indochina had to become an international trusteeship and then independent. In May Churchill wrote to Eden that, from his conversation with the President, 'I imagine it is one of his principal war aims to liberate Indo-China from France.' By then the Foreign Office feared a major crisis in relations with the US over Indochina because they could not conceive of Britain not supporting the restoration of French rule after the departure of Japanese troops. The loss of Indochina would weaken France and 'undermine at the outset the possibilities of friendship with France' for Britain.[105]

No confrontation had materialised by September 1944, by which time France had been liberated and de Gaulle was heading its government and was exercising the tightest control humanly possible over foreign policy. His grand aim, shared by the entire French political class, was to restore the country to great-power status as being in the natural order of the world and, more particularly, as a means of purging the bitter memory of defeat in 1940.[106] His most immediate aim was to secure for France a zone and an equal place in the occupation regime in Germany. Churchill and Eden offered full support for this when they visited Paris in November. They were becoming worried about the burden that occupation of north-west Germany would impose and looked to France to take on part of it. Writing to Roosevelt after the Paris visit, the Prime Minister said: 'One must always realise that before five years are out a French army must be made to take on the main task of holding down Germany.' Somewhat sidestepping the French aspect, the President noted in his reply: 'You know, of course, that after Germany's collapse I must bring American troops home as rapidly as transportation problems will permit.' Churchill replied in alarm that the 'holding down' of Germany would require the combined efforts of Americans, British and the French, whose army would need time to re-equip. Roosevelt's not reassuring reply was that France would surely be able to re-equip itself rapidly from captured German weaponry.[107]

Though the question of a French zone in Germany remained to be decided, de Gaulle knew that he could not expect British support for another item on his agenda, the detachment of Germany west of the

Rhine (consisting entirely of territory that was to be part of the British zone) and the annexation by France of the coal-producing Saarland. He successfully sought an invitation from Stalin to visit Moscow in December. At Soviet insistence, the resulting treaty between the two countries consisted only of verbiage about postwar cooperation and an undertaking not to make a separate peace with Germany that had very little importance by late 1944. There was no support for de Gaulle's Rhineland–Saar aim, even though the General offered unconditional support for whatever territorial changes against Germany that the Soviets might make in the east. Stalin appeared uninterested in de Gaulle's offer of a share for Russia in governing the Ruhr industrial area, probably doubting whether the Frenchman could deliver on the promise. Franco-Soviet relations declined after that. De Gaulle resented Stalin's failure to try to secure an invitation for him to attend the Yalta or Potsdam conferences; after France had been admitted to the European Advisory Commission in late 1944 the Soviets colluded with the Anglo-Americans to shift really important discussions on Germany and Poland away from that body; and, by the time of Potsdam, the French doubted whether the USSR wanted there to be a second great power on the continent of Europe.[108]

De Gaulle had to be a distant observer while Churchill, for his own, British reasons, worked to achieve one French war aim, an occupation zone in Germany and equal French participation in the control machinery for Germany as a whole. As Roosevelt's confidant, Harry Hopkins, noted, 'Winston and Anthony fought like tigers for France' at Yalta over this.[109] Roosevelt and Stalin agreed out of 'kindness'. The conference was followed by maddeningly extravagant French demands regarding the size of their zone, which would have taken it to the border of the Soviet zone, cutting off the British from the US zone, and bringing about, in the words of an official, the union of 'the France of De Gaulle with Russia'. France had to make do with a more limited zone composed of territory from the British zone and what the Foreign Office considered to be a 'very stingy' offer of land from the American zone, though the French would be advised to accept it as the Americans 'will run out very soon'.[110] There was a final, and characteristic, episode in mid-1945 when the issue of a French sector in the occupation regime in Berlin had to be resolved. The US and Russia declined to give France anything. Britain gave up half its previously agreed sector in the city, only to receive a protest from France that the sector offered to it included 'particularly unpleasant' districts.[111] In the interval between zone and sector, the San Francisco conference to found the United Nations had been held. The acme of power and prestige in that body was permanent membership of the executive body, the Security Council. At the previous conference on planning for the UN at Dumbarton Oaks near New York in 1944 France had been offered permanent membership 'in due course'. At San Francisco it was accorded immediate and foundation membership.[112] Coinciding with the end of the war in Europe, France was being restored to at least the symbols of great power status in recognition of its past and potential future strength much more than its actual strength in 1945.

Notes

1. Brian W. Bloet, *Geopolitics and Globalization in the Twentieth Century* (London: Reaktion Books, 2001), p. 110.
2. David Reynolds, *The Creation of the Anglo-American Alliance, 1937–1941: A Study in Competitive Co-operation* (London: Europa Publications, 1981), pp. 50–4.
3. D. Cameron Watt, *Succeeding John Bull: America in Britain's Place, 1900–1975* (Cambridge: Cambridge University Press, 1984), p. 73.
4. Ian Cowman, *Dominion or Decline: Anglo-American Naval Relations on the Pacific, 1937–1941* (Oxford: Berg, 1996), p. 121.
5. Quoted in Ivan Maisky, *Memoirs of a Soviet Ambassador: The War 1939–43* (London: Hutchinson, 1967), p. 22.
6. Wm. Roger Louis, *Imperialism at Bay: The United States and the Decolonization of the British Empire, 1941–1945* (Oxford: Clarendon, 1977), pp. 129–32.
7. Ibid. p. 378.
8. Sir Oliver Franks, *Central Planning and Control in War and Peace* (London: Longman, 1947), p. 21.
9. Martin Kitchen, *British Policy towards the Soviet Union during the Second World War* (Basingstoke: Macmillan, 1986), p. 150.
10. Minute by Strang, October 1939, National Archives (London), FO 371/23058 no. 17104. On Foreign Office worries about Soviet aspirations to 'bolshevise an exhausted Europe' see Sir Llewellyn Woodward, *British Foreign Policy in the Second World War*, single vol. edn (London: Stationery Office, 1962), pp. 8, 17.
11. Anthony Eden, *Freedom and Order: Selected Speeches, 1939–1946* (London: Faber, 1947), p. 110. The transition politically to a sense of implacable hostility to Germany is discussed extensively in Anthony Glees, *Exile Politics during the Second World War: The German Social Democrats in Britain* (Oxford: Clarendon, 1982). Its implications for the conduct of war between the two countries is the subject of a Rand Corporation report: Frederick M. Sallager, *The Road to Total War* (New York: Van Nostrand Reinhold, 1969).
12. For a recent discussion see Martin H. Folly, *Churchill, Whitehall and the Soviet Union, 1940–45* (Basingstoke: Macmillan, 2000), pp. 35–8, 83–102.
13. Glees, *Exile Politics*, p. 62.
14. Article by Tom Bower in *The Times*, 16 March 1985.
15. Martin Gilbert, *Finest Hour: Winston S. Churchill, 1939–1941* (London: Heinemann, 1983), pp. 943–4, 994, 1031; Aaron Goldman, 'Germans and Nazis: the

controversy over "Vansittartism" in Britain during the Second World War', *Journal of Contemporary History*, vol. 14, 1979, p. 165; T. D. Burridge, *British Labour and Hitler's War* (London: Deutsch, 1976), p. 111; Kitchen, *British Policy*, p. 109. For further detail on the Eden–Stalin discussions see Chapter 5 below.

16. For Eden see Victor Rothwell, *Britain and the Cold War, 1941–1947* (London: Cape, 1982), p. 26, and the Earl of Avon, *The Eden Memoirs: The Reckoning* (London: Cassell, 1965), pp. 475–6; National Archives (London), minutes of Armistice and Post-War Committee, 4 January 1945, CAB 87/69; Richard Lamb, *The Ghosts of Peace, 1935–1945* (Salisbury: Michael Russell, 1987), pp. 238–43; Foreign Office memorandum, 27 December 1944, CAB 87/68 no. 127.

17. Keith Sainsbury, 'British policy and German unity at the end of the Second World War', *English Historical Review*, vol. 94, 1979, pp. 789–90.

18. This emerges from the committee's minutes in the CAB 87 series cited in note 16 above; see also Kenneth Harris, *Attlee* (London: Weidenfeld, 1982), p. 211.

19. Hubert Gladwyn, *The Memoirs of Lord Gladwyn* (London: Weidenfeld, 1972), pp. 131–2.

20. Glees, *Exile Politics*, pp. 120, 200–1; Goldman, 'The controversy', pp. 156–7.

21. Glees, *Exile Politics*, pp. 152–6; Donald C. Watt, 'The European civil war', in Wolfgang J. Mommsen and Lothar Kettenacker (eds), *The Fascist Challenge and the Policy of Appeasement* (London: Allen and Unwin, 1983), pp. 16–17.

22. Rothwell, *Britain and the Cold War*, pp. 27–8; Lamb, *Ghosts*, pp. 226–7.

23. Rothwell, *Britain and the Cold War*, p. 29; Lamb, *Ghosts*, pp. 285–9, 296–303.

24. Rothwell, *Britain and the Cold War*, pp. 50–1; Goldman, 'The controversy', p. 173; minute by Roberts, 20 September 1944, FO 371/39116 no. 12405.

25. Hedva Ben-Israel, 'Cross purposes: British reactions to the German anti-Nazi opposition', *Journal of Contemporary History*, vol. 20, 1985, pp. 423–38. This may be compared with the almost total lack of first-hand knowledge of Germany among the most outspoken pro-German publicists in Britain before and immediately after the First World War. A. J. P. Taylor, *The Troublemakers: Dissent over Foreign Policy, 1792–1939* (London: Hamish Hamilton, 1957), pp. 115, 177.

26. Glees, *Exile Politics*, pp. 190–2; Rothwell, *Britain and the Cold War*, pp. 22, 29, for Strang's contempt for the German opponents of Hitler.

27. Minutes of committee, 11 August 1943, FO 371/34461 no. 12405.

28. Rothwell, *Britain and the Cold War*, pp. 48–9.

29. Ibid. pp. 38–9; John Colville, *The Fringes of Power: Downing Street Diaries, 1939–1955* (London: Hodder, 1985), p. 313.

30. Lamb, *Ghosts*, pp. 307–12.

31. 'Anglo-Soviet political conversations at Moscow, October 9–October 17 1944', record of meetings on 9 and 17 October, copy in Ismay papers (King's College, London University), VI/10.

32. Avon, *Reckoning*, pp. 378–9. When addressing Churchill, Eden, probably against his better judgement, expressed support for dismemberment. David Carlton, *Anthony Eden; A Biography* (London: Allen Lane, 1981), p. 211. In a speech at Edinburgh on 8 May 1942 Eden stated that if any anti-Nazi Germans wished to be taken seriously, they would have to overthrow Hitler and set up a 'German state which is based on respect for law and for the rights of the individual'. Eden, *Freedom and Order*, p. 159. This seemed to imply non-dismemberment in return for an anti-Nazi coup since it would have been a strange sort of reward to enforce dismemberment on a regime that had restored legality and individual rights.

33. Burridge, *British Labour*, pp. 169, 172; ministerial committee on Armistice

Terms and Civil Administration, minutes 3 April 1944, CAB 87/84; Armistice and Post-War Committee, minutes 20 July 1944, CAB 87/66; memoranda by Attlee and Eden, 11 and 19 July 1944, CAB 87/67 nos. 43 and 47.

34. Sir Llewellyn Woodward, *British Foreign Policy in the Second World War: Volume V* (London: Stationery Office, 1976), pp. 45–6, 212–13; Harris, *Attlee*, p. 211.

35. Committee on Post-War Settlement, 11 August 1943, FO 371/34461 no. 12172; minute by Roberts, 28 July 1944, FO 371/39079 no. 9626.

36. Armistice and Post-War Committee minutes, 20 July 1944, CAB 87/66.

37. Rothwell, *Britain and the Cold War*, pp. 68–73; Michael Balfour and John Mair, *Four-Power Control in Germany and Austria, 1945–1946* (London: Oxford University Press, 1956), pp. 273–94 (but Mair is wrong to argue on pp. 273–4 that Britain issued 'declarations of an official determination to restore Austrian independence' before October 1943; the statements that he cites were a commitment to no more than that Nazi rule there must end); Armistice and Post-War Committee minutes, 23 November 1944, CAB 87/66.

38. Minute by Roberts, 1 December 1942, FO 371/31519 no. 1464.

39. Woodward, *British Foreign Policy V*, pp. 250–5, 259–60.

40. On the wish for a short period only of military occupation, see memorandum by Chiefs of Staff, 12 December 1943, CAB 87/83 no. 20; and minutes of Armistice and Post-War Committee, 21 September 1944, CAB 87/66.

41. Woodward, *British Foreign Policy V*, p. 50.

42. Minute by Con O'Neill, November 1944, FO 371/26559 no. 16074.

43. Minute by Roberts, 6 August 1941, FO 371/26559 no. 7108.

44. Nicholas Pronay and Keith Wilson (eds), *The Political Re-education of Germany and Her Allies after World War II* (London: Croom Helm, 1985), pp. 5–7 (introduction by Pronay).

45. Rothwell, *Britain and the Cold War*, pp. 184–6; Vojtech Mastny, *Russia's Road to the Cold War, 1941–1945* (New York: Columbia University Press, 1979), p. 58.

46. Articles by Gottfried Niedhart and James S. Herndon in Mommsen and Kettenacker (eds), *Fascist Challenge*, pp. 286–319.

47. Avon, *Reckoning*, pp. 291–2; Harrison quoted in Glees, *Exile Politics*, p. 160.

48. Donald Gillies, *Radical Diplomat: The Life of Archibald Clark Kerr, Lord Inverchapel, 1882–1951* (London: Tauris, 1999), pp. 138–9.

49. Elisabeth Barker, *British Policy in South-East Europe in the Second World War* (London: Macmillan, 1976), pp. 131, 133.

50. Ibid. pp. 48–51, 173–6.

51. Ibid. pp. 139–43, 206–7, 233.

52. Ibid. pp. 163, 182–3.

53. V. Trukhanovsky, *British Foreign Policy during World War II, 1939–1945* (Moscow: Progress Publishers, 1970), p. 341.

54. Armistice and Post-War Committee minutes, 23 August 1944, CAB 87/66.

55. Gladwyn, *Memoirs*, pp. 112–18; Woodward, *British Foreign Policy V*, pp. 3–18.

56. Minute by Jebb, 1 May 1943, FO 371/34458 no. 4611; War Cabinet minutes, 5 October 1943, CAB 65/40; John Harvey (ed.), *The War Diaries of Oliver Harvey, 1941–1945* (London: Collins, 1978), p. 304 (entry for 6 October 1943).

57. Balfour and Mair, *Four-Power Control*, p. 32; Rothwell, *Britain and the Cold War*, p. 50.

58. Woodward, *British Foreign Policy V*, p. 182.

59. Memorandum by Law, 14 April 1944, CAB 87/84 no. 23.

60. Memorandum from German Department of Foreign Office, 15 July 1944, FO 371/39116 no. 9330; minute by Harrison, 9 December 1944, FO 371/39226 no. 16074.

61. Armistice and Post-War Committee minutes, 20 July 1944, CAB 87/66; Grigg to his father, 9 September 1943 and 30 July 1944, and Grigg to Field Marshal Montgomery, 25 July and 6 December 1944, Grigg papers (Churchill College, Cambridge), 9/6 and 8.

62. Gillies, *Radical Diplomat*, pp. 159–60.

63. Memorandum by Orme Sargent, 5 February 1942, in Graham Ross (ed.), *The Foreign Office and the Kremlin: British Documents on Anglo-Soviet Relations, 1941–45* (Cambridge: Cambridge University Press, 1984), document 6, p. 87.

64. Woodward, *British Foreign Policy V*, p. 79; Colville, *Fringes*, p. 570.

65. Lord Strang, 'Prelude to Potsdam: reflections on war and foreign policy', *International Affairs*, vol. 46, 1970, pp. 441–54, especially pp. 442, 453.

66. This account of the zonal division of Germany is largely based on Tony Sharp, *The Wartime Alliance and the Zonal Division of Germany* (Oxford: Clarendon, 1975), chs I–IV.

67. Kurt Koszyk, 'The press in the British zone of Germany', in Pronay and Wilson (eds), *Re-education*, pp. 110–11.

68. Glees, *Exile Politics*, pp. 202–3.

69. Avon, *Reckoning*, pp. 515–16; Mastny, *Russia's Road*, pp. 127, 242; Rothwell, *Britain and the Cold War*, pp. 43–4, 66–7; Frank King, 'Allied negotiations and the dismemberment of Germany', in Walter Laqueur (ed.), *The Second World War* (London: Sage, 1982), pp. 362–72; Armistice and Post-War Committee minutes, 27 July 1944, CAB 87/66; memorandum for committee by Eden, 19 March 1945, CAB 87/69 no. 40; text of Yalta agreement on German dismemberment in Diane Shaver Clemens, *Yalta* (London: Oxford University Press, 1970), p. 304.

70. G. M. Alexander, *The Prelude to the Truman Doctrine: British Policy in Greece, 1944–1947* (Oxford: Clarendon, 1982); William Roger Louis, *The British Empire in the Middle East* (Oxford: Clarendon, 1984).

71. For the wartime origins of the western European group idea see Rothwell, *Britain and the Cold War*, ch. 8; see also Woodward, *British Foreign Policy V*, pp. 189–90.

72. Quoted in Roy Douglas, *From War to Cold War, 1942–1948* (Basingstoke: Macmillan, 1981), p. 61.

73. Avon, *Reckoning*, p. 445; Woodward, *British Foreign Policy V*, pp. 204–5; Kitchen, *British Policy*, pp. 200–1; Folly, *Churchill, Whitehall and the Soviet Union*, p. 119.

74. Armistice and Post-War Committee minutes, 31 August 1944, CAB 87/66.

75. Woodward, *British Foreign Policy V*, pp. 205–10; Rothwell, *Britain and the Cold War*, pp. 33, 118–23; Ross, *The Foreign Office and the Kremlin*, document 27, pp. 157–66; Sir Llewellyn Woodward, 'Some reflections on British policy, 1939–45', *International Affairs*, vol. 31, 1955, pp. 273–90, especially pp. 284–5.

76. David Dilks (ed.), *The Diaries of Sir Alexander Cadogan O.M., 1938–1945*, (London: Cassell, 1971), p. 778.

77. The most detailed recent examination is Folly, *Churchill, Whitehall and the Soviet Union*.

78. Gladwyn, *Memoirs*, pp. 144–5, 156.

79. Memorandum by Sargent, 'Stocktaking after VE Day', FO 371/50912 no. 5471.

80. Woodward, *British Foreign Policy V*, p. 202.

81. Minute by Troubeck, February 1944, FO 371/39091 no. 2261.

82. Foreign Office memorandum, November 1944, CAB 87/68 no. 118.

83. Report by Joint-Intelligence Sub-Committee, September 1944, CAB 87/68 no. 80.

84. Commentary by Grigg on the Non-Fraternisation Order, March 1945, Grigg papers, 9/9/20.

85. Michael Balfour, 'Re-education in retrospect', in Pronay and Wilson (eds), Re-education, p. 140.
86. Armistice and Post-War Committee minutes, 17 May 1945, CAB 87/69.
87. R. T. Thomas, Britain and Vichy: The Dilemma of Anglo-French Relations, 1940–42 (London: Macmillan, 1979), pp. 7–9.
88. J. F. V. Keiger, France and the World since 1870 (London: Arnold, 2001), pp. 137, 174–6.
89. Thomas, Britain and Vichy, pp. 39, 53–6.
90. A. W. DePorte, De Gaulle's Foreign Policy, 1944–1946 (Cambridge: Harvard University Press, 1968), pp. ix–x, 13–15, 22.
91. Thomas, Britain and Vichy, p. 121.
92. On this see DePorte, De Gaulle, pp. 35, 280–1.
93. Thomas, Britain and Vichy, pp. 120–4, 162, 165. More than fifteen years after the end of the war, the Foreign Office's Official Historian could still express moral indignation about the evil of dealings with Darlan. Woodward, British Foreign Policy in the Second World War, p. 211.
94. Most notably François Kersaudy, Churchill and De Gaulle (London: Collins, 1981). De Gaulle's importance is illustrated by the index entry for him in a wartime publication by the Free French movement: 'The references to General de Gaulle are too numerous to be given separately.' Felix de Grand'Combe, The Three Years of Fighting France, June 1940–June 1943 (London: Wells Gardner, Darton, 1943), p. 202.
95. Elisabeth Barker, Churchill and Eden at War (London: Macmillan, 1978), pp. 97, 128, 137–8.
96. Sharp, The Zonal Division, p. 55.
97. W. Averell Harriman and Elie Abel, Special Envoy to Churchill and Stalin, 1941–1946 (New York: Random House, 1975), p. 231; DePorte, De Gaulle, pp. 47–9. At the Tehran conference Stalin and Molotov expressed savage contempt for France, and Stalin agreed with Roosevelt that Indochina must not revert to French rule. Harriman and Abel, pp. 265–8, 275–6. De Gaulle's March 1944 speech provoked a Soviet protest. Georges-Henri Soutou, 'General de Gaulle and the Soviet Union, 1943–5', in Francesca Gori and Silvio Pons (eds), The Soviet Union and Europe in the Cold War, 1943–53 (Basingstoke: Macmillan, 1996), p. 316.
98. Steve Weiss, Allies in Conflict: Anglo-American Strategic Negotiations, 1938–44 (Basingstoke: Macmillan, 1996), p. 17.
99. Norman J. W. Goda, Tomorrow the World: Hitler, Northwest Africa, and the Path toward America (College Station: Texas A. & M. University Press, 1998), pp. 171–4, 181–2; Robert Dallek, 'Roosevelt and De Gaulle', in Robert O. Paxton and Nicholas Wahl (eds), De Gaulle and the United States: A Centennial Reappraisal (Oxford: Berg, 1994), pp. 50, 55, 58; Arthur J. Dommen, Conflict in Laos: The Politics of Neutralization (New York: Praeger, 1971), p. 19.
100. Andrew Shennan, Rethinking France: Plans for Renewal, 1940–1946 (Oxford: Clarendon, 1989), pp. 67, 141, 146–55; John W. Wheeler-Bennett and Anthony Nicholls, The Semblance of Peace: The Political Settlement after the Second World War (London: Macmillan, 1972), p. 109.
101. Norman Rich, Hitler's War Aims: The Establishment of the New Order (London: Deutsch, 1974), pp. 215–16; Keiger, France and the World, pp. 139–40. Darlan had been more ambitious for France than most leading Vichyites, whose idea of a 'National Revolution' centred on recasting France as a semi-authoritarian state within a fascist, German-dominated Europe, and with any notion of

recovering full independence relegated to a distant future. Shennan, *Rethinking France*, pp. 7–8, 22–4.

102. Steven Casey, *Cautious Crusade: Franklin D. Roosevelt, American Public Opinion, and the War against Nazi Germany* (Oxford: Oxford University Press, 2001), pp. 110–17, 121–3; Thomas, *Britain and Vichy*, pp. 153–7, 162–3, 174–7; Weiss, *Allies in Conflict*, p. 75.

103. Henry Kissinger, *Diplomacy* (New York: Simon and Schuster, 1994), p. 396.

104. Winston S. Churchill, *The Second World War Volume Three: The Grand Alliance* (London: Reprint Society edn, 1952), p. 623.

105. Louis, *Imperialism at Bay*, pp. 40n, 277–8, 356.

106. DePorte, *De Gaulle*, pp. 35, 81–90; Shennan, *Rethinking France*, pp. 8–13.

107. Herbert Feis, *Churchill, Roosevelt, Stalin: The War They Waged and the Peace They Sought* (Princeton: Princeton University Press, 1957), p. 472.

108. Sharp, *The Zonal Division*, p. 169, on Foreign Office opposition to France being allowed to pursue 'a divergent policy on Rhineland affairs as they did after the last war'; DePorte, *De Gaulle*, pp. 57–8, 63–83, 94–101; Soutou in Gori and Pons (eds), *The Soviet Union and Europe*, pp. 318–26.

109. Robert E. Sherwood, *The White House Papers of Harry L. Hopkins: Volume II, January 1942–July 1945* (London: Eyre, 1949), p. 849.

110. Sharp, *The Zonal Division*, pp. 172, 179–80.

111. Ibid. pp. 188, 193–9.

112. DePorte, *De Gaulle*, ch. V, on France and the founding of the United Nations.

4

The United States

THE SETTING FOR AMERICAN WAR AIMS
AND EARLY DEVELOPMENTS

President Franklin D. Roosevelt was a leader of immense importance, but he was not the be-all and the end-all of US Second World War war aims. Henry Kissinger has described him as embodying a foreign policy and a body of war aims in which there was only a little of 'personal idiosyncrasy' and much that 'vented the attitude of a people with more faith in the inherent goodness of man than in geopolitical analysis', leading to a desire to 'bring about a world community compatible with America's democratic and social ideals as the best guarantee of peace'. The appearance that he was imbued with a vague, if not woolly, idealism is indicated by his first statement of American aims, though they could not be called war aims because the US was still at peace, in January 1941. This enunciated Four Freedoms – of speech, worship and from want and fear. In fact this was the first, and necessarily vague, salvo by the President to stake out a claim for the eventual peace settlement to be on American terms. He followed it by sending his confidant, Harry Hopkins, to advise the British Foreign Office that the President would take it amiss if Britain issued any competing statement of war aims. This private warning to a semi-ally was the counterpart to many public presidential identifications of the individuals who stood in the way of the realisation of these freedoms. They were 'the Nazi masters of Germany', whom he denounced countless times by name between late December 1940 and early December 1941, and with whom negotiation was pointless and appeasement senseless.[1]

Thus Roosevelt was leading America towards the destruction of the Nazi regime as a US aim even while three-quarters of Americans were, according to opinion polls, opposed to going to war with Germany. Excluding the Far East, which is largely dealt with in another chapter, American war aims may be divided into two categories: those that the majority of the American people could accept with enthusiasm or at least without much questioning, and those that required a revolution in American thinking. Foremost among the former was the quest for economic advantages for the United States. If Gabriel Kolko's assertion that US foreign policy in the Second World War was in essence 'a foreign economic policy' goes too far, then David Reynolds's view that wartime American economic imperialism was a subconscious temptation rather than an actual policy does not go far enough.[2] American foreign policymakers in the 1930s had been obsessed with a search for foreign commercial opportunities in the context of an American economy that seemed incapable of fully recovering from the abyss into which it had fallen after the Wall Street crash in 1929. Many of them feared that, without such recovery, the American people would turn to the horrors of 'national planning, self-containment and eventually socialism' (Secretary of State Cordell Hull) for the US. In this febrile atmosphere, the view had become entrenched that the manifest political differences between Britain and Germany were not matched in the economic sphere. The one with preferential trading arrangements with its Dominions and the other intent on controlling a closed European economic bloc were both guilty of 'economic totalitarianism' (US ambassador to Britain Joseph Kennedy). The smallest losses to even potential American economic penetration were lamented, and help to account for the sharpness of the American protest against the Soviet annexation in 1940 of the Baltic republics of Estonia, Latvia and Lithuania with their tiny and almost poverty-stricken economies. Their annexation meant their loss to the closed economy of the Soviet Union.[3]

Against this background, the US sought many advantages after agreeing in principle to provide economic aid, without which the British war effort could not have continued, in the Lend-Lease scheme that was passed by Congress in early 1941. For instance, as a precondition for aid Britain was required to divest itself of many of its investments in the US, including the Courtaulds company's subsidiary, American Viscose, which produced 60 per cent of American rayon output and accounted for half the parent company's income. (It should be added that some British economic officials in wartime Washington have testified that there was an element of generosity in the Americans with whom they negotiated that is not preserved in the documentary record.[4]) Lend-Lease was designed to aid the British war effort while also denying Britain any possible opportunities to resist US economic war aims. The same ambition was also a factor in the thinking that informed the American side at the celebrated meeting between Churchill and Roosevelt and their delegations off Newfoundland in August 1941. This should not be exaggerated. The political purposes of this meeting, which were the main ones, are discussed elsewhere in this chapter, and Roosevelt spent little time discussing policy, either political or economic, with his entourage on the outward voyage.[5] His most animated discussions with Churchill were on the Far East, and when Roosevelt raised the subject of the need to abolish imperial economic ties he did so in a spirit of playful teasing, though Churchill's response was truculent.[6] The American side had to make do with a vague commitment (one point out of eight that issued from the conference) about the desirability of trade liberalisation without prejudice to existing commitments. Even that was publicly presented by Churchill and Roosevelt as primarily a reassurance to the German and Italian peoples that their countries would not be excluded from world trade if only they became peaceloving.[7] It could hardly have been otherwise given the President's patrician disdain for trade, and the impossibility for the Americans of demanding precise economic commitments from Britain at the same time as they were not only refusing to discuss with it political aims but were also insisting that it should not enter into arrangements with 'any of its allies' (i.e. the Soviets) without American knowledge and agreement. Cadogan of the Foreign Office reassured Sumner Welles of the State Department that Britain had entered into no war aims commitments with anyone except for an 'oral statement' to Yugoslavia to 'reconsider' the Yugoslav-Italian border when it had been trying unsuccessfully to draw that country into the war a few months earlier.[8]

As the United States moved ever closer towards involvement in a war that was certain to be an ordeal that would cost huge numbers of American lives, the senior State Department official Adolf Berle could tell *Fortune* magazine in October 1941 that the then prevailing international situation involved 'the opportunity to create the most brilliant epoch the US has yet seen. It is entirely feasible to make the country at once more prosperous and more free than it has ever been.'[9] He and those who thought like him, including Cordell Hull, took the view that any actual war with Germany and Japan would have to be accompanied by a sort of cold war against Britain and the Soviet Union, which were assumed to be intent on thwarting an American economic agenda that gained legitimacy and nobility from seeking only equal rights for all countries in international trade and commerce. The Anglo-Soviet alliance treaty of May 1942 consisted of generalities that the State Department suspected of masking an intention to divide Europe into British and Soviet spheres of influence that would negate what Hull later told Eden in 1943 must be a new order 'based on liberal commercial policies'. William C. Bullitt was unusual in foreign policy circles in having some understanding that, if the British were toying with such an idea, it was for reasons of postwar security, including a desire to contain Germany and awareness of Soviet strength, and not from motives of economic greed.[10] These suspicions contributed to a policy of keeping Britain on the shortest of economic leashes by manipulating Lend-Lease aid, dollar balances (Britain's were not to be allowed to rise much above one billion) and exports to make it difficult for Britain to resist American economic aims both while the war was going on and afterwards.[11] Britain had some influence in shaping a planned institution, the International Monetary Fund (IMF), which had the aim of reducing problems in the international economy after the war. To a significant extent, the IMF was born out of the stormy relationship between an American official, Harry Dexter White, and an Englishman, John Maynard Keynes, though the outcome, as described no doubt accurately by White, reflected not so much the relative power of their two intellects as that of their two countries: 'It is part compromise, but much more like the American plan.'[12]

Perhaps the most important single American war aim directed against Britain related to Middle East oil supplies. In 1943 a fear swept across the US that the country's own oil reserves were nearing exhaustion, and a Petroleum Reserves Corporation was set up to acquire foreign oil reserves. In 1943 a new chief administrator of US economic operations in the Middle East was sent out with instructions to maximise America's share of the region's oil resources.[13] The visit of an American mission to London in April 1944 succeeded in preventing this issue from seriously threatening relations, and resulted in a de facto division in which Saudi Arabia became American for oil purposes while Britain stayed on in the other two great Middle East oil producers, Iran and Iraq, though it was alarming that in the former the Soviets were demanding oil concessions by 1944.[14] The Roosevelt administration was apt to assert that its quest for oil concessions would bring political emancipation and social improvement to the inhabitants of the oil-producing countries. In January 1944 Roosevelt wrote to Hull about Iran as a unique challenge to the US to use its expertise (but not any significant amount of money) to raise a people, 99 per cent of whom were 'in effect in bondage to the other one per cent'. The President described himself as 'rather thrilled with the idea of using Iran as an example of what we can do by an unselfish American policy' of promoting social reform.[15]

The fundamentally commercial motives underlying this solicitude were rendered doubly ironic by the fact that Zionist pressures in the US were impelling it towards support for a political change that all Arabs and Muslims regarded with abhorrence: the creation of a Jewish state in Palestine. This was a case of a British First World War aim becoming an American Second World War aim. During their gardening weekends together, Eden told his friend, the American ambassador John G. Winant, that he had an important negative war aim which was that the current war should not produce any anti-Arab commitment like the Balfour Declaration of 1917 in the previous conflict. Winant formed the impression that, for Eden, this was a major preoccupation. [16] He had reason to worry. In wartime America Republicans and Democrats were running neck and neck in opinion polls and actual election results, and consequently engaged in a steadily escalating bidding war for the votes of pro-Zionist Jews.[17] Bodies like the Zionist Organisation of America professed neutrality in US domestic politics, but that was clearly conditional on the absence of any discernible differences in the two parties' support for what was referred to as 'a Jewish Commonwealth in Palestine'.

Anti-British American economic war aims reached their nadir in the matter of Argentinian beef. The wartime British (and some later historians) found it particularly difficult to distinguish between obsessive self-righteousness, the desire for economic gain and suspicion of evil British intentions in America's demand for a boycott of Argentina on the grounds that its government was fascist, even though it supplied Britain with two-thirds of its meagre supply of beef. Genuine revulsion against the regime in Buenos Aires, a desire for economic opportunities and a suspicion that Britain wanted to absorb Argentina completely into a closed British economic bloc all played their part.[18] American hopes of bending Britain to its will economically were most likely to be realised when Britain was asked to relinquish only half an asset, as in the case of Middle East oil, and if Britain was offered in return something that it could not otherwise have except at great cost, notably the atomic bomb. Donald Cameron Watt has stated that the wartime Quebec agreements on nuclear sharing that held out the prospect of a British atomic bomb on the cheap were, for Roosevelt, 'only the final hook with which he hoped to secure British good behaviour after the war's end'.[19]

In teaching Britain, and especially Churchill, the rudiments of such good behaviour in an (American) new world order, the President was conscious that he had a pupil who was both apt and backward. On the one hand, Churchill could not be faulted about his support for a permanent Anglo-American relationship, which he expounded during visits to the US in May and September 1943 and in which he gave no indication of having any worries about the unequal nature of such a relationship, which could only be one in which America would be effectively in command. Gladwyn Jebb, a senior Foreign Office official and a publicist for British membership of a united Europe after he retired from diplomacy, was not the only one to be appalled in Britain then or later.[20] On the other hand, Roosevelt was dismayed by Churchill's inability to understand that the American people would only truly support the alliance with Britain if it subscribed to idealistic war aims as they were conceived in the USA. This caused him worry to the end. In January 1945 the *New York Times* published a leak of an actually false message from president to prime minister, warning that the mood of the American people could change 'as mercurially as the English weather if the American people once get the idea that this war . . . [is] just another struggle between rival imperialisms'. The leak was probably made deliberately as a warning to Britain, one which avoided being offensive to Churchill personally.

At the Yalta conference a month later, Roosevelt's warning to Stalin that the American people would not understand anything that fell short of a 'meeting of minds' among the leaders of the great powers might equally have been addressed to Churchill.[21] Stalin perhaps sighed and 'remarked that the weakness of the democracies lay in the fact that the people did not delegate permanently rights such as the Soviet government possessed'.[22]

To return to Roosevelt and the Anglo-American relationship, national security gradually became more important in US war aims and economic objectives (discussed above) and anti-imperialism (discussed below) less; and Britain had a vital role to play in American national security. With its own insular position and its many strategically located colonies, Britain was needed to ensure that many potential threats to US security emanating from outside the western hemisphere could be dealt with before they impinged upon the territory and population of the US itself. In the words of the historian Martin J. Sherwin, Britain was to be 'America's outpost on the European frontier, the sentinel for the New World in the Old'.[23] This meant that Britain could not rationally be denied assistance in any economic difficulties that might arise after the war. President Truman, though not an Anglophile, greatly regretted that he had to couple the termination of Lend-Lease aid to Russia after Japan surrendered, which he wanted, with termination of aid to Britain, which he would have liked to continue.[24] Above all, Roosevelt took the view that the potentially high-risk obligation that he was asking Britain to undertake on behalf of America meant that it was entitled to have the atomic bomb with which to defend itself if some future isolationist US administration left it in the lurch. The British themselves were not above aiding the President in the evolution of his thinking on this subject by threatening to divert resources from their war effort into making a purely British atomic bomb, even though there was clearly no possibility of such a project reaching fruition until some time after the latest conceivable date for German defeat.[25]

Roosevelt had a tendency to keep his own counsel and to be more revealing of his true thoughts to selected foreign visitors such as Soviet foreign minister Molotov and the British economist, John Maynard Keynes, than to those in his administration. Consequently, much American war aims work below the supreme level started off in a vacuum. The head of what should have been the most relevant department, Secretary of State Cordell Hull, rationalised this by convincing himself of the importance of abstract principles. In his memoirs he was to reaffirm that principles needed to come first: 'If the principles were strongly enough proclaimed and adhered to, the details would find readier solution when the time came to solve them.'[26] On 22 December 1941 Hull secured presidential approval for the setting up in the State Department of an Advisory Committee on Post-War Foreign Policy, which was to include representatives from other government departments, Congressmen and some private individuals. Its remit was to consider what would theoretically be best in postwar aims without reference to what was going on in the war. It met as sub-committees between May 1942 and July 1943, when Hull, finally tiring of first principles, disbanded it and informed his senior officials that the time had come to move into the real world of war aims, which would involve negotiations with allies and, in effect, with such features on the Washington landscape as the White House. It would be easy to mock this effort, as does its State Department officer-turned-academic historian: 'Apparently none of the planners, including Secretary Hull, had a glimmering of what the real pattern of the international system would look like in the decades immediately following the war ... American responsibility in maintaining an international settlement was such a radical change in our historic position.' Consequently, it anticipated only a limited measure of long-term American involvement in the world through the United Nations organisation. 'In sum, the postwar world was to be cleaned up in an optimum manner and then set free to operate according to its nature, with an international organisation as a regulating mechanism.'[27] The most noteworthy of the sub-committees was the one on Security Problems, which, under the chairmanship of Norman Davis, had White House connections. While acknowledging the need for a 'diplomacy of principle' in which moral norms would replace power politics, it recommended requiring Germany and Japan to surrender unconditionally in order not to repeat the error of November 1918 when an armistice had enabled Germans to convince themselves that they had not really been defeated. Finally, as an 'interim' measure before the UN fully flowered, there would be merit in a 'two-bloc system' of which one bloc was made up of the principal victorious powers and the other consisted of the remaining states.[28] There is more below in this chapter on such a 'system'; and further developments in American bureaucratic war aims planning are examined in Chapter 6.

ANTI-IMPERIALISM IN US WAR AIMS

Anti-imperialism as a war aim was axiomatic and congenial in relation to allies as well as to the enemy powers. The rhetoric of Roosevelt's presidency was uncompromising in its anti-imperialism from the start. In a speech in his home state of New York in the summer of 1936 he noted with pride that he had removed all restrictions on the independence of Cuba and went on: 'We seek to dominate no other nation. We ask no territorial expansion. We oppose imperialism ... We believe in democracy; we believe in freedom.'[29] American hostility to imperialism grew in intensity during the interwar period. It has been argued that America's own imperialism 'died during childhood' in the early twentieth century, and that disillusionment with the country's colonial experiment in the Philippines, annexed from Spain in 1898, was the main contributing factor.[30] And yet the peacetime Roosevelt administration embarked on an imperialist venture of its own in relation to annexing small islands in the central Pacific that were strategically placed for air routes. These were claimed by Britain or New Zealand, giving the appearance of a clash of imperialisms. In April 1939 Britain and the US resolved their dispute over two islands, Canton and Enderbury, by proclaiming them a condominium.[31]

By contrast, there were some British-owned islands, those in the West Indies, that Roosevelt positively wanted Britain to keep on the grounds that they were political and financial 'headaches'. What he did not say was that their largely black populations would have added to America's perceived racial problem if Britain had left and they had gravitated into the US orbit. They would have become like the inhabitants of Puerto Rico who had unrestricted access to the US and who were reported in 1945 to have the highest rate of population growth ever recorded in the world. This caused Roosevelt to joke to a friend about the advantages of sterilisation for America's Caribbean colony.[32] If Roosevelt was in any sense a racist, it stemmed not from bigotry or hatred but from fear and, in particular, from his awareness of world demography; non-whites already outnumbered whites and would outnumber them even more in the future. His solution was conciliation and the hand of friendship. In June 1944, speaking specifically about the 'yellow race' (though other remarks make it clear that he applied the same principle to 'the brown people in the East'), he remarked at a White House dinner that, 'It will be to the advantage of the white race to be friends with them and work in cooperation with them, rather than make enemies and have them eventually use all the machines of western civilisation to overrun and conquer the white race.'[33]

To Roosevelt after Pearl Harbor victory in the war would be incomplete if it did not bring with it timetables for the end of European colonial empires. A visit to the British West African colony of the Gambia after the Casablanca conference in early 1943 confirmed his suspicions about British colonial exploitation. A full year later, still indignant, he waxed eloquent to a press conference about the iniquity of what he had seen in a colony in which 150 whites lorded it over 'about three million' Africans. (The actual population of the Gambia in 1943 was around 200,000.) Perhaps because of his ancestry, Roosevelt had a soft spot for Dutch rule in the Netherlands East Indies (modern-day Indonesia), but only on the premise that Holland would, after its own liberation from German occupation, grant independence to two of the three largest islands in the East Indies, Java and Sumatra. In the third, Borneo, the President conceded that it would take time to educate the 'headhunters' to prepare them for statehood.[34]

Decolonisation of European empires as a war aim was not a special enthusiasm of Roosevelt's within the American political world. The powerful (until his abrupt fall in 1943) Under Secretary of State, Sumner Welles, was even more strongly in favour, and made it the theme of his address on one of the most sacred dates in the American calendar, Memorial Day, which commemorates the dead of the Civil War, in 1942 to proclaim that: 'Our victory must bring in its train the liberation of all peoples. Discrimination between peoples because of their race, creed or colour must be abolished. The age of imperialism is ended.' He combined this denunciation of European imperialism with an equally vehement indictment of the folly of American isolationism, which was 'the bitter fruit of our own folly and our own lack of vision'.[35] Not everyone agreed. Another senior man in the State Department, Stanley Hornbeck, a Rhodes scholar, saw much to admire in the British Empire, while the General Board of the US navy wanted it to continue as being in America's strategic interest.[36] Roosevelt's anti-colonial aim was also impeded by a degree of presidential carelessness. As already noted, he attributed to the Gambia fifteen times more inhabitants than it actually had. On another occasion he included the independent kingdom of Thailand in a list of south-east Asian countries that should become independent. Towards the end of his life he bracketed the fairly small Pacific island of New Caledonia, which remains a French overseas territory to the present day, with Indochina as front-rank candidates for early independence.[37] Adding to the inconsistency, he had told Molotov in 1942 that Indochina would be incapable of independence within the foreseeable future, and would need international trusteeship of indefinite duration.[38] He also seems to have had no conception that French Indochina consisted of a patchwork of colonies, protectorates and ethnic groups that could not possibly have become independent as one state except on the presumably undesirable basis of the largest group, the Vietnamese, ruling the others.

More fundamentally, the anti-imperialist aim collided with other, emerging American aims and with the opposition of the colonial powers, especially Britain. The former related to strategic places, mostly islands, that were to be used to protect the United States from future aggressors. The driving factors were nightmare memories of the Pearl Harbor catastrophe and a preoccupation with air routes for both civilian and military use. The requirement was for bases and for air transit and landing rights outside the formal base network. To the east of the North American continent the US wanted bases on the Atlantic islands of Iceland and the Azores as a minimum, and then landing rights at various points across north Africa and southern

Asia from Casablanca to Manila. In addition, in 1945 six areas of Latin America, including the whole of Mexico, were designated as vitally important to the US either for strategic reasons or for their raw materials, so that attack on them would be equivalent to attack on the US itself. To a historian of these developments, they were 'a natural evolution of the Monroe Doctrine, accentuated by Axis aggression and new technological imperatives'.[39] The use of force or harsh threats to acquire these assets was ruled out. Host governments' consent would be essential; they would have to be persuaded that an American presence would also be in their interest. Thus, in Iceland the base was to be nominally operated by a civilian company under contract to the US air force. In the Azores the base would fly the Portuguese flag and its manning would include a detachment of Portuguese troops.

Aims pursued with such delicacy were unlikely to arouse much controversy. More problematical was the situation in the other great ocean, the Pacific, with its thousands of small islands and populations which, a few years earlier, would have been referred to without embarrassment as being at an early or primitive stage of development. With America at war this changed. At the start of 1942 Roosevelt declared at a press conference that the Atlantic Charter, with its promises of democracy, 'referred to the whole world' in answer to a question about whether its principles also applied to the Pacific. The State Department marked the end of the year by decreeing that even the term natives must not be used; it was replaced by 'local inhabitants'.[40] And yet the long and bitter battles of the war from Pearl Harbor to the conquest of Okinawa in 1945 led to the conviction that the US needed, and was morally entitled to, the Pacific as 'our lake', as one member of an official planning committee called it in 1943.[41] The moral argument was actually easier to apply to the north and central Pacific than to the south, which never became a major war zone. Roosevelt had authorised the annexation of some islands in the south Pacific before 1939. In 1944 he vetoed any more such annexations as incompatible with America's anti-colonialist and anti-imperialist war aims.[42] Elsewhere in the Pacific, ideas occasionally expressed of requiring France or Britain to give up some of their colonies were completely unrealistic given proclaimed American aims of non-aggrandisement. As US naval strategist Admiral Richard Byrd, who was well acquainted with Roosevelt, put it in a letter to the President in April 1944: 'We cannot allow ourselves to be charged with imperialism, aggrandisement or the abandonment of the tenets of democracy in taking islands from our weak or prostrate allies. Nor can we disturb the solidarity with our more powerful allies by aggressive or tactless methods.'[43]

The matter of some form of US colonial expansion resolved itself into one of the future of the island groups of the Marshalls, Marianas and Carolines that Japan had seized from Germany in the First World War and had subsequently held under League of Nations mandate; and the island chains to the north of the Japanese main islands (the Kuriles), to the south (the Ryukyus) and to the south-east (the Bonins), which were Japanese in population and which had been regarded as integral parts of the Japanese state. Deciding about these three chains was less urgent than the Mandates. The general view was that the US would have the right to dispose of them as it saw fit in its strategic interests, and that the Kuriles and Bonins would be worth having, the former as an extension of America's Aleutian islands, two of which had been occupied by Japanese forces out of the Kuriles in 1942, though formal Japanese sovereignty could be preserved as a sop to Japanese sentiment. The US also wanted forward bases on the Philippines and Taiwan. It was not anticipated that there would be any difficulty in securing these in a spirit of friendship from the Philippines (grateful for having been granted independence) and from China (grateful to the US for being instrumental in bringing about the return of the island after half a century of Japanese occupation), though if China did object the United States would have to accept its decision. Notably absent was any interest at this early stage in acquiring the Ryukyus, including the largest island, Okinawa, which was later to become America's insular fortress in the Far East. In late 1943 Roosevelt was so uninterested in the Ryukyus that he offered them to China in his talks with Chiang Kai-shek in Cairo. Whether he knew that the entire population was Japanese is unclear. He also seems to have been keen on the return to Russia of the southern half of the large island of Sakhalin, acquired by Japan in 1905. All this would have reduced Japan to its core before it began modernisation in the third quarter of the nineteenth century.[44]

The Mandated Islands stranded the US between the rock of anti-imperialism and the hard place of the necessity to acquire strategic assets. Second World War American planners felt that they had reason to curse their predecessors at the end of the Spanish-American War in 1898 who were now regarded as having made the opposite of the right decisions by annexing the Philippines, which had proved a profiless burden, while making no claim to Spanish island possessions in the Pacific (except for Guam), allowing the remaining islands to fall like ripe plums to Germany and then to

Japan. During the second half of the great Pacific war these islands were to be conquered by the US in some of the bitterest fighting of the conflict. This might have seemed to be decisive for their future, as indeed American military and naval leaders thought that it should be. The problem was that their annexation by the US would have been contrary to proclaimed anti-imperialist war aims. It was reinforced by the American political mindset which, as British observers noted usually with scorn, was weak on pragmatism. It started with general principles, and these had to be all-embracing and without exception. Thus in 1942, and admittedly before many American lives had been lost in the Mandated Islands, Roosevelt told the visiting Molotov that they 'were small, but they ought not to be given to one nation. The Japanese should, of course, be removed, but we [US] did not want these islands and neither the British nor the French ought to have them either.' He went on to suggest a joint long-term trusteeship over the islands by the three or four victorious great powers. This implied a willingness to keep the US free from the stigma of colonialism at the price of giving the Soviet Union a position of some power in the western Pacific.[45] (The President may also have hoped that this remarkable offer would also cause Stalin to appreciate that there were alternatives to annexations and exclusive spheres in areas of traditional interest to Russia.) The doctrinaire Cordell Hull was to regret to the end of his life that the US had compromised its principles by taking exclusive control of the Mandated Islands. However, Roosevelt and others of his advisers eventually formulated a solution that was as pragmatic as anything that could have emanated from the British political mind. The US would rule the islands as sole trustee for the United Nations and, in addition, it would be a special or strategic trusteeship under which no other country would have any power to prevent America from making whatever military use it might choose of these islands.[46]

Encouraged by their success over the Marianas, the Marshalls and the Carolines, in early 1945 the War and Navy Departments raised demands in Washington that Okinawa and the other Ryukyu islands should also become a strategic trust territory of the United States, and that rapidly became official US policy.[47] Few in the world in 1944 or 1945 would have been much concerned with the rights of Japan or the Japanese inhabitants of the Ryukyus. The Mandated Islands were a more sensitive matter, partly because their Micronesian populations were obviously innocent of any offence and partly because of their proximity to Australia, for which Roosevelt envisaged a role in the east Asia-Pacific not dissimilar to the one that he assigned to Britain in relation to Europe in the global grand strategy of postwar American national security. While Australia, and also New Zealand, were actually content for the US to control permanently the former Mandated Islands and were immeasurably relieved at the ejection of the Japanese, they did not wish to pass under American domination. In January 1944 the two countries signed the Canberra Pact, in which they insisted on their right to be consulted over the peace settlement, and outlined plans for a regional defence zone in the south-west Pacific that would have comprised themselves, Britain, France, the Netherlands and Portugal but not the US. For perhaps the first time in its career as a superpower, but certainly not the last, the US responded to fears by small allies that it might become overbearing with a mixture of exasperation and incomprehension. Again it was a portent of the future that the smaller ally, Australia, soon repented of its temerity in provoking the US and switched to entreating America to undertake very wide postwar defence commitments in the region.[48]

To return to relations with the largest of the colonial powers, the American aim of making the abolition of colonial empires into a general allied war aim collided with the predominant, though not universal, view in the British political elite that the preservation of the British Empire was, as the arch-imperialist politician Leo Amery put it to his fellow imperialist, Lord Cranborne, in 1942, the fundamental British aim in the war: 'After all, smashing Hitler is only a means to the essential end of preserving the British Empire and all it stands for in the world. It will be no consolation to suggest that Hitler could be replaced by Stalin, Chiang Kai-shek or even an American President if we cease to exercise our power and influence in the world.'[49] If US anti-colonialism was the thesis and Amery's views the antithesis, the synthesis that came about at the end of the war might appear to be largely antithetical in character. The US abandoned pressure on Britain to schedule dates for the independence of at least its more socially advanced colonies, and accepted that no colonies of European states should be placed under international supervision other than the former German colonies that had become mandates of the League of Nations, and possibly also some other former Japanese (besides the islands in Micronesia) and Italian dependencies, which should become trusteeship territories of the new United Nations with that organisation's Trusteeship Council exercising much stronger supervisory powers than its League predecessor had done. And yet the reality was that American wartime pressure did a great deal to reinforce nascent demands for advances towards independence in many colonies. Britain felt obliged to state much more clearly than before that colonial rule could have no justification unless the colonial populations were seen to be making social and economic progress and such progress would inevitably lead to demands for political freedom, at least in many cases.[50] In late 1942 Churchill spoke uncompromisingly both in public and private in defence of British imperialism in response to a torrent of anti-imperialist statements from the US administration and in the American media during the preceding year. Yet even he was, by the time of the Tehran conference in November 1943, speaking of some decolonisation as long as it was not seen to be resulting from outside pressure. Addressing Roosevelt and Stalin, 'He said a portion of the British Empire might eventually be released but that this would be done entirely by Great Britain herself, in accordance with her own moral precepts.'[51]

American anti-colonial pressures on Britain lessened during the last two years of the war as postwar national security became the overriding aim, and they were clearly not the main reason for postwar British decolonisation policies, beginning with the independence of India and Pakistan in 1947. Still less do they account for eventual French decolonisation. Even so, there were to be virtually no formal colonies left within thirty years of the end of the Second World War, and America's anti-colonial war aim influenced the way that that came about, and indeed the basic fact that it did come about.

WINNING THE NATION TO INTERNATIONALISM AND THE PROBLEM OF GERMANY

Turning to war aims that lacked roots in American history, the most important was the assumption of some form of leadership role in world affairs. Another was the issue of what to do with powerful enemies that were deemed so evil and dangerous that their very existence as independent states had to be temporarily suspended. Japan is largely reserved for another chapter. The previously somewhat neglected subject of American war aims towards Germany has now found its historian in Steven Casey.[52] As for internationalism, many Americans were obstinately uninterested in foreign policy issues and aims even while the country was at war. Although most of those questioned by opinion pollsters were able to give a response to very broad questions such as whether the US should join an international security organisation, further questioning revealed staggering levels of ignorance. Thus in a January 1942 poll less than 23 per cent of respondents had heard of the Atlantic Charter that Churchill and Roosevelt had so recently enunciated and less than one third of those could name even one of its points. Near to the end of the war in Europe, 90 per cent in an opinion poll favoured American entry into a world organisation, but only 50 per cent had heard of the Dumbarton Oaks conference, which had received immense publicity when it had been held a few months earlier, and only 30 per cent knew that its subject had been the planning of an international organisation.[53] American political leaders had little choice but to address themselves primarily to those, at most a bare majority of the adult population, who were willing to take any kind of informed interest in foreign affairs and who included a large majority of the better educated and more affluent elements in the population. The inevitable concentration on winning the support of these was pursued alongside an uneasy awareness that there was a culturally (and often economically) deprived mass of people who somehow also had to be won over, even though they had literally no idea of what was going on. In an effort to reach out to such people in rural areas a government pamphlet in 1943 resorted to the argument that nations needed to come together for the same reason that pigs huddled together on a cold night.[54]

Most people, certainly in the democracies, conceived of war aims primarily in terms of domestic policy. In the US in 1943 in a Gallup poll 58 per cent of respondents identified jobs as their main postwar priority, and only 13 per cent 'lasting peace'.[55] In the US there was also an issue that was absent from Britain at the time, which was race. Leaders of the massively underprivileged black minority worked to make racial equality a US war aim. They encountered much resistance, but also achieved a degree of success that was more real than apparent at the time.[56] The domestic and the foreign sometimes interacted. A favourite argument of some pre-Pearl Harbor isolationists was that going to war to solve other countries' problems was a way of avoiding America's own. Interventionists countered with the argument that a Fortress America could not solve its domestic problems or remain democratic in a largely totalitarian world. Much of the American public was sceptical towards both camps, having heard similar arguments before, during the First World War.[57] Roosevelt took refuge in the notion that, if he had 'his people', the liberal intelligentsia, on his side he would be safe, though he also had an elaborate apparatus for gauging the entire spectrum of public opinion.[58]

It was against this challenging backdrop that Roosevelt embarked upon two war aims that had little popular support when America entered the war: the imposition of draconian peace terms on Germany, and a decisive break with isolationism in favour of an engagement with the world that did not have much in common with the country's earlier flirtation with internationalism, Wilsonianism. Roosevelt frankly expounded his complete disillusion with Woodrow Wilson's central creation, the League of Nations, in his talks with Molotov in late May and early June 1942. He gave a detailed account of his own dealings with the League, which he dismissed in scathing terms. He clearly implied that no successor organisation bearing any resemblance to the League could be a real improvement. He also told Molotov that he suspected Churchill of hankering after precisely such a reconstituted League, and said that he hoped that America and Russia would form a united front to compel Churchill to fall into line so that the three powers could police the world.[59]

In relation to Germany, the essential precondition for the US to play a large part in deciding its postwar fate was for America and its British ally to be in occupation of much of the Reich when the war ended. At a very early stage of US belligerency the High Command of the American army made representations to the President that a communist Germany, conquered by the Red Army, would be disastrous, and that US grand strategy must have as its central objective ensuring that at least the greater part of Germany was in western allied hands at the time of surrender. Though Roosevelt readily agreed, the army continued to hammer at this point during 1943. They made no apologies for straying on to what might seem political terrain on the grounds that Russian control of Germany might result in a third world war, involving them, or, less dramatically, that Soviet–American postwar relations could only be healthy on the basis of equality, which would be absent if Soviet Russia controlled most of the continent of Europe. Again, the President agreed.[60] He also wished to preserve Italy from communism, and, at the Quebec conference in September 1944, agreed with Churchill that four American divisions should be rushed into Austria to occupy it before the Soviets if Germany suddenly collapsed.[61]

All of the above smacked of balance of power politics of the kind that Wilson had abhorred. In another respect, Roosevelt had something in common with the equally towering figure of America's other, most recent war president. They both came to a deeply adverse view of the Germans as a people. Roosevelt had become convinced of Hitler's insatiable aggressiveness even before war started in Europe.

In January 1939 he told the Senate Military Affairs Committee that his administration had 'rather definite information' that Hitler's aim was 'world domination', to be achieved by isolating America and making gains in its outer security zone.[62] He did not explain the extent of the latter; he may have meant Latin America and strategic Atlantic islands. At that time he was at one with most of the American public in distinguishing between the Nazis and the mass of the German people, who were looked upon as essentially kind and peaceloving, so that a peace settlement with a post-Nazi Germany should impose few penalties. All the evidence available to the President indicated that most Americans remained wedded to this view after Hitler's declaration of war on the US. Opinion polls in the summer of 1942 gave 74 per cent of respondents blaming the German government for the war and only 5 per cent the German people; 18 per cent blamed both.[63] Roosevelt himself became not only steadily more convinced of the detestable nature of Nazism, but also increasingly pessimistic about the extent of its support among the German people. (This is not to overlook that he had blind spots. For instance, he had little understanding of the centrality of anti-Semitism in Nazi ideology.[64] This was ironic in the light of Hitler's belief that Roosevelt worked for Jews.) Indicative was his secret delight at the high civilian casualties caused by the allied bombing of German cities from 1943, coupled with orders for the state's propaganda machine to inform the American people that only military targets were being attacked and that civilian casualties were few. These were simply lies, but the President feared a storm of protest if the truth were told about the bombing.[65] Roosevelt was so impressed by the bombing that, as early as 1942, he favoured an immediate resumption of it as the best means of bringing Germany to heel if, after the war, it showed any signs of Weimar Republic-style secret rearming.[66]

The doctrine of the Unconditional Surrender of the enemy powers, which the President proclaimed at Casablanca on 24 January 1943, served several purposes, one of which was to avoid the need to announce war aims in relation to Germany. Stated harsh terms might, no doubt, have strengthened German resistance, though evidence from, for example, German prisoners of war under interrogation indicated that their readiness to fight for the Nazi Reich was itself unconditional.[67] Unconditional Surrender kept the door open for harsh peace terms that many Americans, and especially Roosevelt's supporters in the liberal intelligentsia, would have abhorred. He had mentioned the need to avoid such a confrontation with liberal opinion to Molotov in May 1942.[68] The point was reinforced by the favourable, almost rapturous reception that greeted the book, *The Time for Decision*, which former Under Secretary Sumner Welles published in 1944, in which he argued that, apart from the Saar, which would pass to France, Germany should lose no territory except East Prussia, which would become part of Poland, with the latter compensating Germany by ceding to it West Prussia, a province that Poland had been given in 1919 in the Treaty of Versailles! Admittedly, Welles did make the radical proposal that Germany should be divided politically into three states, though economically it would remain united. Also, his proposals for Germany were only part of a Wilsonian blueprint for peace in which there could be no world hegemony, to be exercised by a chosen handful of states. Roosevelt rejected a proposal from one of his advisers that he should issue a public rebuttal of Welles's 'harmful' book, fearing that most public opinion would take the author's side.[69]

Within a year of America going to war Roosevelt was a convert to the partition of Germany. On 2 December 1942 he told the visiting leader of the Polish government in exile, General Sikorski, that, 'Germany must surrender unconditionally. We must then dismember her, and subject her to the harshest possible quarantine, if need be for thirty years.'[70] With what was for him remarkable attention to detail, he presented Churchill and Stalin at the Tehran conference in November with a plan for division into five states after all German territories east of the Oder and one of the two Neisse rivers had been ceded to Poland, with also special international regimes in the Kiel Canal area and Hamburg (for their strategic importance) and the Ruhr and Saar (for their production of most of Germany's coal and steel).[71] This was to go hand-in-hand with massive controls on German industry. After the success of the Normandy landings, US government propaganda took up a new theme of the complicity of German big business in Nazi war crimes, though this still fell far short of any wholesale condemnation of the German people. Then came the Morgenthau Plan. Treasury Secretary Henry Morgenthau drew it up in great haste in the weeks preceding the Anglo-American summit at Quebec in September 1944. He had been dismayed the previous month when he became aware of the State Department's strong preference for generous economic treatment of Germany, which was based on the argument that peace would be best served not by destroying the German industrial economy but by moving it from 'self-sufficiency for war' to integration 'into an interdependent world economy', and he had been incensed by a draft army handbook on occupation policy that called for Germans to receive higher rations than people in neighbouring countries that the Nazis had ravaged on grounds of 'efficiency'. In early September Morgenthau recorded in his diary the President as endorsing his contention that it was 'a fallacy that Europe needs a strong industrialised Germany'. According to Morgenthau, Roosevelt said, 'I agree with this idea . . . Furthermore, I believe in an agricultural Germany.' (It is worth pausing to note that in its call for the Germans as a people to return to the land, the report curiously echoed one of the Nazis' central myths. The consequences of such a return, stated the report, would be 'to redeem this virile, capable people from their worship of force and their lust for war'. To make this a Nazi principle it would only be necessary to substitute 'strengthen' for 'redeem' and 'in' for 'from'.) A little earlier Roosevelt had spoken favourably to Morgenthau about castrating German men 'so they can't just go on reproducing people who want to continue the way they have in the past'.[72]

It is not surprising that, in such a frame of mind, Roosevelt should have endorsed Morgenthau's 'pastoralisation' plan for Germany. Besides appealing to his germanophobia, it seemed to offer a solution to a conundrum that had been worrying him since his conversion to draconian peace terms. This was the problem of enforcing them, given his conviction that Congress and the public would not allow American forces to remain in Europe for more than a short time after the end of the war. German heavy industry could be destroyed even in a short time, and then the British and Soviets would have sufficient force, even without American aid, to stamp on any German attempts to rebuild such industry and rearm. Even Roosevelt appreciated that the plan would stand no chance of implementation unless it could be kept secret until after Germany's defeat and then be implemented before its opponents could mobilise. The leak of the plan to the press in late September 1944 doomed it. The highly adverse public reaction caused the President to disavow it and, campaigning for re-election for a fourth term as president, to offer a hope to the Germans that the plan would have denied them. In a major speech in October he stated that the Germans would have to work long and hard to justify his 'belief' that, ultimately, no people could be wholly depraved. Safely re-elected, he somewhat backtracked. In two press conferences in December he sought to explain away the Atlantic Charter of 1941. At the first he even tried to deny that it existed as a document; there were ony a few 'scraps of paper'. At the second, he described it as an objective like the Ten Commandments that it might take millennia to achieve. He may have been trying to prepare the American people for conduct from the Soviets and even the British, whose intervention in

Greece was attracting much criticism in liberal quarters, that contravened principles of freedom and democracy. However, he also wanted to free himself from the Charter's promise of equal economic treatment for post-Nazi Germany. That promise had corresponded with his thinking about the German problem in 1941; it had long since ceased to accord with his thinking about it by 1944. During the last months of his life he continued to seethe with private anger and even hatred against the Germans. Yet at the Yalta conference he advocated only modest dismantling of German industry and for consideration of reparations and the dismemberment of the country to be deferred. He took an even more modest line on those two issues on his return home, and spoke of Nazism as a cancerous growth whose removal from the German body politic would allow new, healthy growth.[73] In that way Roosevelt rather insincerely left the door open for liberal treatment of western Germany after the war.

INTERNATIONAL ORGANISATION
AND RELATIONS WITH THE SOVIET UNION

Roosevelt was less willing than over Germany to bow to public opinion in relation to his most important war aim of fashioning a new international order. Nearly four months before American entry into the war he and Churchill signed a joint declaration of 'certain common principles . . . for a better future for the world' that a London newspaper had the brilliant idea of christening the Atlantic Charter.[74] In the entire democratic world for the rest of the war this document enjoyed iconic status. However, few individuals can have felt less enthusiasm for it than its two principal progenitors. Although the historian David Reynolds can majestically describe it as 'a community of Anglo-American values to complement the new Atlanticist framework for U.S. security', some of its roots were more prosaic. In August 1941 the two men still thought that it was more likely than not that Hitler would soon win his war in Russia, and would then become more explicit about German aims in his New Order. Roosevelt wanted to pre-empt him with a cohesive set of democratic aims, and Churchill was ready to oblige to bring America closer to joining the war.[75] Churchill's reservations were obvious to all. He denied that its third provision, on the right of 'all peoples' to self-determination, had any relevance to the British Empire, and he wanted nothing to come from the fourth point about the removal of barriers to international trade if that weakened the Empire as an economic unit. He expatiated on these reservations in a major parliamentary speech shortly after returning from the meeting off Newfoundland.[76]

Roosevelt's problems with the Charter were, first, that he feared that it could be taken as binding the US to a promise on which it could not deliver to ensure that countries liberated from Nazi tyranny by the Soviets, in the event that they were victorious, had the freedom to choose their own forms of government, and did not undergo territorial changes except with the consent of the populations affected (points two and three). Gradually he also came to regret the economic equality principle because, as noted above, it made discrimination against Germany difficult. Finally, he disliked the eighth and last principle, not because of what it actually said but because of what was widely inferred from it. The clause called for the disarmament of aggressor countries, which he fully endorsed, but also for 'a wider and permanent system of general security', which he did not like because it implied a Wilsonian successor to the twenty-eighth president's brainchild of the League of Nations. It proved not to be enough that Roosevelt had successfully resisted Churchill's arguments for the principle actually to include a reference to 'effective international organisation'. Public opinion tended to read the principle to mean that there should be such a body. The United Nations Declaration signed in Washington at the start of 1942 reinforced this impression, though again Roosevelt had initially wanted it to relate only to unity during the current war.

Roosevelt had revealed his true thinking to Churchill during the recesses of the conference when he confided that he had no faith in a revived League, and preferred 'an international police force composed of the United States and Britain' to keep order in the world. He meant it. He had said the same to J. M. Keynes in May, and, in the relaxed atmosphere of a dinner party in Washington shortly after the Atlantic meeting, he repeated to his guests his view that the two countries would have to police the world.[77] Expanded to include the Soviet Union and China, this became the Four Policemen, whose importance in Roosevelt's vision of American war aims cannot easily be exaggerated. Neither can the President's reluctance to go above a membership of four. He remarked to Molotov in May 1942 that: 'If there were a great number of participants in the proposed association at the first stage of its operations . . . there was the possible danger that a large number of police could start fighting among themselves.'[78] Aware of the monumental difficulties of translating this vision into reality and concerned not to divert attention from concentration on the war, the

President laid down a line for his administration to follow within less than three months of the start of US belligerency that 'all the details of geography, and of forms of government, and boundaries, and things like that' could be made to await the peace, and rightly so 'as long as you have principles'.[79] Some members of the administration, such as the almost obsessively principles-minded Cordell Hull, found it not uncongenial, as well as their duty to their chief, to adhere to this line. For Roosevelt it was increasingly camouflage as he worked to achieve a system of international security in which only the Four Policemen would really matter.

Many criticisms of the policemen concept have been made. These include its refusal to allow almost any role in world security to countries other than the four; and the absurdity of including China when it was weak and when, paradoxically, many American policy-makers from Roosevelt himself downwards suspected that it might eventually develop aggressive intentions towards the US as part of an upsurge of 'violently anti-foreign' sentiment, while still failing to displace Japan as the regional superpower in east Asia.[80] These criticisms are dwarfed by the one that the entire concept was based on a deluded notion of the Soviet Union as a country with which fruitful cooperation would be possible in peace as in war. There is certainly a remarkable contrast between Roosevelt's attitudes to Hitler's regime and Stalin's. Whereas he had a full, or almost full, understanding of the unmitigated loathsomeness of the Nazi regime, there is no known statement by him expressing revulsion or indignation about the purges and other atrocities that Stalin had inflicted on the Soviet peoples, even though evidence about them was abundant, if widely denied.[81] Roosevelt, a naturally loquacious if also devious and secretive man, seems to have conditioned himself not to say anything adverse, even in the most intimate of circles, about Stalin or the Soviet regime. This does not mean that he was deluded, or even that he had serious illusions. At the same time as he, on the long journey to Tehran in 1943, was making jibes to his entourage about Churchill but not Stalin, he approved the army's Rankin plan for American troops to be rushed into north-west Germany in the event of an internal German collapse. The sole purpose was to keep the Red Army out of north-west Germany, which Roosevelt defined generously to include Berlin.[82] Most probably, Roosevelt thought that Stalin was a more traditional sort of tyrant than Hitler, which was arguably correct, and that there would be opportunities for cooperation with a post-Stalin Soviet Union that were unimaginable in relation to the Germans, poisoned by master-race ideology. The end of the Cold War makes it almost too easy to say that Roosevelt was ultimately proved right about Russia, though obviously not about Germany.

The notion that Roosevelt placed a naive trust in Stalin is, therefore, at best exaggerated. Contributing to an oral history project in the 1950s, the journalist Walter Lippmann, who had known Roosevelt fairly well, conceded that the President had miscalculated the extent to which he could win Stalin over, but continued: 'He distrusted everybody. What he thought he could do was outwit Stalin, which is quite a different thing.'[83] Stalin, needless to say, had the same ambition towards Roosevelt and towards anybody else whom he could not deal with by crushing them or buying them. During the first two years or so of American belligerency the need to be ready-witted was increased by the necessity of keeping a Russia hard pressed by the Germans in the war. This dictated indifference to Stalin's past misdeeds and to his aims for the future. Interviewed in 1981, Averell Harriman, Roosevelt's choice as ambassador to Moscow, said that he accustomed himself to think of Stalin not as a tyrant or a criminal but as 'simply the leader of a country we had some very important business with'. He continued: 'In 1941–3 we were not interested in what Stalin's peace policies might turn out to be. We were at war with Hitler. We were interested in Stalin's *war* policies, and that was enough to keep us busy. Later on, I was much concerned about Stalin's plans for a post-war European settlement.'[84] Then concern about Russian weakness was replaced, with little or no intervening phase, by fear of the Soviet Union emerging from the war so powerful that it would, internationally, be a law to itself, at least in Europe. This was the keynote of the discussions in Washington that preceded the conference of the American, British and Soviet foreign ministers in Moscow in October 1943.[85] One of the shrillest expressions of this fear is contained in a policy document that was drawn up by the Joint Chiefs of Staff in May 1944. They warned that there were severe limits to what the US could do to restrain the Soviets in Europe even if the greater part of Germany had been denied them and even if America was politically willing to fight Russia. Turning to another possible eventuality, a war between Britain and Russia, they asserted that: 'Having due regard to the military factors involved . . . we might be able to successfully defend Britain, but we could not, under existing conditions, defeat Russia. In other words, we might find ourselves engaged in a war which we could not win.'[86] While the military planners lamented their impotence, there were indications of the American people losing faith in Russian intentions. Public opinion polls on whether the Soviets could be trusted to continue cooperation after the war produced a 56 per cent positive response in June 1944, falling to 47 per cent in October. One acute observer of the American and international scene could in 1945, after reviewing post-Stalingrad Soviet policy, write: 'Hence arose the spectre of the "third war" which has been haunting the world now for two years.'[87] Among many American citizens this 'spectre' resulted less from any detailed knowledge of the international scene than from a fundamentalist anti-communism for which there was no real parallel in democratic west European countries. Only a few months after the war had ended a tidal wave of anti-communism, for which Soviet policy was, at most, a catalyst, was to sweep across the country. Its historian has called it 'a genuinely comprehensive social movement'. Roosevelt either did not understand this aspect of the national collective mind or, more probably, shrank from considering its implications.[88]

Partly, but not chiefly, because he underestimated the strength of the hand at his disposal, Roosevelt played a political game with Stalin in which his main technique was to concede to the Soviet Union on smaller war aims so as ultimately to achieve his own grand objectives. He hoped that American–Soviet cooperation, together with Britain, in policing international security would eventually cease to be a matter of bargaining over specifics and become instinctive. His thinking was not unlike that of the British statesman Lord Castlereagh, who had hoped that the coalition that defeated Napoleon could be continued in peace conditions, and who saw no insuperable obstacle to cooperation between liberal, free-market Britain and autocratic Russia with its serf-based economic and social system. He buttressed this thinking with the strong hope that the American and Russian social systems would gradually converge as the state continued to take a greater role in the US, building on his New Deal work, while the Soviet state almost inevitably became less overbearing on the Russian people. As early as 30 June 1939 he had granted an interview to the Soviet ambassador in Washington, Constantine Oumansky, in which he said that one of the keys to improving Soviet–American relations was that 'American public opinion should be given evidence that the USSR has embarked on the road of democratisation and thus is drawing nearer the USA in spirit.'[89] (The Soviet rulers would have preferred a different sort of convergence of a kind evidenced in Vyshinsky's remark, quoted in several books, at the Yalta conference that, 'The American people should learn to obey their leaders.') Harriman, in whom the President confided many of the thoughts discussed above, shrewdly noted that, whereas Churchill was interested in the settlement of specific problems as ends in themselves, Roosevelt was more interested in such deals as a means to a greater end.[90] It follows from all this that the criticism levelled against Roosevelt by historians like Keith Sainsbury and Mark Stoler and the statesman-historian Henry Kissinger that he had golden opportunities to drive a hard bargain with Stalin on war aims on an occasion like the Tehran conference in 1943, when the Soviets were reeling from a German counter-offensive in the Ukraine and when Stalin himself could say that victory would be impossible without American industrial production, is beside the point.[91] Such an approach would have required Roosevelt to have a completely different mindset from the one that he did have about the future of Soviet–American relations.

Roosevelt obviously had no time at all for those in Washington who wanted the US to dictate war aims from strength to a regime that it should have no hesitation in openly describing as criminal. These included State Department Soviet specialist Loy Henderson and William C. Bullitt, a former ambassador to Moscow and frequent luncheon guest at the White House, whose conversation the President found entertaining but not persuasive. In 1941 Henderson dismissed as impossible any idea of Stalin seeking a separate peace with Germany, and in 1943, before being banished from the capital to a minor legation, he urged 'a truly virile policy of blunt warning' to the Soviet regime that it did not have the 'Freedom to Grab' as a counterpart to the President's proclaimed Four Freedoms.[92]

The first phase of Roosevelt's strategy for the Soviet–American relationship was the one already referred to in which it was all-important to keep Russia in the war and in which detailed war aims were not to be allowed publicly to intrude. In the spring of 1942 Roosevelt rejected a plea from the British ambassador, Lord Halifax, to agree with Russia on war aims to provide a 'political substitute for material military assistance' whose quantities the Soviets would never accept as adequate. Otherwise, Halifax warned, there might be a break between the Soviets and the west which, in its repercussions on Britain, might lead to Churchill's downfall and his replacement by a 'frankly Communist, pro-Moscow' government. The President was sufficiently moved to order that aid to Russia should be given total priority. As the historian of Roosevelt's decision to aid Russia explains it, he hoped that aid would 'secure the confidence' of the Soviets and not only keep them in the war against Germany but also induce them 'to assist in the defeat of Japan and in the negotiation of a sound peace'.[93] At the same time, private hints were conveyed to Stalin that the US would not try to prevent the restoration of the Soviet Union's June 1941 borders, allowing it to retain the huge territorial gains that it had made in 1939 and 1940. In March 1942 Roosevelt told Stalin's new envoy to Washington, former foreign minister Maxim Litvinov, that the Soviet Union could have the 1941 borders, but that the issue could not be publicly raised while the war was going on. 'He himself [Roosevelt] had always thought it had been a mistake to separate provinces from Russia after the [1914–18] war.'[94]

In reality, it was impossible to avoid making this policy public if it continued to be pursued. The administration would have to win over the American public, and Roosevelt became more and more concerned to win domestic support for his war aims as the precondition to achieving anything. To win that support there would, in the first place, have to be a system of international security that was Wilsonian in appearance, though it must not be so in substance. Second, he had to accept that there were limits to what the American people and Congress would accept, notably a much more restricted American military and economic aid role outside the western hemisphere than within it. This was doubly unfortunate to Roosevelt as he became more and more convinced that the Germans were a nation of Nazis and not a nation ruled by Nazis. Third, the Soviet Union would have to give something in return for the recovery of the 1941 borders and other gains besides the blood that it was shedding to defeat Hitler; the American people would not tolerate Munich-type appeasement. It was unfortunate that, in that regard, Hull could fall back on the old American vice of moralising, which Molotov must have found simply ridiculous, and that the administration could offer no satisfaction on one matter that might have made a difference – postwar economic aid. The US did make massive concessions to attract the Soviet Union into the institutions that it was fashioning to regulate the international economy, the International Monetary Fund and the World Bank. (The Soviet state signed itself into these at the Bretton Woods conference in July 1944, but did not ratify its membership.)[95] However, there was no possibility of making to Russia a loan for postwar reconstruction of the kind that it requested, for six billion dollars, on 3 January 1945, with, as ambassador Harriman noted, all the terms laid out in full 'before the potential lender could get a word in'. Roosevelt had already rejected any idea of reconstruction aid to France, Italy or the Balkans, and seems to have been in no doubt that the possibility of persuading Congress to approve even a much smaller loan was non-existent.[96]

To indicate the need for reciprocity to the Soviets, the White House inspired an article by Forrest Davis in the *Saturday Evening Post* in April 1943 which warned Stalin baldly that he could not communise eastern Europe and expect cooperation with the western allies elsewhere. The expectation about this White House-inspired article was that the Soviet embassy would send a translation to the Kremlin and that, it was to be hoped, Stalin would read it and heed the warning in it. To Roosevelt this served a dual purpose. It warned Stalin not to disregard American public opinion; and it was designed to attract him towards a vision of making gains that did not include annexations or exclusive spheres of influence. Between early 1942 and March 1943 he had wished to offer Russia railway transit rights through northern Norway and northern Finland to Narvik, the main port in northern Norway, which would have become a free port. The Norwegian exile government advised him that that would not be acceptable to them, and he shifted his geographical focus to the idea of special rights for the Soviets over Iranian railways to provide access to the Persian Gulf.[97] Another strand in Roosevelt's thinking about postwar east–west cooperation, the perpetual nature of the German menace, was given expression at the Moscow foreign ministers' conference in October at which it was agreed that the Germans should no longer be referred to as 'their present enemies' but as 'their enemies', implying permanency.[98]

At the Tehran conference Roosevelt moved his strategy for winning Stalin over to permanent cooperation into high gear. This included an impish ploy of not only accepting hospitality from the Soviets, but also placing his personal safety in their hands because there were rumours of a German assassination squad at large in Tehran, by agreeing to stay in the Soviet legation compound. No attempt was made to sweep the accommodation provided for hidden microphones, which had been installed in abundance. Every day Stalin listened to translations of the President regaling his advisers with criticisms of Churchill and the advisers themselves for expressing fears about the extent of Soviet ambitions. They were, he accused them, serving British interests, not American. (This to the Anglophobe Admiral Leahy.) Stalin was surprised by the absence of sweeping, but did not suspect a trick, and was inclined to believe Roosevelt's half-truths and fables.[99] In a private talk with Stalin at the conference, the President offered to recognise the annexation of the Baltic republics in return for a referendum that he cannot have expected would be fair or free. Stalin's reply was not encouraging. Undaunted, Roosevelt observed silence while Stalin and Churchill talked about making territorial changes for Poland that would have given the Soviet Union the so-called Curzon Line, leaving it with most of the Polish territory that it had acquired in 1939. This silence implied that he did not dissent, and that was an impression that can only have been strengthened by his celebrated remark that his need for Polish-American votes in the next presidential election made it impossible for him at that stage to endorse the Curzon Line. At this time he entertained the cautious hope that, in return for these territorial concessions, Stalin would allow freedom to the countries of eastern Europe. He may have been heartened by the Soviet ruler's response to a plea from him that when Russia entered the war with Japan and drove it out of Manchuria, China's rights over the territory should be respected. Stalin said that 'respect for the sovereignty of other countries was a cardinal principle with him'.[100]

In any event, Roosevelt had embarked on a strategy for long-term cooperation between Russia and the west from which he had no intention of being deflected. Back in the White House after the gruelling return journey from Tehran, he was explicit in telling a gathering there that Stalin must be allowed to retain all his territorial gains in the eastern Baltic area, including territory wrested from Finland in the Winter War, and the Curzon Line border with Poland which would receive East Prussia from Germany in return. (It is impossible to say with certainty whether the President had registered that, towards the end of the conference, Stalin had stated that northern East Prussia, including its capital at Königsberg, must become part of the Soviet Union.) It is worth noting that Churchill was emboldened nearly a year later to make his abortive deal with Stalin on percentages of influence for Britain and the Soviet Union in south-east European countries by the sense that he had acquired at Tehran and later of a *Realpolitik* trend in Roosevelt that he could not reveal for domestic political reasons with a presidential election fast approaching, though the percentages deal was also an attempt by political means to salvage something from the wreck of unrealised military projects, namely an Anglo-American invasion of the Balkans.[101] Gradually, Roosevelt lost hope for, and any real interest in, preventing complete Soviet domination of eastern Europe, including its largest and (in the US) most politically sensitive country, Poland. In late 1944 Britain rejected a plea from the Polish exile government in London for a unilateral guarantee of Poland's independence within whatever postwar borders might be decided upon. Britain would only offer a joint guarantee with the Soviet Union. When the Poles suggested a guarantee by all three of the great powers, the re-elected

Roosevelt refused, though he did hold out the prospect of American economic aid to Poland. In the winter of 1944–5 his sole interest in any Soviet takeover of eastern Europe resided in his fear of that provoking an adverse reaction among the American public that might result in renewed isolationism and the end of his vision of east–west cooperation after the war. In his very last weeks he was specifically resigned to the reality of a Soviet-dominated Poland, but hoped that Stalin would help him with his public opinion by somewhat concealing the appearance.[102]

The weakness in Roosevelt's bid to perpetuate the wartime alliance with the Soviets was that it was manifestly, to a large extent, a case of one man going out on a limb. That was certainly how the Soviet regime saw it. In July 1944 ambassador Andrei Gromyko wrote from Washington about how disastrous it would be for Soviet interests if a Republican was elected president in November, though he conceded that that was unlikely.[103] Stalin was convinced that the capitalists who, in his imagination, controlled America from the shadows would never again permit such a person as Roosevelt to become president – someone who might break free from their puppet strings. Reporting to the Politburo on the Yalta conference in 1945, he spoke with real anxiety about Roosevelt's failing health, and continued: 'Let us hope nothing happens to him. We shall never do business again with anyone like him.'[104] Stalin's first reaction to the news of the President's death was to suspect that he had been poisoned by American anti-communists. Declassified Soviet foreign policy documents from the early postwar years are replete with references to an 'arrogant' America under the 'unstable' Truman having abandoned 'the principle of equality in their [Americans'] relations with other countries', and having 'completely broken away from Roosevelt's foreign and domestic policy' in favour of 'an adventurous path of preparations for a new world war'.[105] To the end of the Cold War and of the Soviet Union, Roosevelt was to retain a place of special esteem in the official version of history. In the words of two late-Soviet-period Russian historians: 'Roosevelt managed to overcome many prejudices and attempted to construct the relations between the United States and the Soviet Union on the basis of their mutual interests. Roosevelt's efforts in this regard were highly estimated in the USSR.'[106]

If Roosevelt was unsuccessful in gaining Soviet confidence in the US as a country as opposed to confidence in himself personally, then on a closely related subject, international organisation, matters slipped out of his administration's control to a large extent. In March 1943 a small group of senators led by Joseph H. Ball introduced a resolution in which they advocated 'a collective world security system to maintain postwar peace'. The reception for this in much of the media was highly favourable, and administration efforts to block the resolution were in vain. Churchill did not help with a radio broadcast in the same month, much commented on in the US press, in which he gave his blessing to the concept of a world organisation.[107] Roosevelt was forced into an alliance with internationalist politicians and other public figures who wanted a world organisation in which all power would not be monopolised by four members. They had a common foe in those politicians, mostly Republicans, who wanted America to return to isolationism after the war and whom Roosevelt, in a radio broadcast on Christmas Eve 1943, denounced as 'cheerful idiots' who were determined to learn nothing from the recent past.

During 1944 most of the administration's public war aims focus was on using the coalition referred to above to formulate proposals on an international organisation that the Senate would not reject in the way that it had barred American entry into the League of Nations in 1919. Much work was done to win over Republicans who were not doctrinaire isolationists, and what was beginning to be called a bipartisan policy on this question took shape. There were, in fact, by this time relatively few avowed isolationists, and closet ones concentrated their efforts on denying the President the right to use any American forces for UN duties outside the western hemisphere without Congressional approval. Roosevelt made the rejection of that one of the major planks in his platform for re-election. The key body in the UN was to be the Security Council, which would be Wilsonian in having a majority of members elected from the totality of all or most of the countries of the world in the General Assembly, but Rooseveltian in the four or five most important powers having permanent seats and the right of veto over executive action by the UN, though the US and Britain successfully resisted the Soviet demand that the permanent members should be able to veto even the discussion of a subject. The Senate was finally to ratify US accession to the UN on 28 July 1945 by eighty-nine votes to two, which were, appropriately, cast by legislators from the traditional isolationist bastion of the Mid West.[108]

It was also appropriate in terms of what was to come that, at the conference in San Francisco which was held shortly after Roosevelt died on 12 April 1945 and which finalised preparations for the UN, the Soviet delegates turned down their American hosts' offer of accommodation in hotels in the city, and stayed aboard their ship in the harbour. It is time to turn to the country in which Roosevelt placed so many hopes for the postwar world.

Notes

1. Henry Kissinger, *Diplomacy* (New York: Simon and Shuster, 1994), p. 412; Steven Casey, *Cautious Crusade: Franklin D. Roosevelt, American Public Opinion, and the War against Nazi Germany* (Oxford: Oxford University Press, 2001), pp. 38–9; David Reynolds, *From Munich to Pearl Harbor: Roosevelt's America and the Origins of the Second World War* (Chicago: Dee, 2001), p. 109.

2. Gabriel Kolko, *The Politics of War: The World and United States Foreign Policy, 1943–1945* (New York: Vintage, 1968), p. 171; David Reynolds, *The Creation of the Anglo-American Alliance, 1937–1941* (London: Europa, 1981), p. 165.

3. Richard N. Gardner, *Sterling-Dollar Diplomacy: Anglo-American Collaboration in the Reconstruction of Multilateral Trade* (Oxford: Clarendon, 1956), pp. 12–23, 64, 76–9, 97.

4. Kathleen Burk, 'American foreign economic policy and Lend-Lease', in Ann Lane and Howard Temperley (eds), *The Rise and Fall of the Grand Alliance, 1941–45* (Basingstoke: Macmillan, 1995), pp. 62–3.

5. Theodore A. Wilson, *The First Summit: Roosevelt and Churchill at Placentia Bay, 1941* (London: Macdonald, 1970), pp. 65–6, 71–2.

6. Ibid. pp. 122, 171–2.

7. Gardner, *Sterling-Dollar*, pp. 44, 49. The American government gave maximum, and the British minimum, publicity to the Master Lend-Lease agreement of February 1942 in which Britain went somewhat further in committing itself to multilateralism, especially in relation to dismantling discriminatory tariffs. Ibid. pp. 60–7.

8. Wilson, *First Summit*, pp. 173–85.

9. Lloyd C. Gardner, *Spheres of Influence: The Partition of Europe, from Munich to Yalta* (London: Murray, 1993), p. 118.

10. Ibid. pp. 146–7, 162, 164–6.

11. Kolko, *Politics of War*, ch. 12, 'Great Britain in theory and practice'. The prose is somewhat polemical, but there is much force in Kolko's arguments, which are largely endorsed and treated in greater detail in Randall Bennett Woods, *A Changing of the Guard: Anglo-American Relations, 1941–1946* (Chapel Hill: University of North Carolina Press, 1990).

12. Robert Skidelsky, *John Maynard Keynes: Fighting for Britain, 1937–1946* (Basingstoke: Macmillan, 2000), p. 320.

13. Amos Perlmutter, *FDR & Stalin: A Not So Grand Alliance, 1943–1945* (Columbia: University of Missouri Press, 1993), p. 198.

14. Sir Llewellyn Woodward, *British Foreign Policy in the Second World War* (London: Stationery Office, 1962), pp. 316–18, 385–401.

15. Kolko, *Politics of War*, pp. 305–8; Cordell Hull, *The Memoirs of Cordell Hull: Volume Two* (London: Hodder, 1948), p. 1507.

16. John G. Winant, *A Letter from Grosvenor Square* (London: Hodder, 1947), pp. 67–8. For Eden's alarm at the growing clamour in the US to 'reestablish the Balfour Declaration' see Ritchie Ovendale, *Britain, the United States and the End of the Palestine Mandate, 1942–1948* (Woodbridge: Royal Historical Society/The Boydell Press, 1989), pp. 8–9, 16.

17. Joseph B. Schechtman, *The United States and the Jewish State Movement, The Crucial Decade: 1939–1949* (New York: The Herzl Press/Thomas Yoseloff, 1966).

18. Woodward, *British Foreign Policy*, ch. XXIII.

19. D. Cameron Watt, *Succeeding John Bull: America in Britain's Place, 1900–1975* (Cambridge: Cambridge University Press, 1984), p. 100.

20. On Jebb see Elisabeth Barker, *Churchill and Eden at War* (London: Macmillan, 1978), pp. 206–7.

21. Robert Dallek, *Franklin D. Roosevelt and American Foreign Policy, 1932–1945* (New York: Oxford University Press, 1979), pp. 323–4, 358–60, 421–2, 505, 514.

22. Sergo Beria, *Beria, My Father: Inside Stalin's Kremlin* (London: Duckworth, 2001), p. 105. Nearly two years earlier Maxim Litvinov had told Sumner Welles that Stalin simply did not believe that public opinion played any part in determining American foreign policy, despite all Litvinov's attempts to persuade him that it did. William Taubman, *Stalin's American Policy* (New York: Norton, 1982), p. 62.

23. Martin J. Sherwin, *A World Destroyed: The Atomic Bomb and the Grand Alliance* (New York: Knopf, 1975), p. 113. See also the discussion of Britain's place in an American-ordered world in William T. R. Fox, *The Super-Powers* (New York: Harcourt, Brace, 1944), pp. 57–60, 73–4. American military chiefs were slower than Roosevelt in perceiving Britain's likely postwar usefulness as an appendage of US power. In a major report in July 1944 the Joint Chiefs of Staff foresaw the early end of Britain as any kind of great power, doubted whether it would be able to do more than defend its 'essential sea lanes' in any future conflict, and left it at that. Wm Roger Louis, *Imperialism at Bay: The United States and the Decolonization of the British Empire, 1941–1945* (Oxford: Clarendon, 1977), p. 376.

24. George C. Herring, Jr, *Aid to Russia, 1941–1946: Strategy, Diplomacy and the Origins of the Cold War* (New York: Columbia University Press, 1973), pp. 233–6.

25. Sherwin, *A World Destroyed*, pp. 68, 84–5, 88–91.

26. Hull, *Memoirs*, p. 1116.

27. Frederick S. Dunn, *Peace-Making and the Settlement with Japan* (Princeton: Princeton University Press, 1963), pp. 16, 25.

28. Ibid. pp. 18–19; John W. Wheeler-Bennett and Anthony Nicholls, *The Semblance of Peace: The Political Settlement after the Second World War* (London: Macmillan, 1972), pp. 55–6.

29. Rubin Francis Weston, *Racism in US Imperialism, 1893–1946* (Columbia: University of South Carolina Press, 1972), pp. 263–4.

30. Frank Ninkovich, *The United States and Imperialism* (Oxford: Blackwell, 2001), pp. 214–36, 247–8.

31. Paul Orders, ' "Adjusting to a new period in world history": Franklin Roosevelt and European colonialism', in David Ryan and Victor Pungong (eds), *The United States and Decolonization* (Basingstoke: Macmillan, 2000), pp. 63–84.

32. Louis, *Imperialism at Bay*, pp. 181–2, 486–7.

33. Lloyd C. Gardner, 'How we "lost" Vietnam, 1940–1954', in Ryan and Pungong (eds), *Decolonization*, p. 129; Kissinger, *Diplomacy*, p. 402.

34. Louis, *Imperialism at Bay*, pp. 425, 437.

35. Ibid. pp. 154–5; Robert A. Divine, *Second Chance: The Triumph of Internationalism in America during World War II* (New York: Atheneum, 1967), p. 66.

36. Louis, *Imperialism at Bay*, pp. 6–7, 166.

37. Ibid. pp. 157, 486.

38. Oleg A. Rzheshevsky, *War and Diplomacy: The Making of the Grand Alliance* (Amsterdam: Harwood Academic, 1996), p. 197.

39. Melvyn P. Leffler, 'The American conception of national security and the beginnings of the Cold War, 1945–48', *The American Historical Review*, vol. 89, 1984, pp. 346–400 at p. 355.

40. Louis, *Imperialism at Bay*, p. 185; Lloyd C. Gardner, 'The Atlantic Charter: idea

and reality', in Douglas Brinkley and David R. Facey-Crowther (eds), *The Atlantic Charter* (Basingstoke: Macmillan, 1994), pp. 58–61.

41. Louis, *Imperialism at Bay*, p. 75.
42. Ibid. pp. 268–70.
43. Ibid. p. 271.
44. Ibid. pp. 80–1, 227, 264–5, 280; Leonard Gordon, 'American planning for Taiwan, 1942–1945', *Pacific Historical Review*, vol. XXXVI, 1968, pp. 201–28 at pp. 211–12.
45. Rzheshevsky, *War and Diplomacy*, p. 197.
46. Hull, *Memoirs*, pp. 1466, 1599; Louis, *Imperialism at Bay*, pp. 81–6, 156, 243–55, 373; Orders in Ryan and Pungong (eds), *Decolonization*.
47. Dunn, *Peace-Making*, pp. 56–7, 111–12.
48. Orders in Ryan and Pungong (eds), *Decolonization*; Louis, *Imperialism at Bay*, pp. 289–308, 346–7.
49. Louis, *Imperialism at Bay*, p. 33.
50. Ibid. pp. 63–7, 350.
51. Ibid. pp. 134–5, 147–50, 181, 209–10, 285.
52. Casey, *Cautious Crusade*.
53. Ibid. p. 56; Divine, *Second Chance*, pp. 252–3.
54. Divine, *Second Chance*, p. 102. On the awesome levels of ignorance about foreign policy in the wartime US see also Jacques R. Pauwels, *The Myth of the Good War: America in the Second World War* (Toronto: Lorimer, 2002), pp. 18–19.
55. Divine, *Second Chance*, pp. 134–5.
56. For racial and gender equality in US war aims see David Mayers, *Wars and Peace: The Future Americans Envisioned, 1861–1991* (Basingstoke: Macmillan, 1998), pp. 71–3; and Rhodri Jeffreys-Jones, *Changing Differences: Women and the Shaping of American Foreign Policy, 1917–1994* (New Brunswick: Rutgers University Press, 1995), pp. 98–100.
57. Mayers, *Wars and Peace*, pp. 64–7, 70.
58. Casey, *Cautious Crusade*, pp. 15–19, 121–3; Divine, *Second Chance*, p. 167.
59. Rzheshevsky, *War and Diplomacy*, pp. 174, 223–4. Churchill's response when Molotov mentioned Roosevelt's policemen concept to him in London a few days later, which was that 'all nations might take part in the organisation of a police force', somewhat vindicates the President's suspicions. Ibid. p. 270.
60. Mark A. Stoler, *The Politics of the Second Front: American Military Planning and Diplomacy in Coalition Warfare, 1941–1943* (Westport: Greenwood Press, 1977), pp. 86–91, 105–6, 120–3.
61. Dallek, *Roosevelt*, pp. 410–13, 468–9.
62. Casey, *Cautious Crusade*, p. 9.
63. Ibid. p. 70.
64. Robert S. Wistrich, *Hitler and the Holocaust: How and Why the Holocaust Happened* (London: Phoenix, 2001), p. 200.
65. Casey, *Cautious Crusade*, pp. 103–5.
66. Rzheshevsky, *War and Diplomacy*, p. 223.
67. Casey, *Cautious Crusade*, pp. 132–6.
68. Rzheshevsky, *War and Diplomacy*, p. 173.
69. Divine, *Second Chance*, p. 182. Even without Welles the State Department remained a stronghold of support for moderate peace terms for Germany. Casey, *Cautious Crusade*, pp. 138, 158–9. Hull consistently opposed the dismemberment of Germany. Hull, *Memoirs*, p. 1287.
70. Sarah Meiklejohn Terry, *Poland's Place in Europe: General Sikorski and the*

Origin of the Oder–Neisse Line, 1939–1943 (Princeton: Princeton University Press, 1983), p. 302. It is interesting that Roosevelt was still hankering after the 'quarantining' of countries that had transgressed, which he had first suggested in 1937. At the Tehran conference he advocated the quarantining of 'revolutionary countries' to Stalin, who responded with silence. Valentin Berezhkov, *History in the Making: Memoirs of World War II Diplomacy* (Moscow: Progress Publishers, 1983), pp. 299–300.

71. W. R. Smyser, *From Yalta to Berlin: The Cold War Struggle over Germany* (Basingstoke: Macmillan, 1999), pp. 8–9.

72. Casey, *Cautious Crusade*, pp. 176, 179; Warren F. Kimball, 'The two-sided octagon: Roosevelt and Churchill at Quebec, September 1944', and David B. Woolner, 'Coming to grips with the "German Problem": Roosevelt, Churchill, and the Morgenthau Plan at the Second Quebec conference', in David B. Woolner (ed.), *The Second Quebec Conference Revisited* (Basingstoke: Macmillan, 1998), pp. 8, 69–78.

73. Casey, *Cautious Crusade*, pp. 139–49, 164–74, 181–94, 201–8; Divine, *Second Chance*, pp. 258–9; Gardner, 'Idea and Reality' in Brinkley and Facey-Crowther (eds), *The Atlantic Charter*, pp. 46–8.

74. Text of declaration in Brinkley and Facey-Crowther (eds), *The Atlantic Charter*, pp. xvii–xviii; Wilson, *The First Summit*, p. 222, on the origins of the term.

75. Reynolds, *From Munich*, p. 145; Nicholas J. Cull, 'Selling peace: the origins, promotion and fate of the Anglo-American new order during the Second World War', *Diplomacy and Statecraft*, vol. 7, 1996, pp. 1–28 at p. 1.

76. Louis, *Imperialism at Bay*, pp. 129–30.

77. Divine, *Second Chance*, pp. 43–4; Skidelsky, *Keynes*, p. 116; Warren F. Kimball, *Forged in War: Churchill, Roosevelt and the Second World War* (London: HarperCollins, 1997), p. 201.

78. Rzheshevsky, *War and Diplomacy*, p. 175.

79. Gardner in Brinkley and Facey-Crowther (eds), *The Atlantic Charter*, p. 53.

80. Louis, *Imperialism at Bay*, pp. 73–6; Warren F. Kimball, *The Juggler: Franklin Roosevelt as Wartime Statesman* (Princeton: Princeton University Press, 1991), pp. 137–41.

81. Perlmutter, *A Not So Grand Alliance*, p. 210.

82. Stoler, *Politics of the Second Front*, pp. 138–9; Keith Sainsbury, *The Turning Point* (Oxford: Oxford University Press, 1985), pp. 163–4.

83. Divine, *Second Chance*, p. 157.

84. G. R. Urban (ed.), *Stalinism: Its Impact on Russia and the World* (Aldershot: Wildwood House, 1985), p. 34.

85. Dunn, *Peace-Making*, p. 26.

86. *Foreign Relations of the United States. The Conference of Berlin, 1945, Vol. I* (Washington: The State Department, 1960), p. 265.

87. David J. Dallin, *The Big Three: The United States, Britain, Russia* (New Haven: Yale University Press, 1945), p. 274; Dallek, *Roosevelt*, p. 503.

88. Philip Jenkins quoted in Ralph B. Levering et al., *Debating the Origins of the Cold War: American and Russian Perspectives* (Lanham: Rowman and Littlefield, 2002), p. 45: see also Fraser J. Harbutt, *The Iron Curtain: Churchill, America, and the Origins of the Cold War* (New York: Oxford University Press, 1986), pp. 41–3.

89. Rzheshevsky, *War and Diplomacy*, p. 164.

90. W. Averell Harriman and Elie Abel, *Special Envoy to Churchill and Stalin, 1941–1946* (New York: Random House, 1975), pp. 169–70.

91. Sainsbury, *Turning Point*, pp. 302–4; Stoler, *Politics of the Second Front*, pp. 153–4; Harriman and Abel, *Special Envoy*, p. 277; Charles E. Bohlen, *Witness to History, 1929–1969* (New York: Norton, 1973), p. 155.

92. On Henderson, see H. W. Brands, *Inside the Cold War: Loy Henderson and the Rise of the American Empire, 1918–1961* (New York: Oxford University Press, 1991), p. 105, and Hugh De Santis, *The Diplomacy of Silence* (Chicago: University of Chicago Press, 1980), p. 95. On Bullitt, see Orville H. Bullitt (ed.), *For the President: Personal and Secret* (London: Deutsch, 1973), especially pp. 522, 530. The Roosevelt scholar Warren Kimball discounts Bullitt's influence on the President; see his *The Juggler*, pp. 30–1.

93. Herring, *Aid to Russia*, pp. 59–61, 101.

94. Gardner in Brinkley and Facey-Crowther (eds), *The Atlantic Charter*, p. 55.

95. Robert A. Pollard, *Economic Security and the Origins of the Cold War, 1945–1950* (New York: Columbia University Press, 1985), pp. 15–18.

96. Harriman and Abel, *Special Envoy*, pp. 384–7; Gardner, *Spheres of Influence*, pp. 152, 177–82; Herbert Feis, *Churchill Roosevelt Stalin: The War They Waged and the Peace They Sought* (Princeton: Princeton University Press, 1957), p. 340.

97. Olav Riste, 'Free ports in north Norway: a contribution to the study of FDR's wartime policy towards the USSR', *Journal of Contemporary History*, vol. 5, no. 4, 1970, pp. 77–95. For the *Saturday Evening Post* affair see Divine, *Second Chance*, pp. 114–15. The Soviets would have appreciated the Iranian railways. A major report on war aims drawn up in the Kremlin in January 1944 stated that 'the USSR must be guaranteed free and convenient use of transit routes across Iran and the Persian Gulf'. Francesca Gori and Silvio Pons (eds), *The Soviet Union and Europe in the Cold War, 1943–53* (Basingstoke: Macmillan, 1996), p. 8. What the US was actually doing in Iran in the late war period was downgrading its use as a conduit for aid supplies to Russia to deny the latter any excuse to retain troops in northern Iran. From taking 30 per cent of American aid to the Soviet Union in 1943–4 it was down to 1 per cent by the end of the war. Joan Beaumont, *Comrades in Arms: British Aid to Russia, 1941–1945* (London: Davis-Poynter, 1980), pp. 193–4.

98. Sainsbury, *Turning Point*, p. 67.

99. Vladislav Zubok and Constantine Pleshakov, *Inside the Kremlin's Cold War from Stalin to Khrushchev* (Cambridge, MA: Harvard University Press, 1996), pp. 23–4; Beria, *Beria*, p. 94. Sergo Beria, a technical specialist, was in charge of 'bugging' operations at the Tehran conference, and reported to Stalin in person.

100. Sainsbury, *Turning Point*, pp. 241, 277–9.

101. Gardner in Brinkley and Facey-Crowther (eds), *The Atlantic Charter*, pp. 67–9; Divine, *Second Chance*, pp. 158–9; Harriman and Abel, *Special Envoy*, pp. 268–82; Sainsbury, *Turning Point*, pp. 273–7; Keith Sainsbury, *Churchill and Roosevelt at War* (Basingstoke: Macmillan, 1994), p. 108.

102. Hull, *Memoirs*, pp. 1447–8; George V. Kacewicz, *Great Britain, the Soviet Union and the Polish Government in Exile (1939–1945)* (The Hague: Nijhoff, 1979), pp. 198–205; Dallek, *Roosevelt*, pp. 503, 507–8, 524–5.

103. Perlmutter, *A Not So Grand Alliance*, pp. 267–8, 278; see also Taubman, *Stalin's American Policy*, p. 83.

104. Beria, *Beria*, p. 106.

105. Vladimir O. Pechatnov in Levering et al., *Debating the Origins of the Cold War*, pp. 101, 111, 130, 161.

106. Nikolai V. Sivachev and Nikolai N. Yakovlev, *Russia and the United States: US–Soviet Relations from the Soviet Point of View* (Chicago: University of Chicago Press, 1979), p. 202.
107. Divine, *Second Chance*, pp. 93–7, 114.
108. Ibid. pp. 313–14.

5

The Soviet Union

STALIN AND SOVIET FOREIGN POLICY: IDEOLOGY AND CRIMINALITY

Like German war aims, those of the Soviet Union in the Second World War were largely decided by one man operating within an ideology, though Soviet Marxism-Leninism, as the term itself implies, was less the leader's own construct than German Nazism was Hitler's. Yet in both cases a state's ambitions and insecurities influenced the ideology and the dictator. To begin with the impersonal before proceeding to the personal, the difficulties in evaluating the impact of traditional national interests and ideology are illustrated by the contrasting views of two recent students of the history of Soviet grand policy in international affairs, Caroline Kennedy-Pipe and Condoleezza Rice. To the former, Soviet policy before and during the war was determined primarily by security concerns and nationalist ambitions. Policy was admittedly also influenced by Marxist-Leninist theories, but one of these insisted that the capitalist states were not a monolith united against socialism; on the contrary, there were numerous antipathies between capitalist states so that cooperation between a socialist state and one or more that were capitalist was entirely possible.[1]

To Rice, by contrast, Soviet thinking about international relations was fundamentally different from any other because it was 'from the beginning influenced by a holistic and universalist ideology, a belief system that not only viewed politics, society, economics, and warfare itself through the lenses of class struggle, but also forecast (and strove to realise) a transcendence of existing power relationships'. It was messianic and embraced 'the hope of converting the entire world into its own image'. It would be, at best, 'too simple' to say that 'ordinary' national interests overrode ideological imperatives. 'Stalin believed that the capitalist powers, given a chance, would seek to destroy the Soviet Union. The "international system" was not the guardian of Soviet interests, it was a threat to them. For Stalin, any cooperation with the West had to be tactical; integration into the international system was suicidal, as this would bring about dependence upon those whose primary goal was the destruction of socialism. There is absolutely no evidence that the alliance experience in World War II had mitigated this view.' Only under Stalin's successors after 1953 was there some modification of this view, chiefly because of a fuller understanding than he ever had of nuclear weapons.[2]

Whether its importance was fundamental or relatively marginal, it is appropriate to try to delineate what Marxist-Leninist ideology was during the time of Stalin's rule over the Soviet Union. The creation of a single, socialist world state was an obsession of the Bolsheviks at the time of their seizure of power in Russia in 1917. Less was heard of this in the 1930s, but it was still reaffirmed as an ultimate goal. By then it was axiomatic that the capital of this world state would be Moscow. As early as 1932 tourist guides to that city were urging upon visitors that they should, 'Feast your eyes on this scene, for you are looking at the future political capital of the world.' The language and symbols of nationalism became more and more prominent in the Soviet Union, as did a Great Russian ethnic bias.[3] In the mid-1920s Stalin evolved a doctrine that the 'complete' victory of socialism in the Soviet Union alone was entirely possible ('socialism in one country'), but that it had to be followed by the 'final' victory of socialism throughout the world. This was elevated to the status of infallible dogma in 1938 in the form of a letter by Stalin to an obscure official (if he really existed) called Ivanov, the commonest of Russian names.[4] Another Soviet doctrine, first formulated in 1924, was that of 'the weakest link in the chain' by which communist parties could take power anywhere, as easily in the rural poverty of India or China as in industrialised Germany or Britain.[5] Yet another of Stalin's ideas, and one to which he gave expression as early as 1917, was that Russia might have a role in bringing socialism to other countries that could not achieve it on their own. He reaffirmed this concept a number of times in the 1930s, and it was to find expression in his celebrated wartime remark to Milovan Djilas that: 'This war is not as in the past; whoever occupies a territory also imposes on it his own social system.

Everyone imposes his own system as far as his army has power to do so. It cannot be otherwise.'[6]

Running somewhat counter to these theories, the young Soviet state evolved a practice of being willing to work with, and even fight alongside, some capitalist states against others that appeared more dangerous. As early as 1920, the jargon-obsessed Bolsheviks defined this as 'peaceful coexistence with bourgeois states'. Stalin's own prewar contribution to the theory of peaceful co-existence was to define it as something that might 'postpone' the 'inevitable' final showdown between capitalism and socialism. It may also be relevant that in the increasingly Stalin-dominated condition of Soviet politics after 1924 references to the Marxist concept of the withering away of the state ceased except as something that might happen after 'an entire historical era' and perhaps not even then.[7] Theory mattered to Stalin, even if his understanding of it was crude and involved a capacity for self-deception that has been described as typical of the Soviet political mind.[8] It is also instructive to note what he wrote in 1913 about the functions of a diplomat in words that harked back to Jacobean England rather than to Marx: 'A diplomat's words have no relation to action – otherwise what kind of a diplomat is it? Words are one thing, actions another . . . Sincere diplomacy is no more possible than dry water or iron wood.'[9] Had Stalin heard of Sir Henry Wotton and his famous dictum of 1604 that an ambassador was an honest man sent to lie abroad for his country? It hardly seems possible, and yet he certainly had some knowledge of the history of the British Isles in the seventeenth century. In October 1944 he described Oliver Cromwell to Churchill as the only man who had known what to do with the Irish because 'force was the way in which to deal with such people'.[10] No doubt influenced by his historical studies, he had become convinced by the mid-1920s that the acme of statesmanship was to encourage potential enemies to go to war with one another. The Soviet state should enter at the last possible moment in order, he pronounced in 1925, to be 'the decisive weight on the scales, a weight that must tip the balance'. By 1934 he was looking forward to a new war because, 'War will surely unleash revolution and put in question the very existence of capitalism in a number of countries as was the case of the first imperialist war [1914–18].' In September 1939, while publicly calling for the war to end, he really wanted the Soviet Union and the communist parties to do what they could to make the belligerents fight each other harder and harder; the last thing that Stalin desired was a phoney war.[11]

Stalin had an eclectic knowledge of history as well as thinking himself a genius on a wide range of other subjects from the art of war to linguistics. In reality, the area of human activity in which he most excelled was criminality. This is a subject that is often dismissed as irrelevant to his foreign policy aims or as too embarrassing to bring into the discussion, though there is seldom any reluctance to shy away from Hitler's criminality in any discussion of the Third Reich. Yet criminality was so prominent in Stalin's life that it would be difficult to argue that it did not impinge on everything that he did. This was a man who, as a young adult, arranged the murder of the village priest who may have been his real father (and who had paid for him to be educated or, better semi-educated).[12] The paradox is that Stalin combined paranoia and a criminal mindset with real, if flawed, abilities as a statesman and ones that improved, even dramatically improved, with experience. To take the testimony of two western diplomats who observed him at first hand, one, the American George Kennan, found him quiet, sensible and sometimes remarkably acute in discussion, a master tactician and in that sense a great man, though utterly evil. The other was the London Polish government's ambassador to Moscow in 1941–2, Stanislaw Kot, who had every reason to detest him but who was impressed by his 'clear and sober understanding' of political issues. He kept Soviet diplomats on their toes by his thorough preparation on every issue (as well as by other means, including fear), and 'stood head and shoulders above the Allies'.[13] It is also relevant to war aims that Stalin drew a distinction between the international communist movement, of which he was determined to be the master, and the major capitalist countries from which he sought not servility but recognition of his regime's equality and legitimacy. Interviewed in 1981, the Yugoslav former communist Milovan Djilas perceived this; for personal psychological reasons the once obscure Georgian needed such recognition, whereas, 'Our conflict [that of the Yugoslav communists] with Stalin was solely due to Moscow's ambitious nationalism expressed in a form of imperialism under the guise of Communism. Without that I doubt whether we would have clashed with the Soviet leadership.'[14] This interpretation is not unchallenged. In what is in many respects a superb book, William O. McCagg presented a picture of Stalin in the middle years of the 1940s as a man of peace, fighting heroically to restrain wild 'insurrectionists' in the world communist movement who wanted the war with Nazi Germany to be quickly followed by a final world war with Anglo-American capitalist imperialism. This is much exaggerated, a case of Kremlinology gone awry. McCagg provides much valuable information about Stalin's paranoia and jealousy in relation to the slightest real or (usually) imagined stirrings of independence among communists, for example against 'pedants' in the Soviet Party itself who made too much use of quotations from Marx and Engels and too little of ones from his own more contemporary teachings; and about Stalin's petty insults about the achievements of the Yugoslav communists, against which Tito was eventually to rebel.[15] However, the Stalin versus insurrectionists theory fails because of the ease with which the dictator exercised control over foreign communists with their love – 'no other term is accurate'[16] – for the Soviet Union under his rule.

The criminal side to Stalin's mind affected his war aims in two principal ways. The first, which worked in conjunction with Marxist-Leninist ideology, was an obsessive belief that western leaders, with the possible and partial exception of Roosevelt, were no different from himself and were therefore constantly on the look out for means to doublecross him, so that neither their commitment to the common cause nor their proposals about the postwar future could be believed in without grave reservations. This counted for more than Stalin's Marxist belief that the war aims of the capitalist western powers were fundamentally economic.[17] Stalin was incapable of believing that Britain and the US would never, because of basic conviction, make peace with any Nazi regime. He did accept that they had probably ruled out peace with Hitler. Despite this he had, before the decisive Soviet victory at the battle of Kursk in July 1943, been keen on having Hitler assassinated. The survival of the Soviet Union was at stake, and Hitler's demise could be expected to wreak havoc with the German war effort. After Kursk, he ordered his security and special operations chief, Beria, to end all planning to kill the German, who now had to remain alive as 'the last obstacle to a separate peace between the Western powers and Germany'.[18] The fear of those powers switching sides remained with him till literally the last days of the war in Europe. Thus, in April 1945, Soviet forces in Austria constructed defence works on the border of territory that they had occupied that included anti-aircraft guns, despite the fact that the Luftwaffe had almost ceased to exist.[19] Second, Soviet war aims could have an outright criminal component. This applied to Stalin's proposal to Churchill and Roosevelt at the Tehran conference that their agreed aim of destroying German militarism would be furthered by the execution of 50,000 German officers. It is indicative of the gulf between Stalin's mindset and that of Churchill in particular that the latter not only exploded against this at the time but that it also continued to prey on his mind for the rest of the war. The idea of killing prisoners of war aroused his deepest revulsion, and it must have been what he had in mind when he said in a speech in February 1944 that 'unconditional surrender means that the victors have a free hand. It does not mean that they are entitled to behave in a barbarous manner.' In Moscow eight months later to seek a deal on territorial war aims, he had every interest in not irritating Stalin, but still raised the issue again by warning that mass executions of Germans after surrender would be absolutely unacceptable to the British people.[20] According to figures drawn up for the Soviet government after the last German prisoners of war had been repatriated in 1955, the number of German officers who died in Soviet captivity during and after the war was 4,505.[21] Although this figure refers only to men who lived to reach the POW camps, it is still less than one third of the number of Polish officers who were murdered on Stalin's order in 1940. Churchill continues to receive criticism for his part in the wartime policy of bombing German towns and cities. It is worth remembering that it was probably in part because of him that the world was spared the horror of a mass slaughter of the German officer corps.

To Stalin, killing Germans, or anyone else, was a pragmatic matter, unencumbered by moral considerations. At an early stage of the Soviet–German war Stalin set his sights on depriving Germany of its easternmost province, East Prussia. At midnight on 8 September 1941, in an air-raid shelter in Moscow, 'the Boss', as recounted by Georgi Dimitrov, declared that: 'If we win, we'll give East Prussia back to Slavdom, where it belongs. We'll settle the whole place with Slavs.'[22] His diplomatic dealings with the Anglo-Americans on this will be discussed below. It started to become possible to translate the air-raid shelter vow into reality in January 1945 when the Red Army began its conquest of the province. Nothing was done to restrain the soldiery from committing atrocities. Understandably incensed by all that they had seen of Nazi bestiality, and having been fed on a diet of anti-German hate propaganda for nearly four years, they were particularly angered by evidence that the prewar German standard of living had been much higher than theirs. West German researchers were to estimate that in late 1944 and 1945 277,000 East Prussian German civilians out of a total population of 2.5 million died as this unique outpost of north European Protestant civilisation vanished without trace. It must be said that a Russian did not need to be a Stalin type to rejoice at this. The Moscow University historian Arkady Yerusalimsky wrote in his diary on 10 April 1945 that: 'Eastern Prussia, historically the citadel of Prusso-German reaction

and aggressive eastern policy, is lost to German militarism forever.'[23]
To Stalin and his associates atrocities were a good means of initiating
the degermanisation of East Prussia by killing some of the inhabitants and giving the remainder an incentive to flee. It worked. In the
high summer of 1945 George Kennan flew low over East Prussia in an
American plane, and was appalled to observe how the once-neatly
maintained and highly productive farmlands of the province had
been transformed into an uninhabited wilderness in preparation for
resettlement by Russians and Poles. Atrocities also occurred with no
restraining hand from above in areas like Silesia that were intended
to become Polish. In February, as the Soviet army approached
territory that it was intended to leave as German, the policy of
encouraging atrocities was modified and in April it was terminated
altogether, though unofficial horrors continued, especially rape on an
epic scale.[24]

As a rule, Stalin knew better than to try to involve his colleagues in
the Grand Alliance in criminal enterprises in the way that he
demanded of his underlings that they should become involved and
even show enterprise in adding a few victims of their own. His foreign
minister (officially People's Commissar for Foreign Affairs), Vyache-
slav Molotov, had to be a man of two worlds. The fact that he once
supplemented a death sentence against an 'enemy of the people' by
ordering that the man's wife should also be executed has become
notorious as a symbol of the depravity that prevailed in Stalin's
entourage. Yet Molotov was a man with whom Cordell Hull, the
almost uncharmable American secretary of state, could declare it a
pleasure to have done business, and who had the finesse, in discussing with Churchill a recent meeting with Roosevelt, carefully to
omit the information that the President had included British Malaya
in a list of colonies that he regarded as in need of placing under
international control. Molotov correctly anticipated that the Prime
Minister would respond furiously when he mentioned only that
Roosevelt had referred to French and Dutch colonies and not also
to a British colony.[25] In 1944 Stalin suggested to Tito that it would be
useful for windowdressing purposes to allow King Peter II to return
to Yugoslavia; he could eventually be assassinated after he had
served his purpose.[26] He would have known better than to mention
any such idea to any western visitor. He had an acute sense of what it
was wise and what it was unwise to say to such dignitaries, and the
remark about killing 50,000 German officers was a rare slip.

What is more important is whether he also had an accurate sense
of the limits to which he could carry Soviet war aims without courting

disaster, and the answer must be that he had. Partly because he knew
that he had seriously miscalculated in his dealings with Hitler in 1940
(on which see below), he was determined not to run risks in terms of
the war aims that he presented to his British and American allies. In
an interview with an American news magazine after the war, Anthony Eden said that during his first wartime meetings with Stalin in
1941 the Soviet leader had remarked that Hitler was clever but that
he did not know when to stop. Noticing that Eden was smiling, Stalin
went on: 'I know why you're smiling. You think that if we are
victorious I shall not know when to stop. You are wrong. I do
know.'[27] Eden's recollection accords with contemporary evidence.
Shortly after returning to London from his visit, the Foreign Secretary
gave an off-the-record briefing to the editor of the *Manchester
Guardian*, W. P. Crozier, in which the latter recorded him as saying
'that we had to make up our minds about Russia. Either she was
International Communist in her intentions or she was Peter-the-Great
Russia. Personally, he was convinced that Stalin's policy was that of
a Peter-the-Great Russia and that we could, and therefore we must,
live with her in Europe . . . Stalin had convinced him that Russia was,
and would be, reasonable in her aims.' Opinions will, of course, vary
about a man as important as Tsar Peter. Crozier, the liberal journalist,
murmured that Peter's ambitions for the expansion of Russia had not
been modest. To Eden he was a positive figure, and Stalin had risen in
his estimation from the time exactly a year earlier when he had
written that Stalin was 'the true lineal descendant of Chenghiz [sic]
Khan and the early Tsars'.[28]

WAR AIMS TO THE SOUTH AND THE NORTH

This study will now examine themes of caution and continuity in
Russian/Soviet aims in two areas of direct concern, the regions of the
Danube delta and the Straits between the Black Sea and the Aegean
and the Mediterranean, and of the Baltic and Scandinavia. Succeeding sections will consider Soviet aims in central Europe (including
Germany and Poland), and how the Soviet Union visualised its
postwar relationships with its two great wartime allies, Britain
and the United States.

Stalin's aims in the Black Sea–Straits region were the purest
continuation of those of Russia under the last tsar. Not satisfied
with his 1915 agreement with Britain and France by which Russia
was to receive Constantinople (Istanbul), Nicholas II noted margin-

ally on a document in August 1916 that 'Turkey must be finished off.' That country would almost certainly have ceased to exist as an independent state if tsarist Russia had survived.[29] During the latter half of 1940 Stalin's demands to Hitler included that Germany should concede to him a free hand in Romania and Bulgaria, though he also wanted much more than that including a free hand in Finland and acceptance by Germany that the Soviet Union had major interests in Yugoslavia. In Romania Stalin's particular interest was to secure control of the rivers in the Danube delta, while control of the rest of that great river within Romania would be vested in a commission of only two members, the Soviet state and Romania. His interest in Bulgaria was not in the country itself but in Bulgaria as a staging point for Soviet control of Istanbul and the Straits. Stalin told the Bulgarian communist leader Dimitrov, who was exiled in Moscow, that he intended to give the hinterland of European Turkey to Bulgaria and to do away with the rest of the Turkish state which he described as a weak and almost illusory entity. Seriously out of date in his knowledge, he listed the presence in Turkey of 1.5 million Armenians as one of the sources of weakness, which pointed to much of eastern Turkey becoming part of the Armenian republic of the USSR. His native Georgia would also gain much. The main aim, however, was to turn the Black Sea into a Russian lake and to control the Straits, which Stalin regarded as essential for the security of his state.[30] What stood between Stalin and this 'sick man of Europe' analysis of Turkey's future, or lack of one, was Hitler. When Molotov visited Berlin in 1940 the Fuhrer asked for acceptance that the Soviet Union had no role to play in Europe west of its expanded borders, and that it must abandon its ambition to exercise power over the Straits. It should look to Iran, the Persian Gulf area and India for its future territorial expansion. Molotov replied that he could not yield or compromise on any of his demands from Finland to the Straits, including that Germany must withdraw its guarantee of Romania's independence while consenting to Russia giving its own version of a guarantee of independence to Bulgaria. Such demands were far in excess of any that Stalin was to present to Churchill and Roosevelt during the time of the Grand Alliance, and they were probably decisive in convincing Hitler that he would have to annihilate Russia sooner rather than later. Stalin's later caution about war aims owed much to his belated awareness that he had overreached himself with Hitler in 1940.

At the time, Molotov left Berlin empty handed, his sole victory a gastronomic one in that he had eaten carnivorously as Hitler's lunch guest while the vegetarian Fuhrer had munched lettuce. ('It seemed a rabbit was sitting next to me eating grass.')[31] After this visit, Stalin blithely resumed pressure on Romania and Bulgaria. Having seized some Romanian islands in the Danube delta before the Hitler–Molotov meeting, he occupied some more after it, to Hitler's fury.[32] It was, however, Bulgaria that bore the main brunt of Soviet demands in the last weeks of 1940. Speaking in the language of pure Russian nationalism and reminding Bulgaria that it owed its very existence to Russian victories in the Russo-Turkish war of 1877–8, the Soviet government demanded that Bulgaria should accept Soviet troops on its soil so that Russia would have whatever force was necessary to secure its legitimate interests in the Straits region. In return the Soviet Union would refrain from all interference in Bulgarian internal affairs – not aiding the country's substantial and notoriously blood-thirsty communist party – and would revert to the 1878 treaty of San Stefano policy of promoting a greater Bulgaria. In the words of an official Soviet note to Bulgaria, 'Russia, in the form of the Soviet Union, maintains that policy [of 1878], fully supporting Bulgaria's territorial claims against its neighbours' – that is, Turkey, Greece and Yugoslavia. The Bulgarian government, not wanting more territory for less independence and possibly none at all, turned in alarm to Berlin. Stalin realised too late in early 1941 that he had made demands that he had no means of enforcing, and that he had given Hitler an excuse, and even a reason, for turning against Russia.[33]

During the desperate first two years of the war with Germany, Stalin subordinated his ambitions in the Straits to the cause of survival. Turkey was now a country to be wooed, not erased from the map. He feared that if it was not drawn into the war on the allied side it would enter it on the German.[34] Instead of making territorial demands on it he became eager to offer it more territory than it already had. In particular, he wished to offer it Rhodes and the other Dodecanese islands, whose population was Greek but which had been occupied by Italy since 1912, and islands in the eastern Aegean that were already part of Greece. Speaking to Eden in December 1941 he professed to feel sympathy with Turkish complaints that foreign ownership of these islands hemmed in their great ports – Istanbul and Izmir. Eden refused to agree to such a betrayal of Greece. The Soviet Union continued to press its allies to offer inducements to Turkey to enter the war up to and including the conference of the three foreign ministers in Moscow in October 1943.[35] A change occurred at the Tehran summit conference a month later when Stalin, despite being far from confident about the military situation, raised the issue of warm water ports that his country legitimately needed. There was something about the phrase 'a warm water port for Russia' that aroused the sympathies of western statesmen. Churchill made an incautious remark that Russia was entitled not to have its 'nostrils pinched' by being denied completely free access to the Turkish Straits and to the waters between the Baltic and the North Sea. In 1944, with military fortunes truly improving, the Soviet Union snubbed a Turkish move to improve relations, and by the summer seemed positively anxious to keep Turkey out of the war to weaken that country's position when the time came for postwar arrangements to be made. Soviet ill-will against Turkey long remained great, and a curious legacy of it was that in postwar Soviet history books and school textbooks the country was depicted as an ally of Hitler's Germany in everything but name, which had only been deterred from launching a treacherous attack by the presence of huge contingents of the Red Army on the Caucasus frontier with Asiatic Turkey, and which, by implication, was in need of belated punishment.[36]

In March 1945 Russia denounced its treaty of non-aggression with Turkey, perhaps in part in response to the Turks' temerity in declaring war on Germany and Japan the previous month, and renewed its demand for a base at the Straits. The stage seemed set for a major challenge to Turkey's independence. Instead, the Soviets backed down when, to their surprise, their demands on Turkey were opposed by the US as well as Britain. This required a psychological effort, of which there are plentiful indications in Molotov's recollections, dictated in old age at sessions that stretched over many years.[37] He explained that his primary task as foreign minister 'was to expand the borders of our Fatherland', and that in this he was both following his own inclinations and serving Stalin, who was somewhat agitated in 1945 that he had made territorial gains in the north, the west and the east but not to the south against Turkey or Iran. Stalin had also said that historically Russia had won wars and then had failed 'to avail itself of the fruits of victory'.[38] Molotov himself became agitated when his scribe asked him why, in that case, the Soviet state had not pressed on and realised its aims in the Straits. The British navy had been in the Straits to keep out Soviet ships (stated in 1972 and 1975). Others had rejected the argument that Russia was entitled to share control of the Straits 'in honour of the victory gained by Soviet forces' (1978). 'If we had gone ahead, everyone would have come down on us' (1982). Pressing the demand would have provided the capitalist powers with a pretext to commit 'joint aggression against us' (1972, 1981). It could only have been different 'if Turkey had been a socialist state' (1978). Molotov seemed to be saying that Soviet power at the Straits was hardly more realistic than the recovery of Alaska, sold by Russia to the US in 1867: 'I wouldn't mind getting Alaska back . . . Just thoughts and nothing more. To my mind, the time hadn't arrived for such tasks' (1981).[39] Basically, Molotov was saying that the Straits demand had to be dropped because it was too risky. In 1974 he was explicit about the general principle involved: 'Of course, you had to know when and where to stop. I believe in this respect, Stalin kept well within the limits.'[40]

Turning to Scandinavia and the Baltic, the concept of war aims as falling within the art of the possible is again in evidence. The north also provided an object lesson in the dangers of overambition even more dramatic than Stalin's folly in demanding to Hitler that he be given the eastern Balkans and the Straits in November 1940. This was the Soviet Union's nearly disastrous experience in the war against Finland that had been launched a year earlier with the expectation of easy victory and the possible consequence of the incorporation of the entire country into the USSR. Molotov had privately looked forward to such incorporation as a step towards the time when 'the Soviet system . . . shall reign everywhere'.[41] In actuality, Finnish resistance, heavy Russian losses and the prospect of Britain and France going to war with the Soviets on Finland's behalf induced Stalin to agree to a peace treaty in March 1940 under which Finland lost one-ninth of its territory but retained its independence and was able to join the German onslaught against Russia after 22 June 1941, in what the Finns referred to as the Continuation War.

Finland could hardly have done anything else. Malevolent Soviet aims against it did not cease with the signature of the peace treaty. In June 1940 Molotov told the puppet foreign minister of Lithuania that the imminent incorporation of his country into 'the honourable family of Soviet peoples' would soon be followed by that of Finland. In November of that year the Soviet General Staff drew up a new war plan for the conquest of all Finland, and the Finns had reason to be grateful to Hitler for warning the Soviets against a new war with Finland at an early date when Molotov visited Berlin that month. Finland went to war in 1941 with the nation united on the recovery of the 1939 borders and divided about whether more territory should be annexed. Those who favoured the latter course drew attention to kinship ties with the native peoples of Soviet Karelia and to the strategic advantages of borders that were short ('a short border – a long peace') and that included barriers provided by nature, the White

Sea, Lake Onega and the Svir river. The assumption was that a Russian state would remain in existence. The Germans had carefully held back from giving the Finns any indication that their war against Russia would be one of unrestrained barbarism and annihilation.[42]

In British official quarters between 1941 and 1944 it was generally assumed that the Soviet Union would resume the unfinished business of the Winter War and take complete control of Finland. As late as August 1944 a Foreign Office briefing memorandum for the War Cabinet predicted that Finland would be the one country in Europe that the Soviets would insist on controlling completely, if not actually annexing.[43] This was confounded within weeks when the Soviet government invited a Finnish delegation to Moscow and offered armistice and preliminary peace terms that took the 1940 settlement as their basis, and in whose negotiation Molotov treated the British ambassador in the Soviet capital as a serious, if inevitably not equal, partner. (Britain was at war with Finland, the US was not.) The two men even reached an agreement, which was concealed at the time from the Finns, about compensation for the Canadian nickel-mining company that had operated in the Petsamo area bordering the Arctic Ocean, which was the one additional piece of territory to what it had gained in 1940 that the Soviets now demanded from Finland. Molotov proved responsive when the British insisted that an important principle of the rights of private property under international law was at stake. More important, Britain helped in persuading the Soviet government to back down from two earlier demands that would have threatened Finland's independence. One of these was that the Red Army should have the right to enter the country if Finland could not itself immediately expel all German forces from its soil. It was now given a period of grace to do that. The other was that Russia reduced its demand for reparations from $600 million to be paid over five years to $300 million to be paid over six years. The latter amount could be paid, albeit with pain; the former would have been impossible and would have afforded another excuse to intervene.[44]

Two features of the Soviet settlement with Finland are of particular interest. First, the Soviets insisted that a large area only a few miles to the west of the Helsinki suburbs at Porkkala must be leased to them as a 'new Gibraltar', in the words of Marshal Voroshilov, to enable them, in conjunction with their control of Estonia on the south shore of the Gulf of Finland, to exercise complete control over the approaches to Leningrad. In 1940 they had taken a base further to the west at Hanko for the same purpose; that was now relinquished. This clearly was to them a genuine issue of defensive security.[45] Second,

Molotov told the Finnish armistice delegation in Moscow 'that Lenin-grad officials and the population of that area had pressed for the occupation of [the whole of] Finland as the only solution. The Soviet government had to look at things on a broader perspective and commence negotiations in spite of this pressure, however under-standable it might be.'[46] This statement can be accepted at essentially face value from a man who, as noted, had himself been eagerly anticipating the annexation of Finland some five years earlier. Soviet relative generosity in the preliminary peace of September 1944 was partly military-strategic. After colossal losses and with Germany still fighting as determinedly as ever, the Soviet Union could have ill afforded to devote large forces to the conquest of Finland. However, relations with important countries also mattered in producing mod-erate war aims towards Finland. The Soviets did not wish to alienate Sweden, whose anxieties about a Soviet-controlled Finland were great. The US, and Roosevelt personally, had often expressed a friendly interest in Finland, though there had been a deafening silence from Washington when it had been suggested that America might help Finland financially to meet the cost of reparations when the subject had been raised earlier in 1943–4. Finally, there was Britain, which was pleasantly surprised by the way in which it had been treated as a negotiating partner in the armistice discussions as well as impressed by the professionalism with which Molotov had performed his leading role in them.

Relations with Britain really mattered to Stalin. Two months after the armistice, in November 1944, a Soviet deputy foreign minister, Solomon Lozovsky, had warned the Yugoslav communist Kardelj about Stalin: 'You see he still thinks that England is the centre of world imperialism, the main enemy of the proletariat, and that America plays a secondary role.'[47] The essence of the situation was that during the time of the Grand Alliance Stalin was unwilling to pursue war aims that would poison relations with his great allies or even with an important neutral like Sweden. Nor, in the case of Finland, was this a case of holding back to wait for a favourable moment to seize control. The Soviets demanded that Finland should legalise the Communist Party, but the latter was warned by the Leningrad boss and party grandee Zhdanov not to expect any outside help to attain power. The Soviets regarded the Finnish communists with contempt as hopelessly weak. As the months went by after the armistice, it became clear that Finland was safe if it delivered reparations goods to Russia and adopted a foreign policy that was unequivocally favourable to Moscow.[48] Molotov consoled himself with the loss of what he had once desired with the comment that Finland was 'a peanut'.[49]

Elsewhere in the Scandinavian region, middle-ranking figures in the sprawling and ill-coordinated Soviet bureaucracy recommended an abundance of grandiose war aims. In the case of Norway, these included that country giving up its exclusive sovereignty over the Arctic archipelago of Spitsbergen and replacing it with Soviet–Norwegian joint sovereignty; outright Soviet annexation of Bear Island between Spitsbergen and the mainland; Soviet annexation or lease of the easternmost region of continental Norway between the Tana river and Norway's border formerly with Finland, now with Russia, which the Germans had used in their unsuccessful offensive to capture the Russian Arctic port of Murmansk in 1941; and Soviet military and naval bases elsewhere in northern Norway to counter a predicted postwar British protectorate over the rest of the country. It is not difficult to understand the attraction of these ideas to Soviet officials concerned exclusively with north Russian and Arctic affairs. To the leadership, their pursuit was out of the question because of the damage that would be done to wider Soviet foreign policy interests. The only partial exceptions were Spitsbergen and Bear Island, in which the Soviet Union and the Russian Empire before it had an internationally acknowledged interest.[50]

As to the Baltic Sea, individual officials during the war expressed enthusiasm for the annexation of several major islands, including the Aland group (Finnish), Rügen (German) and Bornholm (Danish). Any move to acquire the Alands was ruled out by the extreme Swedish sensitivity about them and by the general policy towards Finland discussed above. Rügen was virtually part of the German mainland to which it was connected by a causeway built by the Nazis. The island of Bornholm, which is considerably to the east of the rest of Denmark, was under Soviet occupation from May 1945 to April 1946 when it was evacuated in return for a facesaving undertaking by Denmark not to allow it to become a British base, something that neither Britain nor Denmark had remotely contemplated. The Soviet leadership's maximum aim in relation to the Baltic was that it should be barred to the warships of countries that did not have seaboards on it. Influence over Denmark, with its position at the entrance to this sea, was the key to realising that. During the last months of the war the Soviets adopted a menacing attitude to the Danish resistance's representative in Moscow, though this was accompanied by intimations that Denmark could redeem itself by adopting an understanding approach to Soviet security concerns. Between February and May

1945 the Soviet navy's newspaper ran a series of articles on the theme that the lands along the southern shores of the Baltic had once been Slavonic, and that, whereas the Soviet Union was entitled to complete predominance in the eastern Baltic, the situation in the west was more mixed but included legitimate Soviet security interests in its ingredients. It was predicted that the fight to liberate Denmark would be long and hard. In fact, the only operation of any kind was the bombing of Bornholm by the Russian air force after the German surrender. That was the crux. If the Red Army had entered Denmark in the course of military operations against the Wehrmacht the Soviet Union would have been able to claim a voice in the future not perhaps of Denmark itself but in the Danish waters between the Baltic and the open sea. That did not happen. Egged on by Churchill, the British military commander, Field Marshal Montgomery, reached the port of Lübeck before the war ended and blocked the Red Army's road to Copenhagen. After that, the Soviets accepted effectively that they were in no position to pursue war aims of almost any kind in the western Baltic region.[51]

WAR AIMS TOWARDS GERMANY

In war aims towards Germany there was some parallel between Stalin's and those of Britain before Roosevelt tied the latter's hands with his Unconditional Surrender coup at Casablanca, by which an unrepresented Soviet Union was not bound. For both Britain and the Soviet Union, the stakes were of the highest order. In his radio broadcast on 3 July 1941 Stalin proclaimed the supreme aim as being survival or at least not becoming the Germans' slaves.[52] For both, an important starting point was moral indignation against Nazi treachery and aggression. The British had in mind Hitler's failure to honour the Munich agreement and his general spurning of appeasement. Stalin seems to have been genuinely hurt and angry about Hitler's invasion in violation of the German–Soviet Non-Aggression Pact of 1939 and his spurning of Stalin's own frantic efforts at appeasement in the months before the invasion. According to his foreign-policy aide and interpreter, Valentin Berezhkov, Stalin had been convinced that Hitler would keep faith with the pact. 'This may seem surprising,' added Berezhkov, with an understatement that sounds more British than Russian. In July 1941 Stalin greeted his first high-level American visitor, Roosevelt's special envoy Harry Hopkins, with a curious speech in which he dwelt on the wickedness of breaking treaties, which had made Germany a pariah, and the need for moral considerations to be paramount in international relations.[53]

Stalin soon reverted to more characteristic *Realpolitik* mode with two broad sets of war aims towards Germany in which anger about the innumerable atrocities committed by the Nazis on Soviet territory played little or no part. One set was for an outcome in which Germany could not be completely defeated, so that there would have to be some sort of compromise peace; the other was for total victory. Stalin may have shared, and would certainly have sympathised with, the British conviction that peace on any terms with Hitler was out of the question. During the first, defensive phase of the Soviet–German war he allowed the Soviet propaganda organs to warn the Germans that they faced the direst fate and punishment. His own pronouncements, which Germans could be expected to regard as authoritative, were much more restrained. They included approval for prewar German policy when it had been righteous, including, specifically, when it had been reasserting Germany's sovereign rights in the Rhineland and uniting with Austria. This hinted to dissident German generals that if they made peace they could maintain troops in the Rhineland and retain the *Anschluss* with Austria.[54] Stalin cannot have had any illusions that even a conservative military government in Germany would make peace on such terms unless it had suffered massive military reverses, of which there was little sign before Stalingrad. He also (correctly) surmised that such a government's preference would be to deal with the western powers, and (incorrectly) suspected those powers of being ready to deal with a post-Hitler, right-wing Germany on terms that betrayed Russia. In his first really high-level talks with a western leader, when Eden visited Moscow in December 1941, Stalin adopted a hard line on Germany which was intended to divert Britain from thoughts of a peace with such a Germany. The draft Anglo-Soviet treaty that Eden had brought with him was not wholly reassuring. Its second clause would have bound both countries not to conclude peace with any German government 'that would not clearly repudiate any aggressive intentions'.[55] Stalin cannot have welcomed this indication that Britain was ready to make peace, in certain circumstances, with a German government, even though it was not different from what he was prepared to do. His hard-line response was intended to deflect Britain from such notions while also giving a genuine indication of his thinking about what to do with a Germany that had been totally defeated. With German troops only a few miles from the Kremlin, he stated boldly that the Soviet Union should annex a portion of

Germany as it had been before any Nazi aggression: northern East Prussia, including its capital, Königsberg, was to become part of Lithuania, 'which is part of the USSR'. (In later Soviet thinking the area was to become part of the main Russian republic of the Union.) The Rhineland, including the Ruhr, Austria and probably Bavaria were to be detached from Germany to become independent states or, in the case of the Rhineland, possibly an international protectorate. 'In any case, Comrade Stalin believed that Poland should be given all lands up to the Oder, and let the rest be Prussia, or to be more exact, not Prussia but the state of Berlin.' Eden, taken aback, apologised for being unable to offer any comment on the subject of Germany's future to which his government had not yet devoted serious attention: 'Here it has fallen far behind the Soviet Government.'[56] (Nearly two years later Molotov was to apologise to Eden for not being able to comment on British proposals for the future of Germany on the grounds of his government having been too busy waging the war to think about the subject in what may have been conscious mockery; Molotov enjoyed inflicting mockery.[57]) Eden did allow himself to say that if Stalin's programme was followed 'an irredentist movement might emerge that will unite the whole country again in the near future'. To which 'Comrade Stalin objected that precisely such reasoning had led us to this war. Did Eden want a new assault from Germany?' The Foreign Secretary, showing signs of confusion according to the Kremlin minutes, replied that it was important not to oversimplify.[58]

This was not the most skilful diplomacy on Stalin's part. During 1942 the British were struck by the contrast between these remarks and the conciliatory ones towards Germany that Stalin made in two important speeches. The British ambassador in Moscow was asked to seek clarification and, in the meantime in October, a suspicious Eden told the War Cabinet that postwar Britain might have to fend for itself without Soviet or American support, in which case: 'We should eventually have to accept the collaboration of Germany, with the feeble hope that the Germans would undergo a change of heart and turn away from aggression.'[59] Relegating this thought to the back of their minds and with their hands somewhat tied by the Unconditional Surrender doctrine, the British applied themselves from early 1943, as described in a previous chapter, to winning Soviet and American support for the division of Germany into occupation zones so that it could be held down for as long as was necessary to prevent it from returning to the international comity as a fascist-militarist state or a communist state or a non-communist state in alliance with Russia. The reality was that the Soviet leaders were as baffled as the

British by the Germans: how to defeat them and what to do with them if they could be defeated. This is evident in what Molotov said to the head of the Czechoslovak government in exile in London, Beneš, in June 1942. The latter sought assurance that the Germans 'as a whole', and not only Nazis, should 'pay dearly for what they have done in this war'. To which, 'Molotov agreed that Germany as a whole was to blame for the war, but it would not be proper now to intimidate the German people by promising them punishment and thus helping Hitler.'[60] Pessimism about the Germans as a people was expressed by Stalin at a meeting in the Kremlin on 21 January 1943 at a time when victory at Stalingrad was within sight. In between making 'a lot of jokes', he said: 'Evidently, the majority of German workers have nothing against being the dominant nation. A minority of them are against it, but they have been suppressed. German soldiers are still not surrendering en masse.'[61]

At this desperate time in the war the Soviets from Stalin downwards were undoubtedly most concerned with their survival and were increasingly worried and angry about the western powers' failure to launch a 'second front' invasion of continental north-west Europe. They were later to calculate that 1,080 days passed between the date of the German invasion of Russia and D-Day.[62] The Soviet view at the time and forever afterwards was that that was many hundreds of days too many. They received a particularly shattering blow on 4 June 1943 when Britain and the US informed them that there would be no second front until May of the following year. Stalin's anger and fear were fuelled by reports from Soviet intelligence that German troops in France and the Low Countries were weak in both numbers and quality.[63] He had little understanding of the difficulties of amphibious operations. He may have tried to initiate peace discussions with Hitler using the Soviet legation in Stockholm, which had been wholly taken over by Beria's NKVD security police, though this remains one of the murkiest of all Second World War topics. On 1 July an article in a Soviet journal declared that Germany deserved a peace without any punishment, and even hinted at allowing it to keep the Sudetenland acquired from Czechoslovakia at Munich. The only German reply was the launching of the massive tank offensive at Kursk on 5 July, which was to be one of the decisive battles in world history. On the 12th, with the brunt of the German offensive defeated, the Soviets announced the setting up of a National Committee for a Free Germany as a kind of popular front of communist and non-communist German exiles in Russia. Its task, as outlined by Stalin to Molotov, Beria and others in the leadership, was to impress on the Germans that they could avoid 'the dismemberment and destruction of Germany' by overthrowing Hitler and forming the sort of German government, one with a programme 'for restoring the democratic rights and freedoms of the German people, for the establishment of a parliamentary order, and so on', with which a peace treaty could be concluded.[64] There was clearly no idea in this of Unconditional Surrender. It was to be complemented two months later by a League of German Officers, consisting of officer prisoners who had responded positively to 'anti-fascist education'. Stalin had returned to the tactic of wooing German conservatives, especially senior officers. An NKVD general negotiated a deal with this body while it was being set up for possible use in a bidding war with the western powers if the Nazi regime was overthrown in a conservative coup. Under the deal, Germany would be neither bolshevised nor disarmed, and could retain the territorial gains that it had made in 1938.[65] There were also statements that there would be no objection to dealing with others in Germany, including dissident SA men and 'Christians'.[66] Despite the Kursk victory, Stalin was uncertain that the Red Army had the strength to do more than, at most, advance to the 1941 borders, and his faith in the western powers, never high, was at a low ebb.

All these initiatives were barren of results, and Stalin returned at the Tehran conference to a severe line on Germany and the imposition of peace terms jointly by the three allies. He told Roosevelt that he had been alarmed by Churchill in a preceding discussion in which the Englishman had said that 'the maintenance of peace in the future' was not a matter of urgency because Germany would take a long time to recover. Stalin did not agree: Germany would only need fifteen to twenty years. 'The first big war begun by Germany in 1870 ended in 1871. After only forty-two years, that is in 1914, the Germans began a new war, and again after twenty-one years in 1939, they began another. As we can see, the period required for Germany's rehabilitation is decreasing. And it will obviously decrease still further in the future.'[67] The suggestion to kill 50,000 or more German officers, which so infuriated Churchill, was the one concrete proposal that he made for preventing renewed German aggression. On the political structure of a Germany that had by less drastic means been rendered militarily harmless, he was content to let his colleagues make most of the running, Churchill with his two-states solution of the German problem, and Roosevelt with his for five states, plus international control of the Kiel Canal, the Ruhr and the Saar. Stalin said that he wanted terms which 'will leave Russia on the neck of Germany', and that he preferred Roosevelt's plan to Churchill's because the inevitable German urge to reunite could be more easily thwarted in a five-state context. On two important but secondary issues he was definite. The first was that he was willing to agree that Austria should be reconstituted as a separate state. This put a spoke in the wheel of a deal with German conservatives, in which he had not completely abandoned interest. Second, and as if in return for his consent to undoing the *Anschluss*, he reiterated his determination to annex Königsberg and northern East Prussia. In the words of the American minutes: 'He said that acquisition of Eastern Prussia would not only afford the Soviet Union an ice-free port but would also give to Russia a small piece of German territory which he felt was deserved.'[68] With his relish for detail, Stalin must have known that the factual part of this statement was false. Königsberg was not an ice-free port; it is reached by a ship canal that freezes over in winter. Furthermore, he had acquired no less than three genuinely ice-free ports for the Soviet Union in the annexed Baltic republics, none of them at any great distance from Königsberg. Stalin was to persist with his demand for recognition of the Soviet claim to northern East Prussia until Britain and the US gave it their approval at the Potsdam conference in 1945.[69]

It is worth digressing briefly to note that the Stalin regime was always concerned with obtaining international legal recognition for its gains. If possession was nine-tenths of the law, Stalin wanted the other one-tenth as well. At the Yalta conference in February 1945, Stalin informed Churchill and Roosevelt that he intended to ask China to surrender its nominal or residual sovereignty over the Mongolian People's Republic, and asked them to agree in advance that they would recognise such a step if China took it. They did agree. The Soviet Union already had complete de facto control over Mongolia, but that was not enough. Soon after the end of the war, in the course of one of their many verbal jousts, the new British foreign secretary, Ernest Bevin, and Molotov had an altercation in which the latter condemned Britain for imperialist greed. Bevin replied that that came ill from the representative of a country that covered so much of the land surface of the world, to which Molotov retorted that 'this area had been acquired legally'.[70]

Except for Austria and East Prussia, Stalin declined to say much at Tehran about Germany: 'There is no need to speak at the present time about any Soviet desires, but when the time comes, we will speak.'[71] Some historians have read a sinister import into this remark. Probably Stalin was simply leaving Britain and the US to box themselves into a completely intransigent policy on Germany's future that, at a minimum, would rule out a separate peace between them and any German government, and that, at maximum, would enable Russia to make a bid for German support by championing German unity. As Beria was to remark to his son after the war had ended, Russia could offer Germany nothing in material terms but only 'the unity of their state'.[72] The Soviet Union came out against the dismemberment of Germany in March 1945, but, by that time, opinion in British and American ruling circles was also turning decisively against dismemberment.

During the last quarter of 1943 the Soviet government set up two commissions on war aims, one on Peace Treaties and Post-War Construction headed by Litvinov after his recall from being ambassador in Washington, and one on reparations headed by the former ambassador to Britain, Ivan Maisky. It is problematical how much attention should be devoted to their reports or to Litvinov's declassified 1941–2 despatches from Washington, which are available in translation.[73] In the case of Litvinov at least, probably little. Detested by Molotov, he was denied all access to Foreign Ministry documents, relied on his personal library and western newspapers in drawing up his report, and pursued some eccentric lines of argument, for instance that Britain might try to annex Sicily as a colony.[74] The Maisky committee's views stood a better chance of being heeded at the top. It reported in January 1944, and its central recommendation was that everything economic that could be taken out of Germany without causing mass starvation should be taken. It made some effort to work out the cost to date of the war to the USSR in material damage as the appropriate basis for claiming reparations. (Interestingly, there seems to have been no attempt in the Soviet bureaucracy to estimate the human cost of the war in military and civilian casualties.) It arrived at a reparations figure of $75 billion, of which 80 per cent should be extracted from Germany and 20 per cent from German allies. Initially, $17 billion of German resources were to be confiscated; then Germany was to pay $6 billion per annum for ten years; and Germany was to supply five million of its citizens for work in the Soviet Union over a ten-year period. It was calculated that, on average, each of these five million 'labour units' would be worth $750 net per annum to the Soviet economy. They would live and work under the command of the NKVD. In November 1943 Maisky wrote to Molotov that the draconian plans that he was drawing up were based on the absence of 'a real proletarian revolution in Germany'. If one did occur, completely new plans would be needed. Litvinov, in a commentary, hoped that the experience for millions of Germans of forced labour in the USSR would have the effect that they would 'at least to some extent return home with sounder views and attitudes'. Bearing in mind conditions in Soviet labour camps, that was hardly likely. In fact, both Stalin and Molotov thought that these reparations proposals were excessive and would impede the realisation of other plans for Germany.[75]

Soviet aims towards Germany were in a state of constant flux during the later, victorious phase of the war and for some years afterwards. Ironically, the one thing that can be stated with certainty is that Stalin did not seek, and did not desire, what ultimately came about: a two-state division of Germany with a large and rich bourgeois-capitalist state in the west and a communist state, in every way weaker, in the east. If that had been his intention he would undoubtedly not have given almost exactly as much pre-1938 German territory to Poland as was to be left as the Soviet occupation zone, the future German Democratic Republic. Poland would certainly have received much in addition to southern East Prussia and the former Free City of Danzig, which had not been part of Germany after 1919. However, Stalin's inclination seems to have been to give Poland in addition to these only the relatively thinly populated lands of Pomerania, adjacent to the Baltic, and the ethnically mixed Oppeln area on the southern stretch of the prewar border between Germany and Poland. In May 1944 he told a visiting Polish dignitary, Professor Oskar Lange, that he had not yet decided whether to give Poland the great city of Breslau and German lands east of one of the two Neisse rivers, though he added that if Poland did receive them all their German inhabitants would have to be expelled; the Soviet Union would 'find room' for three million of them in Siberia.[76]

That Stalin did ultimately consent to a German–Polish border that was extravagantly favourable to Poland and which went somewhat against his own better judgement owed a great deal to pressure from the Polish communists. Much hated, widely reviled as traitors and always utterly obsequious towards the Soviet Union when in the presence of westerners, they actually included passionate nationalists like Wladyslaw Gomulka who played a weak hand with some skill. Aware that if they needed Stalin, he also needed them, they used the persuasive argument that they could only win enough popular support to rule without permanent Red Army garrisons everywhere in the country if the Soviet Union was generous in its allocation of German territory to Poland in the west to compensate for all that Poland was losing in the east. They pointed out that the anti-communist Polish politicians in London continued to be fixated on the unfeasible goal of recovering territory from the Soviets in the east more than in gaining new lands for Poland in the west, and that the western powers' enthusiasm for large territorial gains for Poland at the expense of Germany was showing signs of lessening as the war drew towards its close. (They had, however, by 1944 swallowed their earlier doubts and endorsed publicly the principle of the 'efficient resettlement' of Germans from territory to be ceded to Poland and of all German minorities 'whose present situation is liable to endanger future peace' in the words of a British government minister, Lord Cranborne.) In July 1944 Stalin concluded a secret agreement with the nascent Polish communist government, the Lublin Committee, in which he promised to seek an Oder–Western Neisse border for them.[77]

There is evidence that he soon regretted conceding Poland so much because, if it would win some Poles over to acceptance of communist rule, it would surely have an alienating effect on Germans, who were widely perceived at this time as being more obsessed with nationalism, including territorial integrity, than any other people on earth. In March 1945, in one of his curious mystical moods that had begun to occur after the start of the German invasion, he spoke to Molotov and Dimitrov about the Germans, who were still resisting stubbornly, in a 'forgive them for they know not what they do' form of words, condemned Britain for its 'vicious' policy ('They are using every means available to destroy their competitor'), and insisted that the provision of food and basic services to the population in areas occupied by the Red Army was a necessity. However, he also reaffirmed that 'Silesia will go to Poland, along with Pomerania and Danzig'.[78] Yet for several months after the end of the war the Soviet government allowed no publicity in their zone of Germany or in the Soviet media about the ceding to Poland of all territory east of the Oder and the Western Neisse. Maps distributed by the Soviets in Germany in the spring of 1945 showed Germany with its 1937 boundaries.[79] The final prize was the city of Stettin at the mouth of the Oder, over which the German and Polish communists played a game of political ping-pong for control in the weeks after the German surrender until Stalin ruled in favour of the Poles, even though the city is to the west of the Oder. Again, the Polish communists triumphed.[80] Walter Ulbricht, top man among the German communists who returned from Moscow, informed his cadres that they would have to find means of persuading Germans that the new border was just and irreversible.[81]

The new border between Germany and Poland was one of the most important results of the Second World War in Europe and one of the most durable. It represented a change in the European political, cultural and ethnic balance that, before Hitler's insane invasion of the Soviet Union, would have been unthinkable except to one faction among Polish nationalists whose leading figure was General Wladyslaw Sikorski. (This group wanted even more from Germany than what Stalin gave the Polish communists, including 'bridgeheads' on the west side of the Oder and the Western Neisse and 'strategic strongpoints' in the western Baltic, including the islands of Rügen and Fehmarn.[82]) However, the particular point that is being made here is that the chief architect of the new border, Stalin, would have designed a more modest structure if he had been planning a separate communist state in east Germany. He seems in 1945 to have envisaged the Oder–Neisse line as the probable border between communism and non-communism in central Europe. He was more and more interested in a single Germany which, if non-communist, was not actually anti-communist. The July 1944 bomb plot that failed to assassinate Hitler alarmed him. After initially being hailed in the Soviet media as heroes and martyrs, the plotters were, within a week, being denounced as reactionaries. This resulted from the realisation that they had wanted a separate peace with the western allies and would not have been averse to joining with them against Russia.[83] Stalin's thinking on dealing with the German problem in this situation was twofold: a heightened emphasis on the preservation of the Grand Alliance long into the peace with the primary purpose of keeping Germany isolated and nipping renewed German aggression in the bud, which is discussed below, and a strategy for directing Germany's postwar development into acceptable channels.

The broad-based Free Germany Committee was relegated to a purely propaganda role, and Stalin started to assign more importance to the German communists as a force to keep anti-Soviet reaction at bay in the whole of Germany. In October 1944 they produced an 'Action Programme of the Bloc of Militant Democracy' which envisaged a one-party political system and state ownership of industry. Stalin thought that this was much too ambitious. He had hopes of the German communists but they were limited ones. He had long scoffed at the German version of revolutionaries for obeying signs not to walk on the grass. Now he had a new jibe that communism fitted Germany like a saddle a cow.[84] In intensive discussions with German communists, led by Wilhelm Pieck, in Moscow in the last weeks of the war, Stalin consistently expressed support for a united, non-communist Germany, a 'bourgeois-democratic arrangement' that would

complete the work that had been begun in 1848. He spoke in favour of
an economically strong Germany to deny the US complete control of
world markets. In such a Germany the US would not fully control
German industry in association with old-style German big-business
plutocrats who had worked with Hitler, and would be denied the
opportunity to entangle a separate west Germany in an anti-Soviet
alliance. In such a Germany as Stalin envisaged, Russia could also
demand reparations from the entire country and not only from its
own occupation zone.[85] In August 1944 the head of the German
section in the Foreign Ministry wrote a paper in favour 'of regarding
Germany as a single economic entity, regardless of the occupation
zones. This will strengthen our position on the question of control of
German industry, which is largely concentrated in the Anglo-American zone.'[86]

SOVIET WAR AIMS AND THE GRAND ALLIANCE

A country fighting, seemingly against the odds, for survival like the
Soviet Union after 22 June 1941 was unlikely to adopt ambitious war
aims. An important initial decision was that any aims must not be of
a character that the Soviets' new 'capitalist' allies would find alarming. On 24 June the British Communist Party was sent a message
ordering it to stop describing the war as one between capitalism and
socialism. For the Soviet Union it was a war of defence, not a war to
extend the social system of socialism. Advocating anything else 'in
the current situation means playing into the hands of the pro-Hitler,
anti-Soviet elements of England'. A similar message went out to the
French Communist Party.[87] Within two weeks of the start of the
invasion the Soviet government sent the British a preliminary indication of war aims of a type that London would be likely to find
reassuring. The USSR favoured the reconstitution of Czechoslovakia
and Yugoslavia and 'an independent Polish state within its national
borders, with the restoration to it of certain cities and regions that are
currently within USSR territory'.[88] This was a trailer for Soviet
advocacy of the 'Curzon Line' eastern border for Poland, under which
Stalin was willing to give up a little of the Polish areas that he had
annexed under the Nazi–Soviet agreements. In July 1941 the Soviet
and Polish exile governments established diplomatic relations with
territorial and many other issues between them unresolved, but the
Soviet Union was committed to the restoration of an independent
Polish state. Stalin chose to raise war aims when senior British and

American emissaries, Lord Beaverbrook and Averell Harriman, visited him in September 1941 to discuss aid for Russia. While aid was Stalin's primary concern, he asked Beaverbrook what British war aims were. (He could not ask Harriman the same question because America was still neutral.) Beaverbrook promised to let him know, but did not and could not since so little had been decided.[89]

Some reference has already been made to Eden's important visit to Moscow in December 1941. He brought with him a draft Anglo-Soviet treaty, whose most important provision was that neither party would conclude a separate peace with Germany. Stalin demanded that any such treaty should include a secret protocol on territorial war aims. In particular, he wanted Britain to recognise the validity of Soviet gains in 1940 from Finland and Romania and the annexation of the Baltic republics. These were two enemies and three states which had, at least in the Soviet view, ceased to exist. He stressed that he sought no immediate commitment on the Soviet–Polish border which would have to be negotiated with Poland and Britain. He concentrated on the Baltic states and Finland because 'it was precisely the question of the Baltic States and Finland [Finland had not figured in the unsuccessful Anglo-French–Soviet alliance negotiations in 1939] that had been the stumbling block in the negotiations of 1939 on the pact of mutual assistance under Chamberlain's Government'. Without British recognition of the Baltic annexations, 'An involuntary impression was created that the Atlantic Charter was directed not against the people who were striving for global supremacy but against the USSR.' Eden replied that it was all a matter of timing: 'This only requires time, a measure of postponement.' Stalin added that any treaty would have to include a clause about non-interference in other countries' affairs. This 'was especially necessary, as many people abroad were saying that the USSR intended "to bolshevise Europe"'. In a separate conversation with the British ambassador, Molotov said that Stalin had remarked to him that if he signed a treaty with Britain that did not refer to frontiers the Soviet people's anger would know no bounds, and 'the people might want such a government to go to hell'. At a final meeting, Stalin stressed to Eden the historical perspective: 'He recalled that Britain had had an alliance with tsarist Russia when it comprised Finland, Bessarabia [annexed from Romania in 1940] and more than half of Poland. Not a single statesman in Britain had thought of protesting against that alliance then on the grounds that the said territories were part of the Russian Empire. Today, however, the question of the Finnish frontier and the Baltic republics seems to be a stumbling-block.'[90]

This was to be one of Stalin's constant themes in presenting Soviet war aims to western leaders, that he was, to borrow a phrase, amazed by his own moderation, particularly in respect of the fact that he did not seek the restoration of the Russian borders of 1914. In the summer of 1944 he told the Polish prime minister, Mikolajczyk, that he was only depriving them of their eastern provinces: 'in 1914 we were much further to the west'.[91] On the same subject of Polish borders he was probably being entirely serious when he told Churchill that the Poles, instead of complaining about the loss of their eastern city of Lvov, ought to be grateful that he was letting them have Warsaw, which had been Russian in 1914.

Eden would probably have acceded to Stalin's demands if it had been for him to decide, but Churchill had a general objection to agreements on war aims, especially given that the new American ally was also strongly opposed.[92] When Molotov next met Eden in London in May 1942 for renewed discussions on a treaty, the Foreign Secretary confined himself to seeking marginal concessions in relation to the recognition of Soviet annexations. One, related specifically to Estonia, was for the right of emigration for those who did not wish to resume living under Soviet rule after the Germans had been driven out. Molotov opposed this as 'alarming for the Estonian people' and as providing propaganda for 'the malcontents, thus artificially creating internal problems for the USSR'.[93]

The problem was temporarily solved when Stalin sent a message to Molotov instructing him to reverse previous policy and accept the original British proposal for a treaty that was general and devoid of references to specific war aims. On Stalin's previous command, Molotov had called that 'an empty declaration', but he now informed his foreign minister that: 'We do not consider it an empty declaration but regard it as an important document. It lacks the question of the security of frontiers, but this is not bad, perhaps, for it gives us a free hand. The question of frontiers, or to be more exact, of guarantees for the security of our frontiers at one or another section of our country, will be decided by force.' Molotov flew on to Washington, where Roosevelt informed him of his concept of peace being safeguarded by the three or four policemen of the Grand Alliance, with all discussion of war aims being left to a later date. Stalin cabled Molotov to inform the President of his enthusiastic support for his ideas: 'Roosevelt's considerations about peace protection after the war are absolutely sound. There is no doubt that it would be impossible to maintain peace in future without creating a united military force by Britain, the USA and the USSR, capable of preventing aggression. It would be good to include China here. As for Poland, Turkey and other states, I think we can well do without them, because the military power of three or four states is quite enough. Tell Roosevelt that you have communicated with Moscow, thought this matter over and come to the conclusion that Roosevelt is absolutely right and that his position will be fully supported by the Soviet Government.' Stalin is unlikely to have been disturbed by a later message from Molotov in which the President was reported as saying that China's policeman role would be marginal and might come to nothing at all though, conversely, France might eventually become a policeman.[94] On a return visit to London before going back to Moscow, Molotov found Churchill more enthusiastic for Roosevelt's idea of not discussing war aims than for his policemen idea. In a farewell speech, Churchill was moved to slip into Marxist terminology; the allies would not cease their efforts until 'the working masses' had been liberated from the dangers of Naz-ism.[95]

Unless almost all the available evidence is to be rejected, Stalin really does appear to have adopted by the middle of 1942 a twin-track approach to war aims to which he was to adhere for the following three years. One track was long-term cooperation with the other two allies for security, particularly against Germany. The other, which will be discussed in a later section, was dominance over key countries on the Soviet Union's borders. Regarding the first track, it is important not to read history – in this case Britain's postwar international decline – backwards and to grasp that there were few signs of Russia assigning a significantly lesser role to Britain than to the US. During the desperate times between the German invasion and early 1944 the Soviet 'parliament', the powerless Supreme Soviet, was summoned only once, and that was to ratify the Anglo-Soviet treaty of alliance of June 1942. When the defeated Republican presidential candidate, Wendell Willkie, visited Moscow in September of that year and made some crass and gratuitous anti-British remarks along the lines that Russia and America did not need 'any other country' his Soviet host, Vyshinsky, rebuked him and advised him that the war would need the efforts of all three allies. At the foreign ministers' conference in Moscow over a year later it was again Vyshinsky in a keynote speech who 'expressed the warmest conviction that the future hope of the world rested in collaboration with the United States, Great Britain and the Soviet Union, and that without such collaboration he feared there would be no future'.[96]

This was partly from belief in Britain as still a world power. Stalin probably shared the notion of the American academic Alexander

Dallin that the Turkish–Soviet border was, for all practical purposes, an Anglo–Soviet border.[97] However, he was also responding to a golden opportunity to become the arbiter of the Grand Alliance that Roosevelt presented to him with his unsubtle (though not unsuccessful) attempts at summit meetings to forge a special relationship with Stalin by coldshouldering Churchill. Stalin sometimes donned the mantle of Britain's special friend and ally. At Tehran, he departed from his general unwillingness to discuss war aims by saying that he 'favoured an increase in the British Empire, particularly the area around Gibraltar'. At the next summit at Yalta, when Roosevelt was negative about a role for Britain in postwar Korea, Stalin said that it should be offered one because it would be offended if it was not. Stalin saw huge advantages in an Anglo-Soviet special relationship because the only long-term alternative was a special Anglo-American relationship, which could only be to the Soviet Union's disadvantage. No doubt he could hardly believe his good fortune that Roosevelt's slights at Tehran and afterwards were goading the entire British political leadership into seeing merit in such an alignment.[98] More generally, Stalin's readiness to work for the Grand Alliance to continue after the war must have been enhanced by the pleasurable knowledge that he had developed diplomatic skills of the highest order, fully equal to Churchill's or Roosevelt's. If he knew how to win over Churchill, he could also show superlative tactical skill in dealing with Roosevelt. A good example is the occasion at the Yalta conference when he chose precisely the right moment to persuade the President to agree to the Soviet formula for dealing with Poland in return for abandoning his demand that each of the sixteen republics of the USSR should have a separate vote in the future United Nations organisation. It may well be that this demand had only been made in the first place as a bargaining chip. If so, Stalin chose the moment of maximum advantage to cash in the chip. Stalin had sensed that this demand, which would have played havoc with their UN project, was an ultimate political bombshell to the American administration, which had codenamed it the 'X matter' and banned all reference to it, though Roosevelt himself had blurted it out to the Brazilian ambassador.[99]

An intentionally dramatic illustration of this new phase in Soviet policy was the dissolution of an old bogeyman of western statesmen, the Communist International or Comintern in May 1943. Stalin had never regarded this body, which had failed to engineer a single communist takeover since its foundation in 1919, with much respect.[100] The great purge of the late 1930s, in which tens of thousands of foreign communists in the Soviet Union, many of them active in it, had been 'repressed', left it moribund, and its importance was played down in the bible of high Stalinism, *The Short Course*, published in 1939.[101] Between August 1939 and June 1941 it had had to do things that made it an embarrassment afterwards, for example the illegal Czech Communist Party used it to broadcast propaganda to the home country in which Czechs had been urged to extend a friendly reception to 'German workers in uniform', that is, Nazi occupation troops. In the spring of 1941 Stalin had been poised to dissolve it as a gesture of appeasement towards Hitler.[102] Its chief function in the war was radio propaganda which could easily be continued after the dissolution, while its more clandestine activities passed to three 'institutes' and to a Department of International Information of the Soviet Communist Party Central Committee.[103] A postwar textbook for Soviet schoolchildren explained that the disbanding of the Comintern 'decisively gave the lie to the bourgeois calumny that the Communist parties acted only on orders from the Comintern and did not serve the interests of their own nations'. The children were reassured that the Comintern had done so much good work during its existence that communist parties had reached the stage where they could 'solve independently the complicated problems facing the working class'.[104] It would be nearer the truth to say that obedience to the Soviet Party had become such an ingrained habit in other communist parties that they could be controlled independently of the existence of such a body as the Comintern. It had never issued a public statement or directive since 1935; incredible as it might sound, it had not even issued a statement in response to the signature of the Anti-Comintern Pact by Germany and Japan in 1936.[105]

Thus it would be easy to explain away the abolition of the Comintern, but it would also be mistaken. Stalin had become disillusioned with the illegal communist parties across Europe because of their failure, except in Yugoslavia, to take pressure off the Soviet Union by mounting serious resistance against the Nazis.[106] That was one more reason for putting a great many eggs in the basket of relations with Britain and the US. At the Comintern school in the east of European Russia, one of the students has recorded that from 1942 lectures regularly 'extolled the firm, unbreakable common alliance between England, the USA and the Soviet Union'. Shortly after the dissolution, the school was closed down, and some little time after that Stalin gave orders to the Foreign Ministry that all documents of any importance that reached it relating to Britain or the US should be sent to him.[107] That Stalin increasingly regarded relations with those

two countries as the basis for the fundamental war aim of providing
the Soviet Union with long-term guarantees of its security is supported by much evidence. The most important date in the Soviet
calendar was 7 November, the date of the Bolshevik seizure of power
in 1917. In his 1941 speech he congratulated the American and British
peoples on having 'elementary democratic liberties' as demonstrated
by the existence of trade unions, 'workers' parties' and parlia-
ments.[108] If there was an element of only faint praise in this, the
Revolution Day address in 1943 was, in the words of one historian,
'open-minded and conciliatory'. It came after the foreign ministers'
conference the previous month and three weeks before the first of the
great summit meetings at Tehran. The atmosphere in diplomatic
quarters in Moscow was euphoric around the sacred date.[109] Stalin
himself was still euphoric in the 1944 Revolution Day address, in
which he declared that the basis for the Grand Alliance 'lies not in
chance and passing considerations but in vitally important and long-
term interests'. It would 'certainly stand the strain of the concluding
phase of the war' – probably a reference to an expected German
attempt to surrender to the western powers only. After the war, Stalin
pronounced, it would be essential to thwart the 'law of history' by
which alliances forged in war dissolved with the arrival of peace. He
uttered one cautionary note: unanimity among the big three was a
'necessary precondition' for the alliance to continue after the war had
ended.[110]

To all this may be added the repeated assertions by the Italian
communist leader Togliatti, in guest lectures in Russia to select
communist audiences before he returned home in the spring of 1944,
that the publicly stated policy of continuing the Grand Alliance
constituted 'not a trick but [something that] corresponds to the most
profound needs of the working class'.[111] Stalin himself, on the
second most important date in his calendar, May Day, used his
1944 address finally to endorse Roosevelt's doctrine of Unconditional Surrender: the German 'wounded beast' must be driven back
into its lair and destroyed. In the same month he told the visiting
Polish-American Marxist academic Oskar Lange that the German
danger would persist after the defeat of Nazism, and that the only
antidote to it was the Grand Alliance, which was not temporary
but, rather, arose from 'a fundamental community of historical
interests'.[112]

WAR AIMS IN EUROPE, EAST AND WEST

The question naturally arises of what form Stalin expected this 'fundamental community' to take. What precise meaning did he ascribe to the precondition of unanimity? Had he forgotten or set aside his message to Molotov in May 1942 that the issue of Soviet borders should be settled by force? Beria's son's view that he wanted the US and Britain to give him a completely free hand to do as he wished within an agreed Soviet sphere of influence is oversimplified.[113] According to two post-communism Russian historians, Stalin attached much value to the reports on war aims drawn up in 1944 by Maisky and Litvinov, to which some reference has already been made, and his policies 'were often in tune with the memorandums of the two strategists'.[114] These men, and especially Litvinov, whose liquidation was Molotov's ambition, would not have survived in Stalin's Kremlin, still less influenced him, if they had not understood his broad thoughts and given them coherent form. In his almost ideology-free report in January 1944 Maisky called, in effect, for postwar Soviet relations with Britain and the US to be a version of the 'competitive cooperation' that has been described as the hallmark of the Anglo-American wartime relationship. Britain, in Maisky's view, might be a useful buttress against the 'dynamic imperialism' of the United States, to the extent that Britain and Russia might even form an entente to resist America's 'imperialist expansion'. Even so, there needed to be no serious conflict with the US for at least a long time. Maisky and Litvinov sketched postwar futures for the European continent that would have precluded 'Cold War' conflict. The former foresaw no real independence for Finland or Romania. (Neither did Britain.) The Poles were entitled to a more genuinely independent state but not one large enough to 'threaten' Russia. Czechoslovakia 'can be an important transmitter of our influence' in central and south-eastern Europe, though Tito's communists in Yugoslavia might have to be sacrificed to gain British acquiescence for Soviet policies in Poland, Finland and Romania, and to forge a postwar Anglo-Soviet entente. Litvinov, who did not report until November 1944, recommended the division of Europe into three spheres of influence or rather two spheres and one non-sphere; there would be a British sphere in the west, a Soviet one in the east, and a non-sphere in between, comprising Austria, Italy, Denmark, Norway and a Germany divided into seven or eight separate states.[115]

By that time Stalin had turned away from thoughts of dismembering Germany but not towards ones of confrontation with the Anglo-

Americans over that country. During the year preceding Litvinov's report he had agreed readily to the British idea of initially dividing a defeated Germany into occupation zones, which meant that if the Anglo-American armies conquered part of the Soviet zone they would have to yield it to the Red Army, but also that if that body entered agreed-upon western powers' zones or sectors (as it did in Berlin and Austria) it would have to retreat. Stalin's thinking was one of a spectrum in which there would be close east–west cooperation in great matters like policy in Germany and greater freedom for him to do as he wished in lesser (to the western allies) matters. Thus, correctly judged by Stalin to be at the opposite end of the range from Germany, was Sub-Carpathian Ruthenia, the easternmost province of Czechoslovakia, which he decided in 1944, as the Red Army entered it, that he wished to annex to the Ukrainian republic of the USSR, even though it had never been part of the tsarist empire and the Czechoslovak exile government was strongly opposed to relinquishing it. From late October, pro-Soviet officials were installed and the Soviet press reported that they were being inundated with pleas and petitions to become part of the Ukraine from the population of what the Soviets now referred to as the Carpatho-Ukraine. The Czech government complained, pointing out that the treaty that President Beneš had negotiated with Stalin less than a year earlier strictly prohibited interference in each other's internal affairs. The Soviet reply, worthy of Orwell or Kafka, was that the spontaneous movement to secede from Czechoslovakia had nothing to do with them, and that they would only be guilty of interference in its internal affairs if they tried to prevent the province from seceding. De facto, the province had been annexed to the Soviet Ukraine by the start of 1945. The matter did not stop there. Stalin feigned outrage that the Czechoslovak government had questioned the purity of the Soviet government's motives in acceding to the wishes of the Carpatho-Ukrainian people, and demanded that it make amends by recognising the communist Lublin government that had been proclaimed in Poland on new year's day 1945, which it did. Stalin seems to have entered the new year in a jocular frame of mind, perhaps because for once the Americans were bearing the brunt of the war in the Ardennes battles. When Roosevelt made a personal plea to him not to recognise the Lublin government he replied that he must because the Supreme Soviet had voted in favour of recognition and he was 'powerless' to override their decision.[116] The transfer of the province was to be formalised in a Czech–Soviet treaty in June 1945, whereupon Molotov sent a message to the Carpatho-Ukrainian people congratulating them on the attainment of their 'age old dream' of joining the peoples grouped in the USSR.[117] Stalin's motives in deciding to annex were twofold. First, he deeply feared Ukrainian nationalism and wished to counter it by including all Ukrainians (or part Ukrainians in the case of the ethnically mixed population of the Carpatho) under direct Soviet control. Second, he wished the USSR to have a border with Hungary, and, in that regard, he showed foresight. His successor and critic, Khrushchev, was to use this border to pour troops into Hungary in 1956 for the bloody crushing of that country's national uprising. Finally, Stalin was right in not anticipating any adverse reaction from the west; the British Foreign Office regarded the annexation with indifference or even understanding.[118]

The Carpatho-Ukraine, northern East Prussia and the Finnish Arctic port of Petsamo were the only additional annexations in Europe that the Soviet Union was to make as a result of the Soviet–German war, and only the first two of these had not been part of the tsarist empire. However, this modesty masks an aim of dominating countries to the west of the Soviet state, both to ensure its security and to place its superpower status beyond question. As the intelligence official Pavel Sudoplatov explained it in his memoirs: 'We needed a buffer between us and the spheres of influence of the other world powers, and . . . Only military strength and domination of the countries on our borders could ensure us a superpower role.'[119] Within this framework, Stalin intended to settle the many territorial disputes of east-central Europe with decisions whose primary purpose was to benefit the Soviet Union. The most important was the border between Germany and Poland, which has already been discussed and over which he grossly favoured the latter country, chiefly because he envisaged a non-communist Germany and a communist Poland, though also because of pique that his efforts to foment rebellion among Germans to overthrow Hitler and make peace on terms not unreasonable to Germany had failed.

The second most important territorial dispute concerned the disposition of the huge province of Transylvania, which was bitterly disputed between Hungary and Romania. Traditionally, the Soviet Union had supported Hungary and, when Hitler 'awarded' three-fifths of the province to Hungary in 1940, the Soviet view was that that was the least to which Hungary was entitled. Both countries joined Hitler's war against Russia, so that there was nothing to choose between them in that respect. As the prospect of defeating Germany ceased to be only a dream, Stalin undoubtedly gave considerable thought to Transylvania as a great prize and one that, this time, he would be the man to award. His eventual decision, that the entire province should again become Romanian, was dictated by his war aims towards the two countries that coveted the great prize. He thought that one country had to receive everything because a compromise like Hitler's in 1940 would satisfy neither. He may have been influenced by the fact that Soviet efforts to recruit Hungarian officers in the prisoner-of-war camps largely failed, whereas captured Romanian officers were more pliable material.[120] However, it was the facts of geography and the fortunes of war that primarily dictated the decision. With its position on the Soviet southern border in Europe, Stalin had sought to turn Romania into (at best for the Romanians) a Soviet client state in 1940. This ambition reasserted itself after Stalingrad. The small band of Romanian communists in Moscow, who were led by Anna Pauker, a rabbi's daughter and a fervent Stalinist despite her husband having been liquidated in the purges, egged him on, urging him to establish a pure communist regime which, since there was almost no popular support for communism in Romania, could only have functioned as a European equivalent of the Japanese puppet state of Manchukuo.

This was the optimum Soviet war aim for Romania in 1943–4. It was even planned to liquidate underground communists in the country in case they had been 'contaminated'. The only power in the land would have been the Red Army, acting through the returned Romanian communist exiles, most of whom were Jews in a country in which anti-Semitism was rife.[121] Stalin was willing to set this aim aside if Romania would leave the war. On 2 April 1944 Molotov issued a statement that the Soviet Union had no desire to intervene in Romanian affairs, and the Red Army stopped its victorious advance at the June 1941 Soviet–Romanian border. Peace negotiations were opened with the government of Ion Antonescu, in which the sole important demand was that Romania should remove German troops from its territory.[122] In fact, Antonescu remained loyal to Hitler, but what had been offered to him came about in August 1944 when a royalist coup brought about a change of sides by Romania in the war at no cost to the Soviets. This triggered the accommodationist model of Soviet war aims towards Romania. Stalin welcomed the development intellectually but not emotionally. He had been looking forward to the virtual incorporation of Romania as a de facto Soviet province like Mongolia in the east. Now it had to be treated with more respect. This included allowing it to seek to reclaim all Transylvania, and to be given it after the Romanian government had been changed to make it largely communist in composition in March 1945.[123] Romania had escaped the Nazi embrace with some heroism in circumstances which, in the short term, enabled it to recover Transylvania, and which, in the longer term, were to enable it to become substantially independent of the Soviet Union from the 1960s to the complete collapse of the Soviet empire in eastern Europe in 1989.

Infinitely less happy was Hungary's experience. In October 1944 the flame of the Soviets' traditional pro-Hungary stance was still flickering. Stalin told the Polish prime minister, Mikolajczyk, that Hungary would soon be an ally, and 'It will change completely when we get there.' He was expecting a repetition of the coup in Bucharest in August, coupled with the capture of Budapest by the Soviet army. Neither happened. The assault on the city failed, and it was the Germans who engineered a coup in which they installed the Hungarian Nazis of the Arrow Cross Party in office. Faced with the prospect, which proved to be all too real, of long and costly warfare to drive the Germans out of Hungary, Stalin decided on a twofold set of war aims towards that country. First, it should lose all Transylvania and all other gains that it had made at Germany's coat tails between 1938 and 1941. This would obviously cause immense nationalist anguish and therefore, second, the country should not become fully communist for a period of ten to fifteen years so that non-communist politicians could be blamed for the complete negation of Hungarian national aspirations. This policy was revealed by the Hungarian communist leader, Mátyás Rákosi, to his fellow Magyar comrades in 1952, by which time Hungary had been completely under communist rule for three or four years, rule that was oppressive even by the general standards of communism in postwar eastern Europe. Hungary had become communist within a very few years of Romania under the impact of the postwar events known as the Cold War.[124] Then, while the Hungarian communists had to rely heavily on brutality to impose their rule, Stalin was not wrong in expecting the restoration of all Transylvania to provide communism in Romania with some basis of popular support.

Besides boding ill for Hungary, Romania's change of sides rendered the German position in Bulgaria and that of the royalist government there untenable. In September it admitted the Red Army and a mixed government including communists was set up, entrenching Soviet power in the country. This was obviously important. Even so, the acquisition of Bulgaria was for Stalin, in the autumn of 1944, a side issue, and not the central preoccupation that it had been for him in the autumn of 1940. There are two related matters. First in 1941 Germany had allowed Bulgaria to annex from Greece the province of

Western Thrace, which gave it a seaboard on the Aegean. The Bulgarian communists joined with others in the governing 'Fatherland Front' to ask for the retention of this gain. Faced with the strongest British demands that the area must be returned to Greece, the Soviets ordered a Bulgarian withdrawal. In May 1944 Eden had written to Churchill that it would be intolerable 'having the Russians on the Aegean', which was clearly what the retention of Western Thrace by a Soviet-dominated Bulgaria would have meant. In 1978 Molotov reminisced that he had sympathised with the Bulgarian plea, which corresponded with what Stalin had offered Bulgaria in 1940, but: 'It was impossible . . . It would have been better. But you had to stay within the limits. Raising this issue would have caused trouble at the beginning of the peace. The English and French would have been opposed . . . It was desirable but not timely.' Second, the British stance on the return of Western Thrace to Greece was linked to its opposition against the idea, which Tito was championing in late 1944, for a South Slav federation, including Greek Macedonia, which would also have brought communism to the shores of the Aegean; Greek Macedonia bordered Western Thrace on that sea. Britain favoured a central European federation that would have been dominated by the anti-Russian as well as anti-German Poles. For the same reasons of *Realpolitik* it opposed a federation in the middle Balkans among peoples (Serbs, Macedonians, Bulgarians) who were identified as Russophile. Stalin himself had mixed feelings about a South Slav federation, which would have threatened to dilute his own new power position in Bulgaria. He could, therefore, readily join with Britain in opposing the idea at this time. The matter was very different from the Bulgarian claim to Western Thrace, which would have suited his purposes admirably but which had to be ruled out to avoid a crisis in Anglo-Soviet relations.[125]

The aim of expanding Soviet power while preserving the Grand Alliance into the period of peace proved realisable with little difficulty in Bulgaria and its region. Britain had no real problem with a Soviet-dominated Bulgaria, and the country hardly entered into American thinking before Truman became president. Likewise, the Soviets could easily refuse to sponsor the greater Bulgaria ambitions of the Bulgarian communists. Such compromises would not be available everywhere. As the war drew towards its victorious climax, Stalin had to worry more and more about the respective merits of preserving the Grand Alliance while expanding Soviet power and attending to his duties, if that is the word to use, as head of the international communist movement.

If the Grand Alliance and Germany were at the top of Stalin's priorities, Poland came a close third. Some consideration has already been given to his aims for Poland's frontiers. In the east, most of the territory gained under the Nazi–Soviet pact partition of Poland in 1939 was to be retained. A little would be returned, partly to make the border correspond with the one, proposed in 1920 by the British Foreign Office, known as the Curzon Line after the then foreign secretary. In the west, Poland was to gain some 40,000 square miles from Germany. The reasons for such largesse have been discussed. It might not have been expected from any study of the record of Stalin's dealings with Poland. He had acquired an animus against the Poles from his role in the Russo-Polish war of 1920, in which his bungling had contributed to Bolshevik defeat. In the late 1930s as many as 110,000 Polish communists exiled in the Soviet Union had been killed in the great purges.[126] In 1938 the Polish Communist Party had been dissolved on the grounds that it had been taken over by 'agents of Polish fascism'.[127] In 1940 he had ordered the murder of some 15,000 Polish officer prisoners of war. After that he seems to have taken the view that the debt dating back to 1920 had been settled and he became less obsessively anti-Polish than Molotov, to whom, to the end of his life, the Poles were 'irrational' and 'always on one's neck'.[128] Even so, Stalin continued to think that force might be necessary to dragoon the 'individualistic' Poles into serving Soviet purposes, and that Poland was less a country than a corridor through which Germany invaded Russia whenever it felt strong enough to do so.

After the invasion of June 1941, the Soviets negotiated the establishment of diplomatic relations with the Polish government in exile in London. However, as early as October of that year the prominent Stalinist Vyshinsky, himself of Polish origin, told the newly arrived Polish ambassador, Kot, that: 'We concluded the Polish-Soviet agreement from sentimental measures rather than rational ones.'[129] The word panic should perhaps be substituted for sentimental. Within less than a year Kot had been recalled, and Polish-Soviet diplomatic relations had become nominal by the time they were formally suspended by the Soviets in April 1943, following the discovery of mass graves of murdered officers at one of the massacre sites, Katyn. Relations were not formally broken off, and Moscow stated that they could be resumed if the London government was suitably 'reconstituted'.[130] This implied that a government in Poland that was not purely communist might be compatible with Soviet aims. Such a government's first action would have had to be recognition of the

Curzon Line as the Soviet–Polish border. The Soviet government made its first public claim to the line in March 1943, as they embarked on the slow advance westwards after Stalingrad. In October this was upgraded to a demand to Britain to extend unconditional recognition to the line as the rightful border.[131] With that condition satisfied, Stalin was ready to consider a mixed government in Poland, partly because of some awareness of the bankruptcy of the policy that he had pursued towards Poland and the Poles before June 1941, and partly because he did not want the satisfaction of Soviet aims in relation to Poland to be achieved at the cost of disrupting the Grand Alliance. How far he might have been prepared to go was not to be put to the test because there was something approaching complete intransigence in Polish exile circles against giving up any territory at all from eastern Poland within its pre-1939 borders.[132]

There is not space here to discuss the Polish issue during the last two years of the war except in outline. Churchill assigned a prominent place in British war aims to the restoration of an independent Poland with a government of its own choice, though in return he was prepared to concede the Curzon Line border. This would have been more realistic if America had been willing to constitute a joint front with Britain on what Russia could do in Poland without alienating Washington as well as London. Stalin himself sought in vain from Roosevelt clear guidance on this. All he received was what the historian William Taubman has called 'a vague invitation to unspecified aggrandisement, along with a plea that Soviet gains somehow be rendered palatable to American opinion'.[133] Roosevelt behaved at his worst over Poland, indifferent to its fate but unwilling to say so, if only because of the Polish-American vote. The Polish resistance fighter and, in later life, academic historian Jan Karski was forced to the conclusion that Roosevelt had simply been lying to him when, at their meeting, he had outlined a glittering future for Poland. The President certainly plumbed the depths of hypocrisy when, in his last election campaign in October 1944, he received a Polish-American delegation seated in front of a large map of Poland showing the prewar borders.[134] Roosevelt was not willing to do anything serious to gain for Poland genuine independence within reduced borders, still less to seek the restoration of the old borders, though he did make a half-hearted attempt to secure Soviet assent for the city of Lvov becoming a Polish enclave, surrounded by Soviet territory, east of the Curzon Line. It is unlikely that he was really disappointed that nothing came of this. At some point in 1944 he told Averell Harriman that he 'didn't care whether the countries bordering on Russia became communised'.[135]

This American non-policy and the refusal of the exiled Polish government to agree to the Curzon Line border combined with events on the ground to create a situation in which, if the Grand Alliance continued into the peace, it would be despite what happened in Poland. A Polish communist party was reconstituted in 1942 under the name of the Polish Workers' Party. Polish communism was actually divided between surviving Polish communists in Russia, often known as 'Muscovites', whose main aim tended to be to retain Stalin's confidence, and those in occupied Poland who, at the end of 1943, under Gomulka's leadership, formed a National Council of the Homeland (NCH), which, actually including only a handful of persons who were in constant danger from the Gestapo, made the breathtaking claim to be 'the real political representation of the Polish nation, entitled to act in the name of the nation and to guide its destiny until Poland's liberation from foreign occupation'.[136] During 1944 Stalin was increasingly attracted to the idea of using this body and the Muscovite Polish communists as the nucleus for the political reconstruction of Poland, especially when the NCH made it clear that it favoured a gradualist and populist approach, while being willing to call upon the services of the Red Army and the NKVD until such time as it was 'able to smash the reaction with our own internal forces'. As has been noted, a communist proto-government for Poland, modestly designated as a committee, was set up in the liberated city of Lublin in June and Stalin had about thirty meetings with members of it during the following six months.[137]

Stalin's readiness to favour the Polish communists was strengthened by the London Polish government's refusal to yield on the eastern borders, and by Roosevelt, who, on the eve of a visit to Moscow by the London Polish prime minister, Mikolajczyk, in July 1944, sent Stalin a message stressing America's complete neutrality in all disputes between Poland and the Soviet Union.[138] After the failure of the anti-communist Home Army's rash bid to seize the initiative by rising against the Germans in Warsaw in the summer, the Polish communists were allowed to make the 'October turn' in policy in which terror tactics were employed against actual or suspected opponents in the eastern and central areas from which the Germans had been expelled. Elections as a basis for deciding the government were ruled out because, as Gomulka said, they would 'give the reactionary forces a legal basis'. The Lublin committee's newspaper described the Home Army as 'accomplices of Hitler' and the NKVD arrested tens of thousands of suspects, a few of whom were hanged or shot.[139] As has already been noted, the Lublin committee became a provisional government at the start of 1945, and the western powers were able to gain only the poorest of deals for Poland at the Yalta conference; the communist government, by that time installed in Warsaw, was to be broadened, and the British and American ambassadors in Moscow were to form a committee with Molotov for the long-distance supervision of the restoration of democracy in Poland. The remainder of the tortuous process by which Poland became fully communist lies outside the scope of this study, including the restoration for a time, beginning in May–June 1945, of a genuine multiparty system which coincided with Mikolajczyk's return and his inclusion in the new Provisional Government of National Unity.[140] With the war in Europe at an end, Stalin undoubtedly wanted a communist Poland, but he hesitated to take all measures to create one because of his continuing interest in preserving good relations with the great western powers.

In Poland's southern neighbour (though never friend), Czechoslovakia, Stalin was willing to refrain from seeking a predominantly communist regime as a Soviet war aim. This stemmed from the pro-Soviet orientation adopted by the Czech government in exile, led by Eduard Beneš, who won some grudging approval, though only as the best of a bad bunch among the exile governments in London. Among these, according to Georgi Dimitrov towards the end of 1942, the Poles were 'hostile', the Yugoslavs in 'utter disorder', and the Free French 'repulsive'. 'The Czechs behave better, although you cannot trust in Beneš's sincerity either.'[141] Stalin did judge Beneš fairly trustworthy when he visited Moscow in December 1943 to negotiate a treaty that was intended to serve as the framework for Soviet–Czech postwar relations. He showed considerable obsequiousness not only to Stalin and Molotov while subjecting them to a monologue of his views about the greatness of the Soviet Union and his own country, the worthlessness of other east European states and the need to keep the west out of the area, but also to the Czech communist leader Klement Gottwald, to whom his message was that the communists should and must be the 'strongest element of the new regime', even though they had polled only 10 per cent of the votes in the last prewar elections in 1935. For their part, the Czech communists were adopting a soothing line in their propaganda, for instance being silent, probably on Stalin's orders, about the nationalisation of the economy. Beneš accepted all Soviet proposals for the treaty; if he had any misgivings, he did not reveal them. Those proposals included a clause authorising Soviet intervention in Czechoslovakia in the event of 'indirect aggression', which could have been nothing more than a change of government that the Soviets did not like, and the removal of the words 'full international' from a reference to Czechoslovakia's sovereignty. In return for this Beneš gained not only the promise of a democratic, multi-party Czechoslovakia, but also Soviet support for his most cherished war aim, which was the expulsion of the three million-strong minority of 'Sudeten Germans' after the war. The Soviets had previously been at best ambiguous about this.[142] On this basis, Czechoslovakia in 1945 was able to resume for a time its life as a democracy, albeit one in which the communists took their pick of ministries (initially interior, defence, agriculture and education).

Interestingly, Stalin asked Beneš in December 1943 if he knew of any Polish politician in London who had the same outlook on relations with Russia as Beneš had. In the early months of 1944 the Soviets explicitly informed the London Poles that the model of Czech–Soviet relations that had just been adopted could also work for Poland.[143] The reality was that the Czech–Soviet treaty of 1943 could not be adapted as a model for Soviet war aims in any other country. Poland was a more typical situation of non-communists pitted against communists. Stalin had striven mightily almost since the 1917 Bolshevik revolution to gain mastery over the international communist movement as well as over the Soviet Communist Party and state. By the later part of the war he had to balance the aim of preserving the Grand Alliance with the desire of foreign communists for power and his own Marxist-Leninist and revolutionary heritage. The later war period saw a widespread upsurge in support for communism, especially in Europe. A Soviet historian proudly noted that in 1939 there were sixty-one communist parties with four million members; in September 1945, seventy-six with twenty million.[144] Stalin certainly regarded a showdown with the opponents of communism as ultimately inevitable. In January 1945 he told Dimitrov that 'the crisis of capitalism manifests itself in the division of the capitalists into two factions, the Fascist and the democratic ones . . . Today we support one of those bourgeois factions in the struggle against the other, but in the future we will also be against this capitalist faction.'[145]

The fundamental question is when he expected this particular future to occur and in 1945 he was certainly in no hurry. His aims in relation to the expansion of communism were calibrated to restrict communists to what was possible in their respective countries, and to work for those objectives in a manner which, at best, would not lead to a breakdown in his relations with the western great powers, and which, at the least, would not involve him in actual conflict with them. He evolved a theory in which there were two models, one based on the 'parity principle' and the other on the concept of the popular front from below. In the former the communists would accept a place as one among all progressive parties and thus a minority. In the latter the communists would share power with other parties, but the political parties as a whole would share authority with other organisations such as trade unions and youth and women's groups, all of which the communists would seek to bring under their control with the objective of overall effective control.[146] In practice, this was to provide only the roughest of guides and was subject to factors that local communists were certain to find congenial, such as the presence of the Red Army and the NKVD, and to ones which would try their patience, though their loyalty to the Soviet regime had very deep roots.

Italy provides a good illustration of Stalin juggling with these considerations. As more and more of the country was liberated from the German occupation that had followed Mussolini's overthrow in 1943, it became clear that the communist party enjoyed massive support. For Britain and the United States the prospect of a communist Italy was obviously intolerable, and their monopoly of military power in liberated Italy gave them a decisive advantage but one which they wished to press without having to resort to force. In a major speech in the Commons on 22 February 1944 Churchill for the first time publicly expressed support for the Curzon Line border and also for the Badoglio government that the western allies had installed in Italy. This was a hint to Stalin, which could hardly have been clearer, that he could have his western border if he cooperated to give his allies a non-communist Italy.[147] There was no possibility of a communist Italy, but Stalin had it in his gift to decide whether that outcome came about in a hard way for the west or an easier one. He gave the west the latter. He sent the Italian communist leader Palmiro Togliatti back home from Soviet exile in March 1944 with instructions to seek no more than communist minority representation in the Badoglio government, and to restrain the revolutionary enthusiasm of the 1.7 million Italians who joined the party after it was legalised in 1944, though that was also Togliatti's own inclination. After his return, he was in constant communication with the Soviet ambassador to Italy for advice, if not actual orders, and in October 1944 the latter wrote approvingly to Molotov that, 'Only the moderating influence of its vanguard, the PCI ... can halt this rush of the masses towards premature insurrection.'[148] Togliatti was not actually totally immune to his followers' mood. In late 1944 he entertained the hope that cooperation between Tito's Yugoslav partisans and Italian communist guerrillas in the north-eastern province of Venezia Giulia might create a 'democratic situation' in one small part of Italy.[149] What was visible to western policymakers was that Soviet policy in Italy was pretty much exactly what they would have wished. In October 1944 the senior Foreign Office official, Christopher Warner, wrote in a memorandum addressed to the Cabinet on Soviet aims that: 'If the Soviet Government are interested in post-war Italy and are resolved to exercise their influence there, this is not merely or even at all because they wish to impose a Communist regime on Italy, but because they will see in a strong Communist party the best guarantee against the danger of Italy being drawn back into the German orbit.'[150] This was a notably generous interpretation. It may be compared with what Stalin said to Togliatti before his departure that he wanted a strong Italy with a strong army and that it was 'the English' who wanted a weak Italy, presumably so that they could turn the Mediterranean into an English lake.[151]

The unprovocative Soviet policy towards Italy took its place beside the policy that was dictated to the French Communist Party, though this was one that took into account the peculiarities of both France and its communist party. Stalin rightly saw scope for a liberated France, unlike Italy, to make an important contribution to the final defeat of Germany. The French comrades must do nothing to impede this by distracting attention to the 'parliamentary cretinism' of constitution drafting or debate about Marxist-Leninist theory. They must curb the expression of their flattering but potentially counter-productive 'inordinate zeal' for all that was Russian, and their admirable but unwise 'revolutionary impatience'. Thorez, the party's leader, was not allowed to return until November 1944, and took with him further instructions, given to him personally by Stalin, for the party to position itself as part of a broad alliance of the left and to play down its separate identity, for instance not reviving the Young Communist League. It should, however, waste no opportunity to argue to the French people that the Soviet Union was its one true friend, and that relations with it should be the cornerstone of postwar French foreign policy: the Anglo-Americans were declared to 'want a weak France as well as a weak Italy'.[152]

Stalin's rejection of insurrectionism in Italy or France, together with his percentages agreement on spheres of influence in south-east Europe with Churchill in October 1944 and the many agreements reached at the Yalta conference contributed to a situation in which the

Cold War was not looking inevitable as the defeat of Germany neared. Everything depended on the willingness and ability of the two players or sets of players to continue to make concessions to one another. In March 1945 Churchill urged upon Eden that Britain should not protest with any vigour against a Soviet-engineered coup in Bucharest that imposed upon what he called 'late Roumanian enemies' a largely communist government, both because he had conceded that country to the Soviets in the percentages agreement in effect in return for a British monopoly in Greece, and because of the need to concentrate on securing freedom for Poland: 'I am anxious to go full out about Poland and this requires concentration at the expense of other matters.'[153] There were plenty of danger signals between the Soviet Union and the west as the war in Europe ended, but Soviet and western war aims were not on any obvious collision course.

Notes

1. Caroline Kennedy-Pipe, *Stalin's Cold War: Soviet Strategies in Europe, 1943 to 1956* (Manchester: Manchester University Press, 1995), pp. 27–9.
2. Condoleezza Rice, 'The evolution of Soviet grand strategy', in Paul Kennedy (ed.), *Grand Strategies in War and Peace* (New Haven: Yale University Press, 1991), pp. 145, 148, 153–4.
3. Elliott R. Goodman, *The Soviet Design for a World State* (New York: Columbia University Press, 1960), pp. 42–3, 65–6, 74, 82, 86–7; Julian and Margaret Bullard (eds), *Inside Stalin's Russia: The Diaries of Reader Bullard, 1930–1934* (Charlbury: Day Books, 2000), p. 109.
4. Goodman, *Soviet Design*, pp. 141–5, 149–53.
5. Ibid. pp. 153–9.
6. Ibid. pp. 161–3, 303–8; Milovan Djilas, *Conversations with Stalin* (Harmondsworth: Penguin, 1962), p. 90.
7. Goodman, *Soviet Design*, pp. 164–6, 171–2, 448–9, 458–64. In the words of another historian the theory was 'recast as a mere scholastic hypothesis'. Paolo Spriano, *Stalin and The European Communists* (London: Verso, 1985), p. 84.
8. Alexander Zinoviev, *The Reality of Communism* (London: Paladin Books, 1985), pp. 273–4.
9. Teddy J. Uldricks, *Diplomacy and Ideology: The Origins of Soviet Foreign Relations* (London: Sage, 1979), p. 149.
10. Martin Kitchen, *British Policy towards the Soviet Union during the Second World War* (Basingstoke: Macmillan, 1986), p. 235. This perhaps recalls Hitler's prewar advice to Lord Halifax to solve the Indian problem by shooting Mahatma Gandhi.
11. Albert L. Weeks, *Stalin's Other War: Soviet Grand Strategy, 1939–1941* (Lanham: Rowman, 2002), pp. 9, 23, 41, 73; Ivo Banac (ed.), *The Diary of Georgi Dimitrov, 1933–1949* (New Haven: Yale University Press, 2003), pp. 115–17.
12. Stalin's criminal career is examined in Roman Brockman, *The Secret File of Joseph Stalin: A Hidden Life* (London: Cass, 2001).

13. George F. Kennan, Memoirs, 1925–1950 (London: Hutchinson, 1968), pp. 279–80; Stanislaw Kot, Conversations with the Kremlin and Dispatches from Russia (London: Oxford University Press, 1963), pp. xxv–xxvi.

14. G. R. Urban (ed.), Stalinism: Its Impact on Russia and the World (London: Wildwood House, 1985), pp. 193, 218.

15. William O. McCagg, Jr, Stalin Embattled, 1943–1948 (Detroit: Wayne State University Press, 1978), especially pp. 60–2, 166–7. On Stalin and Tito in the later part of the war see John Erickson, The Road to Berlin (London: Weidenfeld, 1983), pp. 337–40.

16. Spriano, Stalin and European Communists, p. 189.

17. On this see William Taubman, Stalin's American Policy (New York: Norton, 1982), pp. 84–7.

18. Sergo Beria, Beria, My Father: Inside Stalin's Kremlin (London: Duckworth, 2001), p. 90.

19. Vojtech Mastny, Russia's Road to the Cold War: Diplomacy, Warfare, and the Politics of Communism, 1941–1945 (New York: Columbia University Press, 1979), pp. 270–1.

20. Elisabeth Barker, British Policy in South-East Europe in the Second World War (London: Macmillan, 1976), p. 210.

21. Vladimir Galitsky, 'Uncovering previously unknown statistics', New Times, no. 24, 12–18 June 1990, p. 39.

22. Banac (ed.), Dimitrov Diary, p. 193.

23. Arkady Yerusalimsky, German Imperialism: Its Past and Present (Moscow: Progress Publishers, 1969), p. 338.

24. Figures for civilian deaths in Martin K. Sorge, The Other Price of Hitler's War: German Military and Civilian Losses from World War II (Westport: Greenwood Press, 1986), pp. 126–9; Kennan, Memoirs, pp. 265–6; Mastny, Russia's Road, pp. 253–5, 269; Beria, Beria, pp. 106–7; R. C. Raack, Stalin's Drive to the West, 1938–1945: The Origins of the Cold War (Stanford: Stanford University Press, 1995), pp. 120–1; on rape as an instrument of policy see Norman M. Naimark, The Russians in Germany: A History of the Soviet Zone of Occupation, 1945–1949 (Cambridge, MA: Harvard University Press, 1995), pp. 69–78. Some East Prussians were deported to the eastern Soviet Union, and there is an excellent German documentary film, Kaltes Heimatland (Cold Homeland), about the return of some of them to their former homes in the Russian-annexed part of former East Prussia in the 1990s.

25. Cordell Hull, The Memoirs of Cordell Hull: Volume Two (London: Hodder, 1948), pp. 1174, 1282; Oleg A. Rzheshevsky, War and Diplomacy: The Making of the Grand Alliance, Documents from Stalin's Archives (Amsterdam: Harwood, 1996), pp. 270, 282; Simon Sebag Montefiore, Stalin: The Court of the Red Tsar (London: Weidenfeld, 2003), p. 212.

26. Erickson, Road to Berlin, pp. 381–3.

27. Alexander Dallin, 'Stalin and the prospects for post-war Europe', in Francesca Gori and Silvio Pons (eds), The Soviet Union and Europe in the Cold War, 1943–53 (Basingstoke: Macmillan, 1996), p. 187.

28. A. J. P. Taylor (ed.), W. P. Crozier: Off the Record: Political Interviews, 1933–1943 (London: Hutchinson, 1973), p. 266; Martin H. Folly, Churchill, Whitehall and the Soviet Union, 1941–45 (Basingstoke: Macmillan, 2000), p. 189.

29. David J. Dallin, The Big Three: The United States, Britain, Russia (New Haven: Yale University Press, 1945), p. 157.

30. Gabriel Gorodetsky, Grand Delusion: Stalin and the German Invasion of Russia (New Haven: Yale University Press, 1999), pp. 57–65, 81.

31. Ibid. pp. 72–5; Albert Resis (ed.), *Molotov Remembers: Inside Kremlin Politics: Conversations with Felix Chuev* (Chicago: Dee, 1993), p. 16.
32. Gorodetsky, *Grand Delusion*, pp. 46–7, 83–6.
33. Ibid. pp. 72–5, 78, 81–2.
34. Sarah Meiklejohn Terry, *Poland's Place in Europe: General Sikorski and the Origin of the Oder–Neisse Line, 1939–1943* (Princeton: Princeton University Press, 1983), p. 219.
35. Rzheshevsky, *Grand Alliance*, pp. 11–12, 21; Vojtech Mastny, 'Soviet war aims at the Moscow and Teheran Conferences of 1943', in *Journal of Modern History*, vol. 47, 1975, pp. 481–504.
36. Bruce Robellet Kuniholm, *The Origins of the Cold War in the Near East* (Princeton: Princeton University Press, 1980), pp. 42, 52–3, 57–9, 69–70; Graham Lyons (ed.), *The Russian Version of the Second World War: The History of the War as Taught to Soviet Schoolchildren* (London: Leo Cooper, 1976), pp. 28, 54, 84; Oleg Rzheshevsky, *World War II: Myths and the Realities* (Moscow: Progress Publishers, 1984), p. 127.
37. Resis (ed.), *Molotov*. Naturally, these must be used with caution. Molotov's assertion in 1983 (p. 13) that there had been no secret protocol to the 1939 Nazi–Soviet Non-Aggression pact, by which Germany and Russia partitioned Poland, can only have been a conscious lie. It is less easy to know what to make of his 'recollection', also in 1983 (p. 51), that he had been aboard a train in the US, eating in the dining car, when someone shouted that Roosevelt had died. No one paid any attention except the Soviets present, who were griefstricken. He attributed this to Americans being a callous people who were indifferent to anything that did not affect them 'in their pocketbook'. The reality is that Stalin had rejected repeated pleas from Roosevelt during what proved to be his last days to send Molotov to attend the United Nations foundation conference at San Francisco. He reversed this after Roosevelt died as a gesture of goodwill, and Molotov did not arrive in America until several days after the President's death.
38. Ibid. pp. 8, 53.
39. Ibid. pp. 71–4.
40. Ibid. p. 59.
41. Raack, *Stalin's Drive*, pp. 41–2.
42. Oppi Vehviläinen, *Finland in the Second World War: Between Germany and Russia* (Basingstoke: Palgrave, 2002), pp. 79–84, 91–95, 104–8.
43. Victor Rothwell, *Britain and the Cold War, 1941–1947* (London: Cape, 1982), p. 128.
44. Tuomo Polvinen, *Between East and West: Finland in International Politics, 1944–1947* (Minneapolis: University of Minnesota Press, 1986), chs 1 and 2; Wolfgang Wagner, *The Partitioning of Europe: A History of the Soviet Expansion up to the Cleavage of Germany, 1918–1945* (Stuttgart: Deutsche Verlags Anstalt, 1959), pp. 127–8.
45. Polvinen, *Finland*, p. 25.
46. Ibid. p. 32.
47. Jonathan Haslam, 'Soviet war-aims', in Ann Lane and Howard Temperley (eds), *The Rise and Fall of the Grand Alliance* (Basingstoke: Macmillan, 1995), p. 37. The remark seems somewhat incautious, though it was his Jewishness that was to seal Lozovsky's fate. One of Stalin's last purge victims, he was tried and executed in 1952.
48. Jukka Nevakivi, 'The Soviet Union and Finland after the war, 1944–53', Gori and Pons (eds), *The Soviet Union and Europe*, pp. 93–6.

49. Djilas, *Conversations with Stalin*, p. 120.
50. Sven G. Holtsmark, 'The limits to Soviet influence: Soviet diplomats and the pursuit of strategic interests in Norway and Denmark, 1944–7', in Gori and Pons (eds), *The Soviet Union and Europe*, pp. 112–21; Mastny, *Russia's Road*, p. 232.
51. Mastny, *Russia's Road*, pp. 107–12; Mary Dau, 'The Soviet Union and the liberation of Denmark', *Survey: A Journal of Soviet and East European Studies*, no. 76, summer 1970, pp. 64–81; Tony Sharp, *The Wartime Alliance and the Zonal Division of Germany* (Oxford: Clarendon, 1975), pp. 124–5.
52. R. Craig Nation, *Black Earth, Red Star: A History of Soviet Security Policy, 1917–1991* (Ithaca: Cornell University Press, 1992), p. 122.
53. Valentin Berezhkov, *History in the Making: Memoirs of World War II Diplomacy* (Moscow: Progress Publishers, 1983), pp. 39, 122.
54. Adam B. Ulam, *Expansion and Coexistence: The History of Soviet Foreign Policy, 1917–67* (London: Secker, 1968), pp. 332–3; Robert M. Slusser, 'Soviet policy and the division of Germany, 1941–1945', in Susan J. Linz (ed.), *The Impact of World War II on the Soviet Union* (Totowa: Rowman, 1985), pp. 108–9.
55. Rzheshevsky, *Grand Alliance*, p. 8.
56. Ibid. pp. 11, 13–14, 17.
57. Sir Llewellyn Woodward, *British Foreign Policy in the Second World War: Volume V* (London: Stationery Office, 1976), p. 77.
58. Rzheshevsky, *Grand Alliance*, pp. 17–18; see also V. Trukhanovsky, *British Foreign Policy during World War II, 1939–1945* (Moscow: Progress Publishers, 1970), pp. 213–23.
59. Sir Llewellyn Woodward, *British Foreign Policy in the Second World War: Volume II* (London: Stationery Office, 1971), p. 551; additional information in the same author's single-volume abridgement of this work, *British Foreign Policy in the Second World War* (London: Stationery Office, 1962), p. 435.
60. Rzheshevsky, *Grand Alliance*, p. 287.
61. Banac (ed.), *Dimitrov*, p. 257.
62. Marshal V. Kulikov, 'Internationalist assistance to peoples of Europe', in USSR Academy of Sciences, *The Liberating Mission of the Soviet Union in the Second World War* (Moscow: Nauka, 1985), p. 40.
63. Erickson, *Road to Berlin*, p. 89.
64. Banac (ed.), *Dimitrov*, pp. 279–80.
65. Erickson, *Road to Berlin*, pp. 134–5.
66. Vojtech Mastny, 'Stalin and the prospects of a separate peace in World War II', *American Historical Review*, vol. 77, 1972, pp. 1378–80; Mastny, *Russia's Road*, pp. 70, 80–2, 105–8.
67. Berezhkov, *History in the Making*, p. 293.
68. Slusser, 'Soviet policy and the division of Germany, 1941–1945', in Linz (ed.), *Impact*, p. 113.
69. Herbert Feis, *Between War and Peace: The Potsdam Conference* (Princeton: Princeton University Press, 1960), pp. 222, 235, 299, 347. In his report on this conference to the American people Truman stated that he had been proud to be of help in satisfying the age-old Russian yearning for an ice-free port. After 1945 Soviet reference books were amended to assert that Königsberg (renamed Kaliningrad) was ice-free. Kennan, *Memoirs*, pp. 263–4.
70. Goodman, *Soviet Design*, p. 356; Patricia Dawson Ward, *The Threat of Peace: James F. Byrnes and the Conference of Foreign Ministers, 1945–1946* (Kent: Kent State University Press, 1979), p. 95.
71. Woodward, *British Foreign Policy*, single vol. edn, pp. 553–4.

72. Beria, *Beria*, p. 117.
73. For the committees' reports see Aleksei M. Filitov, 'Problems of post-war construction in Soviet foreign policy conceptions during World War II', in Gori and Pons (eds), *Soviet Union and Europe*, pp. 3–22; for the despatches from Washington, Amos Perlmutter, *FDR & Stalin: A Not So Grand Alliance* (Columbia: University of Missouri Press, 1993), pp. 89–92, 219–49.
74. Filitov, 'Problems of post-war construction', in Gori and Pons (eds), *Soviet Union and Europe*, pp. 5–6; Resis (ed.), *Molotov*, pp. 67–8.
75. Filitov, 'Problems of post-war construction', in Gori and Pons (eds), *Soviet Union and Europe*, pp. 6–7, 17–18.
76. Stanislaw Mikolajczyk, *The Pattern of Soviet Domination* (London: Sampson Low, Marston, 1948), p. 70.
77. Terry, *Poland's Place*, pp. 175–85, 260–72, 307, 347–50, 359–60; Alfred M. de Zayas, *Nemesis at Potsdam: The Anglo-Americans and the Expulsion of the Germans* (London: Routledge, 1977), pp. 9–11; Jan Karski, *The Great Powers and Poland, 1919–1945: From Versailles to Yalta* (Lanham: University Press of America, 1985), pp. 495–6, 504–5, 565, 576–8, 608; Mastny, *Russia's Road*, pp. 299–300.
78. Banac (ed.), *Dimitrov*, p. 363.
79. Raack, *Stalin's Drive*, pp. 133–4. The first public indication of Soviet support for an Oder–Neisse border came in the indirect form of an article calling for it in the newspaper *Pravda* on 18 December 1944 by the propaganda chief of the Lublin committee, who cheekily also demanded Stettin. De Zayas, *Nemesis*, pp. 50–1.
80. De Zayas, *Nemesis*, pp. 99–101, 132; Antony Polonsky and Boleslaw Drukier, *The Beginnings of Communist Rule in Poland, December 1943–June 1945* (London: Routledge, 1980), pp. 120–1.
81. Wolfgang Leonhard, *Child of the Revolution* (London: Ink Links, 1979), p. 337. Propagandists were urged to argue that the Oder–Neisse border was just because the Polish people had resisted Hitler whereas the German people had not. This reflected anger at the almost complete ineffectiveness of the National Committee for a Free Germany and the League of German Officers. Ibid. pp. 259–61, 282.
82. Terry, *Poland's Place*, pp. 4, 68–71, 76.
83. Mastny, *Russia's Road*, pp. 164–5.
84. Mikolajczyk, *Pattern*, p. 87.
85. Mastny, *Russia's Road*, pp. 165–6, 233–5; Wilfried Loth, 'Stalin's plans for post-war Germany', in Gori and Pons (eds), *Soviet Union and Europe*, pp. 23–36; Erickson, *Road to Berlin*, pp. 229–30.
86. Filitov, 'Problems of post-war construction', in Gori and Pons (eds), *Soviet Union and Europe*, p. 20.
87. Banac (ed.), *Dimitrov*, pp. 168–9.
88. Ibid. p. 174.
89. Kot, *Conversations*, p. xvii; W. Averell Harriman and Elie Abel, *Special Envoy to Churchill and Stalin, 1941–1946* (New York: Random House, 1975), p. 91.
90. Rzheshevsky, *Grand Alliance* pp. 28, 32–3, 37–8, 48, 54.
91. Mikolajczyk, *Pattern*, p. 111.
92. For a Soviet view of the pressures operating on Britain in relation to Soviet war aims demands in early 1942 see Trukhanovsky, *British Foreign Policy*, pp. 246–52.
93. Rzheshevsky, *Grand Alliance*, p. 85.
94. Ibid. pp. 122, 173, 197–8, 204, 223–4.
95. Ibid. pp. 282, 297.

96. Taubman, *Stalin's American Policy*, pp. 58, 60.
97. Dallin, *The Big Three*, p. 168.
98. Wm Roger Louis, *Imperialism at Bay: The United States and the Decolonization of the British Empire, 1941–1945* (Oxford: Clarendon, 1977), pp. 285, 457; Sebag Montefiore, *Stalin*, p. 413; Faser J. Harbutt, *The Iron Curtain: Churchill, America, and the Origins of the Cold War* (New York: Oxford University Press, 1986), pp. 43–51, 55–65, 74–80.
99. Erickson, *Road to Berlin*, pp. 496–7; Taubman, *Stalin's American Policy*, p. 89.
100. W. R. Corson and R. T. Crawley, *The New KGB: Engine of Soviet Power* (Brighton: Harvester, 1986), pp. 192, 422.
101. Spriano, *Stalin and European Communists*, pp. 51, 83.
102. Fridrikh Firsov, 'Stalin and the Comintern', *New Times*, no. 18, 2–8 May 1989, pp. 39–42. See also Banac (ed.), *Dimitrov*, pp. 155–7, where dissolution is discussed in April 1941 but with no mention of currying favour with Germany.
103. Spriano, *Stalin and European Communists*, pp. 116–17, 137–8, 141, 175; Kevin McDermott and Jeremy Agnew, *The Comintern: A History of International Communism from Lenin to Stalin* (Basingstoke: Macmillan, 1996), p. 210.
104. Lyons (ed.), *Russian Version of the Second World War*, p. 58.
105. Julius Braunthal, *History of the International: Volume 2, 1914–1943* (London: Nelson, 1967), pp. 528–9.
106. Mastny, *Russia's Road*, pp. 94–6.
107. Leonhard, *Child*, p. 208; Berezhkov, *History in the Making*, p. 306.
108. Dallin, *The Big Three*, p. 260.
109. Nation, *Black Earth*, p. 150; Donald Gillies, *Radical Diplomat: The Life of Archibald Clark Kerr, Lord Inverchapel, 1882–1951* (London: I. B. Tauris, 1999), pp. 150–2; Sebag Montefiore, *Stalin*, pp. 408–9.
110. Mastny, *Russia's Road*, p. 235; McCagg, *Stalin Embattled*, pp. 63–5; Taubman, *Stalin's American Policy*, p. 83.
111. Spriano, *Stalin and European Communists*, p. 188.
112. Mastny, *Russia's Road*, pp. 158–60; Erickson, *Road to Berlin*, pp. 260–1.
113. Beria, *Beria*, p. 104.
114. Vladislav Zubok and Constantine Pleshakov, *Inside the Kremlin's Cold War: From Stalin to Khrushchev* (Cambridge: Harvard University Press, 1996), p. 32.
115. Filitov, 'Problems of post-war construction', in Gori and Pons (eds), *Soviet Union and Europe*, pp. 3–22.
116. Karski, *Great Powers and Poland*, p. 573.
117. Mastny, *Russia's Road*, pp. 227–9; Wagner, *Partitioning of Europe*, p. 107; Walter Kolarz, *Myths and Realities in Eastern Europe* (London: Lindsay Drummond, 1946), pp. 115, 147–52.
118. Rothwell, *Britain and the Cold War*, pp. 192–3.
119. Pavel and Anatoli Sudoplatov, *Special Tasks: The Memoirs of an Unwanted Witness – A Soviet Spymaster* (London: Warner, 1995), p. 102.
120. Mastny, *Russia's Road*, pp. 104–5.
121. Stephen Fischer-Galati, 'The communist takeover of Rumania: a function of Soviet power', in Thomas T. Hammond (ed.), *The Anatomy of Communist Takeovers* (New Haven: Yale University Press, 1975), pp. 310–11.
122. McCagg, *Stalin Embattled*, pp. 48–9; Mastny, *Russia's Road*, pp. 155–6.
123. Erickson, *Road to Berlin*, pp. 188, 335–6; Mastny, *Russia's Road*, pp. 197–9; Banac (ed.), *Dimitrov*, pp. 350–1.
124. Mikolajczyk, *Pattern*, pp. 111–12; Erickson, *Road to Berlin*, pp. 395–7; Mastny, *Russia's Road*, pp. 206–7; McCagg, *Stalin Embattled*, pp. 35–6.
125. Nissan Oren, *Revolution Administered: Agrarianism and Communism in Bul-

garia (Baltimore: Johns Hopkins University Press, 1973), pp. 89–91; Resis (ed.), *Molotov*, p. 65; Barker, *Britain and South-East Europe*, pp. 187, 199–203, 222; Mastny, *Russia's Road*, pp. 200–3; Banac (ed.), *Dimitrov*, p. 377.

126. Sebag Montefiore, *Stalin*, p. 204.
127. Polonsky and Drukier, *Beginnings*, p. 5.
128. Resis (ed.), *Molotov*, p. 54; see also p. 408: 'Bolsheviks among Poles were precious few.'
129. Kot, *Conversations*, p. 67. Soviet agonising after 22 June 1941 about whether it was in their interest to resurrect a Polish state is discussed in Terry, *Poland's Place*, pp. 170–2.
130. George V. Kacewicz, *Great Britain, the Soviet Union and the Polish Government in Exile (1939–1945)* (The Hague: Martinus Nijhoff, 1979), p. 157.
131. John Coutouvidis and Jaime Reynolds, *Poland, 1939–1947* (Leicester: Leicester University Press, 1986), pp. 86–7.
132. Terry, *Poland's Place*, pp. 260–72.
133. Taubman, *Stalin's American Policy*, p. 56.
134. Karski, *Poland and the Great Powers*, pp. 461, 560. On Polish-American political lobbying in 1944–5 see Lawrence Aronsen and Martin Kitchen, *The Origins of the Cold War in Comparative Perspective* (Basingstoke: Macmillan, 1988) pp. 24–5.
135. David Mayers, *The Ambassadors and America's Soviet Policy* (New York: Oxford University Press, 1995), pp. 157–8.
136. Polonsky and Drukier, *Beginnings*, p. 10; see also Mastny, *Russia's Road*, pp. 171–2.
137. Coutouvidis and Reynolds, *Poland*, pp. 131–5, 144–6.
138. Karski, *Poland and the Great Powers*, pp. 519–20.
139. Coutouvidis and Reynolds, *Poland*, pp. 155–61; Nicholas Bethell, *Gomulka, His Poland and His Communism* (London: Longmans, 1969), p. 93; Polonsky and Drukier, *Beginnings*, pp. 34–5, 47–50, 63–5, 83.
140. Coutouvidis and Reynolds, *Poland*, pp. 192–6.
141. Banac (ed.), *Dimitrov*, p. 251.
142. Mastny, *Russia's Road*, pp. 53, 102–3, 133–43; Vladimir V. Kusin, 'Czechoslovakia', in Martin McCauley (ed.), *Communist Power in Europe, 1944–1949* (London: Macmillan, 1977), p. 75; M. R. Myant, *Socialism and Democracy in Czechoslovakia, 1945–1948* (Cambridge: Cambridge University Press, 1981), pp. 37–8.
143. Mastny, *Russia's Road*, pp. 138, 142–3.
144. Rzheshevsky, *World War II: Myths and Realities*, pp. 231–2.
145. Zubok and Pleshakov, *Kremlin's Cold War*, p. 37; Banac (ed.), *Dimitrov*, pp. 357–8.
146. Geoffrey Swain, 'Stalin's wartime vision of the postwar world', *Diplomacy and Statecraft*, vol. 7, no. 1, March 1996, pp. 81–2.
147. Joan Barth Urban, *Moscow and the Italian Communist Party: From Togliatti to Berlinguer* (London: Tauris, 1986), pp. 191–6. The Polish government in London was naturally angered by this, but so also were some Anglo-American figures like the veteran writer on Russian affairs W. H. Chamberlin, to whom it was a proposal to 'underwrite crime'. Karski, *Poland and the Great Powers*, pp. 504–5. It should be added that, by early 1944, Churchill had convinced himself that the cession of prewar eastern Poland to the Soviets was morally justified, as well as expedient, and was a price that Poland should be willing to pay to the USSR for liberating it from Nazi slavery. Kitchen, *Britain and the Soviet Union*, pp. 177–9, 182.
148. Urban, *Moscow and Italian Communist Party*, pp. 184–6, 189–90; Elena Aga-

Rossi and Victor Zaslavsky, 'The Soviet Union and the Italian Communist Party, 1944–8', in Gori and Pons (eds), *Soviet Union and Europe*, pp. 162–4; David W. Ellwood, *Italy, 1943–1945* (Leicester: Leicester University Press, 1985) for a detailed account written before the release of Soviet documents.

149. Spriano, *Stalin and European Communists*, pp. 211–13.
150. Folly, *Churchill, Whitehall and Soviet Union*, pp. 122–3.
151. Banac (ed.), *Dimitrov*, p. 304.
152. Ibid. pp. 304–5, 342–3.
153. Bela Vago, 'Romania', in McCauley (ed.), *Communist Power*, p. 120. On the Churchill–Stalin percentages agreement see Rothwell, *Britain and the Cold War*, pp. 128–36.

6

Japan and the Grand Allies in East Asia

Although details are uncertain, there is strong evidence that in early October 1918 a draft treaty was concluded between German negotiators and not the Japanese government but representatives of the Japanese army in a neutral European capital. This would most probably have been The Hague, where Japan maintained an important legation to safeguard its commercial interests in the Netherlands East Indies (as Indonesia then was) and the well-being of the largest overseas Japanese community in south-east Asia. (A vanished people, the long-established Japanese residents in south-east Asia were to be repatriated after 1945.) The draft treaty would have been the work of military attaches who were answerable only to the army command or to some faction within it.

Under the treaty, which consisted of nine articles and some explanatory notes with texts in German and French, the two countries were to 'restore' Russia to some kind of tsarist regime and then to form a bloc with this 'restored' Russia which would have to accept that the price of its 'restoration' was that it could not be an equal partner. Besides presumably retaining all its gains under the March 1918 treaty of Brest-Litovsk, Germany would acquire a sphere of influence in Russian central Asia and from there its power would radiate into Iran, Chinese Turkestan or Xinjiang and the south of China proper. Japan would have a free hand in north China, Manchuria and eastern Siberia. All three countries would cooperate to expel Britain and the United States from any presence in these areas with the ultimate aim of their complete exclusion from Asia. When this agreement surfaced on three continents and in several capitals in 1919, Japanese diplomatic missions issued confused and contradictory denials.[1]

For Germans the attractions of such an agreement are not difficult to discern in terms of clutching at straws. For any Japanese to enter into such a deal when Germany was within weeks of an armistice that approximated to surrender must seem astonishing. However, Germany's defeat in early October 1918 did not look nearly as certain as it was to do in early April 1945 and the Japanese proponents of the accord misread the signs. They might have understood that Germany had suffered defeats in the west, but they would have seen no reason why it should suffer anything more than local losses in that quarter while retaining and expanding its gains in the east. This was the sort of miscalculation that could happen in a country that had, within living memory, ended centuries of self-imposed isolation with the result that understanding international realities did not always come easily. The particular Japanese who instigated the accord would almost certainly have been the military-oligarchical faction in the Japanese polity grouped around Field Marshal Yamagata Aritomo, one of the last surviving genro, or official elder statesmen, who had shaped Japan's path to modernisation after the Meiji restoration of 1868. This faction, one of the most important in Japanese politics, had probed for opportunities to replace the Anglo-Japanese alliance with a German–Japanese alliance between 1912 and 1914, and, during the war, had belittled Britain and bemoaned or ignored German defeats, and had, until the revolutions of 1917, craved for a separate peace between Germany and Russia so that the ruling oligarchs in all three countries could make common cause against the Anglo-Americans externally and against what Yamagata called the 'low ignorant classes' within their borders.

Some of Yamagata's beliefs were bizarre. He had imagined that after tsarist Russia had broken with Britain and France, it would welcome a Japanese military protectorate over all its territory east of the Urals, in return for which Japan would suppress uprisings there. (By whom? Most of the population of Siberia consisted of ethnic Russians.) During the first year of the war (he died in September 1915) another official elder statesman, Marquis Inoue Kaoru, became fixated on the insane idea that Germany and the United States might form an alliance to partition China with all other powers excluded. Nishihara Kamezo, chief foreign policy adviser to one of Japan's prime ministers during the First World War, Terauchi Masatake, advocated in 1917 that Japan should use an alleged insult against China by the Dutch minister in Beijing as an excuse to finance and supervise a Chinese expeditionary force to 'recover' the Dutch East Indies, which had never belonged to China but which China would then hand over to Japan. Terauchi himself had written to a friend in 1915 that, 'Eventually all of Asia should be under the control of our Emperor.' Yamagata (again) saw an opportunity towards the end of the war in 1918 to 'capture Singapore'.[2]

These science-fiction flights into fantasy by prominent Japanese political figures are the more remarkable in that they occurred not in an atmosphere of war frenzy but in one of serenity. The military phase of Japan's involvement in the First World War largely ended in November 1914 with the capture of the German naval base at Kiaochou (Quingdao) in north China and with the shipping of the garrison to Japan, to be greeted on landing by a representative of the Emperor and by a cheering crowd of wellwishers waving German and Japanese flags.[3] The absurdities referred to above were intermingled with a great deal of realistic and successful Japanese statecraft during the war. They are assembled here not to mock but to show how easily Japanese war aims could descend into unreality. Before further pursuing that point, it is appropriate to note that nothing was more unrealistic than some western assessments of Japan. This would include the grotesque racist underestimation that prevailed in Anglo-American-Dutch circles before Pearl Harbor and even (disastrously) afterwards before Japan struck hammer blows that could not have failed to make an impression on even the most opinionated westerners. (In the case of the Dutch, Queen Wilhelmina recommended in February 1941 in relation to the Japanese that the west should 'drown them like rats'.[4] Against that, one can only applaud the courage of the Dutch government in exile in declaring war on Japan the day after Pearl Harbor instead of waiting like lambs for the slaughter.) Japanese war aims also compare favourably in the rationality stakes with those of Nazi Germany. According to the Nazis, Germany, a highly developed country with a low birth rate, could only survive if it conquered vast territories in eastern Europe and planted them with German farming colonies. This was deluded. By contrast, Japanese war aims were rooted in part in rational concerns about how, in the long term, the country could live at more than a primitive subsistence level.

Japanese war aims in the Second World War can only be understood in the context of the legacy of centuries of cultural isolation and of the particular type of modernisation upon which the country embarked in the middle decades of the nineteenth century after the end of the reactionary Shogunate and the Meiji restoration in 1868. To summarise with great brevity, the model that was usually in the ascendant and which was to triumph completely in the 1930s was based on an ideology of emperor worship (consisting to a large extent of 'invented tradition') and was bureaucratic-oligarchical, militarist and dedicated to a vision of overseas expansion for Japan that recognised few limits. It should be added that there was no lack of exponents of alternatives. In the 1880s the young intellectual Tokutomi Soho wrote a book in which he advocated eschewing militarism and war and becoming a peaceful society devoted to commerce and industry. Tokutomi lived to a great old age (he died in 1957) and was therefore able to witness the realisation of this Japan.[5] In the political world, one of the giants of Japanese history was the wholly admirable (from a British point of view) Baron Kato Takaaki, who wanted to raise the elected Diet in Tokyo to a status equivalent to that of the British Parliament and who wanted Japan to content itself with the sort of imperialism of free trade that Britain had practised in the Far East, though not in Africa or south Asia, where it had practised the imperialism of conquests and annexations.

The pattern of Japanese political history in the Meiji and Taisho periods (1868–1926) was that the forces of oligarchy and expansionist aims were boosted by success in war but found themselves in retreat in long periods of peace. A political football that illustrated this was the question of whether a cabinet could continue if the army or navy minister resigned. These ministers were nominated by their respective services which were able to blackmail the government in office by threatening to withdraw their representatives if such a step automatically brought the cabinet down. Such a provision was instituted in 1900. It was repealed in 1912 and then restored in 1936. This reinforced the increase in the power of the two services that had resulted from the creation in 1933 of an inner cabinet, in which all major decisions were made, of five members. These were the prime, finance, foreign, army and navy ministers, which guaranteed the services a minimum of a 40 per cent share in decision-making. In any case, political parties, some of which were opposed to expansion through war, were in decline in 1930s Japan, and in 1940 were to be formally dissolved and replaced by a brainchild of the army, an Imperial Rule Assistance Association, whose declared purpose was to allow 'leaders and people [to be] coupled together, working smoothly in unison'.

The exponents of oligarchy-militarism were undoubtedly the ones in the Japanese nation who had the most difficulty in understanding international relations, including both the limits on Japan's own capacities and the opportunities and dangers presented to Japan by other countries. There is something almost awe-inspiring in the persistence in error of the militarist right's views about Germany and the United States. Before 1918 it embraced sentiments verging on love for the conservative-militarist German Empire (1871–1918), even though for the greater part of its existence it was headed by a monarch one of whose favourite themes was that of the 'yellow peril'. This carried forward to an exaggerated notion of what Japan could gain from a relationship with the Nazi Reich. Equal obtusity was evident in the right's reluctance to recognise the inevitably suicidal consequences of challenging American power. This stemmed to an extent from the unpalatable consequences of the ideological challenge issued by President Woodrow Wilson, particularly after he took America into the world war in 1917. Wilson advocated an order in which advanced countries, including Japan, should combine internal democracy with a rejection of the use of war and secret diplomacy in external policy. This could produce in Japanese conservatives a hysterical response akin to the Islamic fundamentalist critique of the US eighty years later as when interior minister Goto wrote to prime minister Terauchi in March 1918 that: 'If we probe the real intentions of the US further, it embraces what I call moralistic aggression. It is, in other words, none other than a great hypocritical monster clothed in justice and humanity.' The Japanese people should be indoctrinated so that they would remain unchanged for ten million years. More realistically, later in the same year, a member of the Imperial Privy Council noted with horror that if Japan yielded to Wilsonianism, 'We may no longer demand even an inch of territory . . . It is like saying that we cannot promote any path of development for the Empire except economic relations.'[6]

Such an abandonment of the martial virtues in formulating national aims was anathema to many on the Japanese right. In 1914 the Goto who has been quoted above denounced those who tried to compute the exact economic benefits and costs of expansion in Manchuria as 'bean counters' – a reference to one of the territory's main products, soya beans.[7] A sneaking awareness of the disparity in resources between the two countries could produce astonishing wishful thinking as, at the time when the fleet was sailing towards Pearl Harbor, the prime minister, General Tojo, mused that, although America might be annoyed for a time by what Japan was about to do to it, this would give way to a mood of cordial understanding: 'America may be enraged for a while, but later she will come to understand.'[8]

And yet an external policy based on the peaceful pursuit of commerce was entirely acceptable to a large segment of the Japanese right, consisting of conservative anti-militarists who cordially detested the army's claim to a political role and who regarded territorial expansion by force as foolish and reckless. Including a notable figure like Shidehara Kijuro, they were a dominant influence for a time in the 1920s and took Japan into the Washington agreements of 1921–2. Under these there were to be no further encroachments on the sovereignty or integrity of China (and Japan returned Quingdao, over which it had nearly wrecked the Paris peace conference three years earlier by its refusal to return it to China), and Japan agreed that its navy should be no more than three-fifths the size of those of Britain or the United States, plus non-fortification of insular possessions in the western Pacific.[9] This wing of Japanese conservatism and all liberal and left elements were to be terrorised into submission and silence during the 1930s as Japan adopted expansionist aims to be achieved by war. It would, however, be highly misleading to assert that Japan only adopted such policies because of the triumph of irrational fanaticism and the use of terror by certain factions. Just as the Nazis would very probably never have attained power in Germany but for the world depression of the early 1930s, which began with the collapse of the New York stock exchange in October 1929, so the militarist-expansionist cause in Japan would probably have languished without the same stimulus. Japan actually adopted the gold standard as late as early 1930, partly in response to American pressure to join the standard that regulated the international economy.[10] This added insult to injury when the US and the traditionally free-trading British, as well as other countries, imposed high tariffs and quotas that threatened Japan with economic ruin. Disillusion with the liberal international order extended from economics to politics, including the great liberal experiment of the League of Nations. In Japan in the 1930s, among people who were able to form a view on such matters, there were probably few who did not believe that Anglo-American liberal internationalism was a failure in economics and a sham in politics.

A few figures illustrate the dire impact of the world depression on Japan. Exports fell in value by 43 per cent between 1929 and 1931. Farm incomes fell from an index figure of 100 in 1926 to 33.5 in 1931, and cannibalism occurred in the countryside. This produced a national obsession with the problem of feeding and finding work for one of the most rapidly growing populations in the world, coupled with indignant rejection of advice from outsiders that birth control should be practised more widely. After 1931 Japan actually underwent a remarkable economic recovery. Exports, expressed in volume terms, in 1936 were 202 against an index figure of 100 for 1928, the last year before the world economic crash. By 1936 Japan was accounting for an impressive 6.2 per cent of world exports and a much higher proportion of exports of manufactured goods. This was achieved through a combination of quality and price. Japanese cotton textile exports were little more than half the price of comparable British textiles while radios made in Japan sold in east Asia at one-third of the price of American sets.

The price of this success was horrendous. Wages and profits were greatly reduced, the former from an already low level. The yen was devalued to make exports more competitive, with the result that by 1936 the volume of exports needed to pay for a given volume of imports would pay for less than half as many imports (47 per cent) as it would have done in 1931. Living standards fell to desperately low levels and not only for peasants and workers. The historian and journalist William Henry Chamberlin has left a description of the pitifully frugal fare that was served when the management of a silk manufacturing plant invited him to join them for lunch. To make matters worse, Japanese were acutely aware that their efforts could be undone by the arbitrary decisions of countries with which they traded but over which they had no political or military leverage. In 1935–6 Japan engaged in a trade war with Canada and Australia, whose wheat, timber and wool it needed, and was impotent when Egypt and South Africa imposed huge increases in duties on Japanese textile exports. Nearer home to Japan, in the mid-1930s the British, Dutch and American colonial governments in south-east Asia placed quota and other restrictions on Japanese exports to the territories that they controlled. Japan turned in some anguish to independent Thailand as a trading partner to which it could sell in return for food and raw materials. It even tried unsuccessfully, by bribery and intimidation, to prospect for oil in tiny Portuguese Timor to supplement the meagre 9 per cent of its oil needs that it produced itself.[11] The country's economic prospects seemed dismal in a world that did not undergo radical political change. It cannot be stressed too much that Japanese war aims grew out of a society that was modern and not from the death pangs of a feudal remnant that was struggling to retain some privilege and power. They were fundamentally the result of modern industry, mass culture, political pluralism and new social organisations. The historian W. G. Beasley interprets Japanese expansion as having been primarily concerned with the needs of industry probably from as early as 1905 and certainly by 1918. He has also noted that in 1930 there were three elements in the serving of

those needs: membership of an Anglo-American-dictated international system in east Asia, colonies and spheres of influence, and
an incipient special relationship with China geared to the needs of
Japanese industry.[12]

The economic unattractiveness of retaining the first of these in the
conditions of the 1930s was reinforced by the radical right tendencies
and the often poor capacity to judge international political realities,
to which reference has been made. Messianic chauvinism was on the
upsurge in 1930s Japan. A professor of philosophy referred to 'the
heavenly mission of Japan to tranquillise the whole world'. A Japanese navy ministry publication in 1935 was content to restrict matters
to east Asia in which 'the maintenance of peace' should be the
responsibility of Japan alone. 'If the other powers fail to recognise
the mission of Japan they may well be said to disobey the will of
Heaven.'[13] The only 'other powers' that actually mattered were the
Soviet Union, Britain and the United States. The first of these was
seen as posing an ideological and, increasingly, a military threat. A
decisive settling of accounts with it by war appeared inevitable, and
would have enabled Japan to take de facto control of north China and
Inner Mongolia. In the case of the two English-speaking countries, the
complete exclusion of Britain from the Far East showed signs of
emerging as a Japanese aim during the late thirties. This owed
something to a lingering sense that Britain had betrayed Japan by
terminating their alliance at America's behest in 1922 and to a
stereotype of the British as the archetype of the arrogant white
imperialist. The scholar-diplomat George Sansom wrote from his
office in the embassy in Tokyo in 1939 that Britain 'did not have
any really useful friends' in Japan, that all Japanese wanted a 'new
order' in Asia, and that that new order necessarily 'involves the
ultimate displacement of Great Britain in the Far East'.[14]

In a rare display of unity, Britain, the US and France presented an
ultimatum to Japan in February 1938 – the first to be issued in the
world since the Great War – in which they warned Japan that they
would observe no restraint in naval construction unless it agreed
within fifteen days to abide by internationally agreed limits. Japan
speedily returned an intransigent reply on naval building, and went
on to change the subject by dwelling at length on its economic
grievances, and particularly on its need for a privileged position
in China, 'which is the only chance left for Japan's survival'. It
continued: 'The British possess a great self-sufficient empire, the
Americans have an equally self-sufficient position in the two American continents. They ought to be generous enough to concede to

Japan a place in the Orient that will meet her dire needs.'[15] Unfortunately for the Japanese, with their tendency to hope for a little more from America than from Britain, the US in the late 1930s was the exponent of an ideology of anti-imperialism and was fixated on the idea that 'open door' opportunities for US business were America's lifeline out of economic depression. In late 1937, with China and Japan at war, the latter had informed the US that the open door in China had become anachronistic and needed to be replaced with a 'new order'. The US responded officially that no country had the right to build a new order anywhere except on its own territory.[16] The contrast in ideas could hardly have been starker. In regard to its economic interests, in October 1939 ambassador Joseph Grew in Tokyo warned the Japanese government that the US was opposed to the effort 'to establish control, in Japan's own interest, of large areas on the continent of Asia and to impose upon those areas a system of closed economy'. When Japan openly proclaimed that south-east Asia was coming within the orbit of its ambitions, the State Department, on 23 August 1940, issued a warning that if Japan moved forces into that area a 'time of reckoning' would come.[17]

Despite such warnings, Japan by 1939 was moving almost inexorably towards the elimination of one of the three elements in its previous system of foreign relations as defined by Beasley, the system in east Asia that had most recently been defined by the Washington conference and treaties of 1921–2. It was even more clearly embarked on a redefinition of its relationship with China with the aim of creating an economically and culturally self-contained Sinitic world. One manifestation of this was an insistence in some Japanese quarters, harking back to pre-1868 isolation, that a foreign service of the kind that had been built up since then was unnecessary and dangerous. Knowledge of foreign languages other than Chinese ceased to figure in entrance examinations for the diplomatic service, to be replaced by ones on Japanese history and 'character'. One nationalist critic wrote in 1938: 'It is because Japanese diplomats think with the minds of foreigners that they are inappropriate to guide us on our "headlong" course. Thus, ultimately we must carry out the renovation of Kasumigaseki and change the minds of diplomats into those of Japanese.'[18] Kasumigaseki was the district of Tokyo in which the foreign ministry was situated. To nationalist Japanese it was a code word for cosmopolitanism and a readiness to seek accommodation with the Anglo-Americans. The unique Japanese war aim of banishing a widely used language, English, from the area that it controlled was not easily achieved, much as the language was to be denounced as an obscenity in wartime Japan. The text of the German–Italian–Japanese Tripartite Pact in 1940 was in English, and most Japanese propaganda to occupied south-east Asia during the war was also in that language. Thus, the English-language press in occupied Singapore (renamed Syonon) continued to be published with 'Nippon-Go' language lessons occupying a small amount of space. The ruling Military Administration Department in the occupied city raised no objection to being invariably referred to in these newspapers as 'The MAD.'[19]

Most Japanese in the 1930s were proud of, and were heartened in a time of adversity by, their achievements in their colonial territories, of which the most important were Korea, Taiwan and Manchuria, though the formerly German islands in the western Pacific (renamed Nanyo) rapidly also won a place in the hearts of the Japanese people.[20] Manchuria provided Japan with immense benefits in trade opportunities, tax revenues and emigration opportunites even before it took complete control of the territory from a warlord who hankered after reuniting it with China in 1931–2, and turned it into the client or puppet state of Manchukuo. These benefits increased enormously during the 1930s, and there was every reason for thinking that they could only continue to increase even as Japan's prospects in the wider international economy looked more and more uncertain. On this bedrock of economic advantages, an emotional superstructure was constructed. In 1932 Uchida Kasai, a former foreign minister and one of Japan's most distinguished statesmen, declared in the Diet in Tokyo, in a statement of what came to be known as 'scorched earth diplomacy', that Japan must retain every inch of territory that it had conquered in Manchuria even 'should the country be burnt to the ground'.[21]

The fanaticism implicit in this threatened conflict with the rest of the Asian world, in which nationalism was becoming ever stronger, and with the mighty nation on the other side of the Pacific in which imperialism was becoming even less acceptable than before. It might have been different if Japan had been offering the ethnic Chinese mass of the Manchurian population some form of partnership, but that was not the case. Both in theory and practice they were being offered very little. The image of Manchuria in the Japanese media and in the teaching of children in Japanese schools between 1932 and 1945 was one in which the Chinese inhabitants of Manchuria – more than 90 per cent of the total – figured little, and when they did it was in a lowly and passive role as coolie labour, grateful to Japan for providing them with unskilled jobs, or as peasants, equally grateful to Japan for its settlement among them of rural Japanese with the know-how and the innate racial ability to raise the countryside to a level of productivity that the natives knew they could never themselves attain. The image reflected realities on the ground. The main economic asset of Manchukuo was the South Manchurian Railway, but that, in 1934, did not have one Chinese among its 180 most senior officials and 134 senior engineers and only seventy-one Chinese among its 5,608 clerical workers.[22]

A Manchuria-like aim of transforming the rest of China, or much of it, into a Japanese dependency with the prime objective of economic exploitation developed after war between the two countries started in July 1937. The army successfully pressed in the later months of 1938 for the setting up of a special ministry for China that excluded the foreign ministry almost entirely from Chinese affairs, The moderate foreign minister, Ugaki Kazushige, resigned in protest. He described the new ministry as a second colonial ministry, and compared it with a butcher who displayed a lamb's head to his customers while actually selling them dog meat. The new ministry was officially called the China Policy Board. Recalling the shameful origins of British imperialism in China, one of its activities was the large-scale trading of opium to bring economic gain to Japan. This had a serious effect in the US, which had for long been trying to control and reduce the poppy trade. By 1939, in the words of a historian of this subject, both the Chinese government 'and the State Department were convinced that drug trafficking had become part of the fundamental makeup of the Japanese state'.[23] The Japanese military advance stopped in October 1938 after the occupation of the northern provinces around Beijing, China's economic powerhouse in the lower Yangtse valley and almost all coastal areas as far as the border with French Indochina. The Imperial Japanese Army was in a position to dictate policy on China, but it was not a monolith. There were two Japanese armies in China from 1937, the Central China Area Army and the North China Area Army. The China Area Fleet of the navy also demanded a share in political decision-making. Each area army established a government in its occupation zone in early 1938. The North China one was a fig leaf for a war aim of full permanent Japanese control of an area of strategic importance for Japan for defence against the Soviet Union and one which produced the 'two blacks' (coal and iron ore) that Japan required from China. (It also wanted 'two whites', cotton and salt.)

The emphasis at this stage on an aim of closely controlling only the five provinces of north China closest to Manchukuo was reflected in the share out of Japanese capital for the economic development of occupied China, which prime minister Konoe announced in November 1938. A new North China Development Company was to be allocated 350 million yen, a South China Development Company only 100 million, even though over 75 per cent of modern factories in occupied China were in the designated area of the South China Company, compared with 15 per cent in the designated northern area. The Central China Army in the latter was reduced to making overtures to the Shanghai underworld for funding. To emphasise the point, the north China area was incorporated into the Japanese-Manchukuoan yen bloc that Japan had been constructing since 1931. Nominally, Manchukuo had its own currency, the Manchukuoan yuan, but that was fixed at parity with the yen. The rest of occupied China was given its own inflation-prone currency, the fapi. What all this meant was that, for all practical purposes, Manchuria and north China had been economically annexed by Japan, though not politically or in civil liberties, including the right to strike, which survived in the Japanese homeland to a surprising extent throughout the 1930s. In these mainland extensions of the empire Japan obtained some of its raw material needs without having to spend foreign exchange, and built up an industrial economy that was probably unique in the history of imperialism. This was done on the basis of public–private partnership with public and private capital, private entrepreneurship and technology, and holding companies that each supervised many private companies. Two essential features of this system were ruthless exploitation of the labour force in these industries, and complete and total unconcern with whether those in the occupied population who were not of use to Japan lived or died. Thus in 1939 the army took control of 60 per cent of the rail capacity that had been used to transport food to the great northern cities of Peking and Tientsin and diverted it to transport coal needed by Japan. These practices of exploitation were extended to the whole of occupied China. Thus a Rice Control Commission, which was supposed to buy rice for both the Japanese occupation troops and the civilian population in Shanghai, purchased in 1944, at very low prices, 254,000 tons of which 220,000 were allocated to the army. For the civilian population the only alternatives were resort to the black market or starvation. Exploitation was sometimes modified but only to make it more effective. Thus in 1939 Japan took 92 per cent of the Chinese raw cotton crop for itself, but reduced this to 33 per cent in 1942 to allow Chinese textile manufacturing to revive. However, seven-eighths of the output of Chinese cotton mills were then compulsorily purchased at one-quarter of the black-market price.[24]

Although Japan had occupied most of the economically desirable parts of China by the time that it largely halted military operations in that country in October 1938, it could not rest easy while considerable Chinese resistance continued and China still had a government that was recognised by the vast majority of countries. By 1938 Japanese official propaganda for home consumption was saying that the Chinese deserved to be 'annihilated' for having the temerity to resist. (A great many of the population of the capital, Nanking, had just suffered precisely that fate.)[25] Japanese rulers, even ones as harsh as Tojo Hideki, realised that that was not possible and worked out two sets of war aims for a final settlement in China. One was for a dictated agreement with a client government that had been created by Japan. The other was for Chiang Kai-shek's Republic of China government based at Chungking, though the differences between the two were not great, given Tojo's insistence, after he became prime minister in October 1941, that Japan could yield little in China after suffering 100,000 casualties and spending tens of billions of yen. The terms that Japan offered to Chiang in the period before Pearl Harbor included that China must recognise Manchukuo, must agree to the indefinite stationing of Japanese troops in Inner Mongolia and parts of northern China for 'defence against communism' (admittedly a genuine concern), complete prohibition of anti-Japanese propaganda and all anti-Japanese organisations in China, privileged access to Japanese investment and business, and the free movement of Japanese throughout Chinese territory. Such terms would have left Japan free to do most of what it wanted to do in a postwar China, and hardly supported Tojo's assertion in his speech on war aims to the Diet on 21 January 1942 that Chinese resistance against Japan had become 'meaningless', and that all that Japan wished to do was to enlist the Chinese people 'in the glorious task of constructing the sphere of common prosperity in Greater East Asia by discarding once and for all the time-old dependence upon the United States and Britain'.[26]

The terms on which Japan recognised the government of Wang Ching-wei, who had once been prime minister of China in a Kuomintang government, in November 1940 included a wider permanent stationing of Japanese troops than in the terms offered to Chiang. The troops were to remain until Japan was satisfied that China was fulfilling all its obligations, including a special economic position for Japan in the lower Yangtse valley, the most important part of the country. In October 1943, faced with a bleak war situation, Japan made more concessions to the Wang government, including the return of the foreign extraterritorial enclaves against which the Chinese people had been railing for a century. To prove that it was truly independent the Wang government was accorded the 'privilege', previously denied to it, of declaring war on Britain and the US. If this meant little, it was almost realistic in comparison with the frequent secret negotiations between the Chungking government and Japan from after Pearl Harbor till as late as July 1945, in which, while steadily moderating their terms, the latter still insisted on the retention of Manchukuo and some form of special position for Japan in the Republic of China. The Japanese had little conception that China was only interested in deterring Japan from resuming its advance in China while the US and Japan's other enemies defeated it elsewhere. The victory of the Anglo-Americans held out for China the effortless recovery of all its losses, including Manchuria and even Taiwan, lost in 1895. The Japanese could not accept that, by their policies since 1937, they had exchanged a sustainable empire for one that was, in both its pre- and post-1937 components, unsustainable. In a final burst of military prowess and political irrationality they launched operation Itchiyo in the later part of 1944, in which they scored major victories against Chinese government forces and occupied much additional Chinese territory. It remained beyond their capacity to destroy Chiang's government, and even the humiliation for the latter of suffering defeats while Britain was achieving a great victory on the India–Burma border and the Americans were reconquering the Philippines was cancelled out by the influential 'China Lobby' of pro-Chiang apologists that the Chinese embassy in Washington had engineered into existence and by the general American policy towards China, which will be discussed below.[27]

The supreme expression of overextension was the inclusion of south-east Asia and territories in the Pacific within the ambit of Japanese aims. The idea that Japan should expand into south-east Asia may, with considerable reservations, be dated to 1934 when the Imperial Navy drew up contingency plans for operations in the area and the neighbouring seas. Yet the naval planners, who had a great interest in acquiring the resources of the region, recognised that probably nothing could be done unless 'the complicated political situation in Europe' became so 'complicated' that Britain went to war with, and had to apply most of its resources against, Germany and Italy.[28] (In 1936 Britain and Japan announced naval building programmes costing £600 million and £48 million respectively. Even without American support for Britain, Japan would have had to be bold to challenge a Britain free from European distractions.) The Japanese naval planners hoped that the 'complications' to which they referred would make it possible to pressurise and blackmail Britain into leaving the region without actual war. Then the American giant would have been more likely to remain somnolent.[29]

On 22 December 1938 Konoe proclaimed the New Order in East Asia (NOEA), but went on to discuss it entirely in terms of Japan and its relations with China and Manchuria. Only the name implied that there might be aims that embraced more than those three countries.[30] It required the German victories in western Europe in the early summer of 1940 for Japan to become more serious about southward expansion, not only because of the opportunities offered by British weakness and the collapse of France but also because the establishment of Japanese power in south-east Asia might be expected finally to induce China to yield to Japan. As in what would soon be called the First World War, thinking that was not irrational intermingled with fantasy. In July 1940 the army general staff, taking a new interest in south-east Asia, predicted that Britain, squeezed out of continental Europe and Africa, would look west and form an alliance with the US that would take a firm grip on south-east Asia as an end in itself but also to provide a bridge to control India from the east. 'The upshot will be the establishment of a strong Anglo-American bloc, economic as well as strategic, in the South Seas.' Japan would have no choice but to act to prevent this. The navy repeated its old hope that this should be done by peaceful means 'if at all possible'.[31]

In that same month Konoe returned to office as prime minister for the second time and presided over the drawing up of an 'Outline for Dealing with Changes in the World Situation'. Japanese power was to be extended as far south as the East Indies with the aim of ending Japanese economic dependence on the rest of the world. Expansion was to be in fits and starts that America might be willing to swallow. On 1 August 1940 foreign minister Matsuoka Yosuke gave the world a name for this emerging aim, the Greater East Asia Co-Prosperity Sphere (GEACPS). Privately, he defined it to include the whole of south-east Asia except the Philippines, India, Australia and New Zealand. Even this hotheaded man hoped for American quiescence if it was not itself directly attacked. However, the US responded to the first expansionist move, the sending of troops into northern Indochina with the reluctant consent of the French authorities, by applying economic sanctions against Japan, and Matsuoka's statement caused America to issue the warning about a reckoning to which reference has been made.[32]

Over the next fifteen months Japan worked out plans of rare brilliance that resulted in the conquest of south-east Asia within a few months of the Pearl Harbor attack. It also formulated cunningly worded but futile terms for the resolution of its differences with the United States, terms under which Japan would have given up much in China in appearance and very little in reality.[33] What it did not do was to work out detailed war aims for south-east Asia if it did conquer the area. Plans were drawn up for the maintenance of order and for economic exploitation, both to supply the occupation forces from local resources as in China, and to acquire vital raw materials, including Malayan bauxite and, above all, the oil of the Netherlands East Indies. (Japan did not need Malayan rubber. It could obtain all the rubber that it needed from its ally, Thailand, and from the compliant Vichy authorities in Indochina.) As for political change, a planning document merely stated that the peoples of south-east Asia 'shall be so guided as to induce a sense of trust in the Imperial forces, and premature encouragement of native independence movements shall be avoided'. Otherwise, there was little more than musing about the peoples whom Japan was soon to rule. In November 1941 a propagandist pondered on what his country could do for 'the ignorant but innocent Indonesians', and speculated that it had a moral mission to raise them up. Less idealistically, an army memorandum on occupation policy, drawn up in late November, noted that the south-east Asian peoples were 'of low cultural standards without much hostility towards us'. Once in control, Japan should refrain from 'rash pledges' that might impede it from 'selecting the best possible policies in the future'. Conciliation could bring 'only harm and no good'.[34]

The essential fact was that, before 1939, Japan had been overwhelmingly concerned with the Sinitic world of itself, China and Korea. South-east Asia, except to an extent Vietnam, was not part of the Sinitic cultural world, and Japanese attempts in the 1930s to take an interest, such as building a few mosques in the home country and then inviting leading Muslim clerics from the East Indies to inspect them, had been clumsy and transparent in their purpose.[35] The Sinitic outlook was actually reinforced after Pearl Harbor when it was announced in Tokyo that it was no longer acceptable for the country to be called by a foreign name; it must in future only be called Nippon. The system of dating from the time when the Sun God created Japan, which was now being taught as historical fact in

schools, was introduced for the empire and all its conquests. This
was 660 years before the birth of Christ. Thus Pearl Harbor took
place in 2601. If this betokened an aim of returning to a wholly
Japanocentric past, tokenism is precisely what it was. There was no
return to the lunar calendar of old Japan. Monday continued to be
Monday, March to be March and so on.

Japanese war aims were driven by events and a theory of war aims
was formulated afterwards. Inevitably it tended to be incomplete and
incoherent. This applied to both the NOEA, which was proclaimed in
1938 as a response to a war in China that Japan had not wanted at
that particular time, and to the GEACPS, which was proclaimed in
1940 in anticipation of huge gains for Japan in south Asia and the
Pacific that the German victories in Europe had made a feasible
prospect. In between these, Konoe had founded a 'think-tank' of
intellectuals, academics and bureaucrats with instructions to find
idealistic justifications for non-idealistic aims. It produced ideas that
smacked of the 'Asian values' that were to be widely proclaimed in
east Asia in the late twentieth century: rejection of western indivi-
dualism and the collective ideal in its place. As by far the most
advanced of the Asian nations, Japan had a duty to rescue other
Asians from what was sometimes actually referred to as the 'White
Peril', and a right to claim regional hegemony as its reward. The
Japanese people had a duty to abandon the western import of party
politics and unite behind their leaders, who could not be expected to
tolerate dissenting voices at home while they were fashioning a
regional power bloc under Japan's leadership to complement the
other blocs into which the entire world was ineluctably dividing. The
theory of the NOEA–GEACPS, such as it was, amounted to little more
than a cloak for an elite which wanted to pursue imperialism in an
anti-imperialist age and to establish right-wing authoritarianism at
home.[36]

In terms of a specific programme of aims for the newly conquered
territories, Tojo, in his important speech to the House of Peers on 20
January 1942, clearly delineated a fundamental policy. This was that
the conquests would not be treated as a unity, at least not in
appearance. He hinted at independence for Burma and the Philippines if they showed themselves ready to cooperate with Japan in the
GEACPS, and at the permanent retention by Japan of Hong Kong and
Malaya and Singapore. The Netherlands East Indies – the future
Indonesia – was a particular problem. Its vast size and population
would have made it an embarrassingly conspicuous colony for a
country that claimed to be embarked on a liberation mission. Yet its

oil was regarded as vital for Japan, and especially for the navy, whose views could hardly be ignored at the 'liaison conferences' that determined policy in the confederal Japanese power structure and which could only function if an imperialist demand made by one participant was acceded to by all the others. This was reinforced by the fact that the navy was given the eastern islands of the Indies from Borneo to New Guinea to administer in March 1942 and promptly produced a plan under which they were to be permanent Japanese colonies.[37]

One matter was seemingly easily dealt with. On 18 January 1942 Germany and Japan signed an agreement on global spheres of influence. The line dividing their respective spheres was to cut through the middle of what is now Pakistan and then southwards through the Indian Ocean. In theory, the agreement referred to spheres for military and naval operations only, but the terms of an overtly political division would probably not have differed greatly except that Germany might have claimed some Soviet territory east of the seventieth degree of longitude, which was the precise line that divided the spheres. (Japan took this division of north Asia seriously. Early in 1942 the war and colonial ministries drew up a plan 'for the administration of territories and the common development of Great Western Asia' under which the territories of the Soviet Far East would be annexed to the Japanese or Manchukuoan empires, 'and the Trans-Siberian Railway will be put under the full control of Germany and Japan with Omsk as the dividing point'. Omsk is slightly to the east of the seventieth degree.) Essentially, each of the two countries wanted complete freedom to do what it liked without consulting, or considering the interests of, the other. The Japanese also feared that Germany might have colonial designs in south-east Asia; in particular, if it annexed Holland to the Reich it might then claim that it owned the East Indies. Nine months were to pass after Pearl Harbor before Japan would describe itself as Germany's ally. The most that they could agree upon in early 1942 was that the German navy might operate in the eastern Indian Ocean and the Japanese in the western without the prior consent of the other country. It should be added that there was a leftover from history that Germany and Japan were unable to resolve definitively. This related to the former German colonies in the Pacific. In the negotiations leading up to the Tripartite Pact in 1940 Germany had agreed to Japan retaining the former German islands that it had acquired under mandate, but only if Germany received unspecified compensation. Japan had agreed that the other former German colonies (German New Guinea, German

Samoa) should revert to German rule, though Germany should discuss with Japan their final disposal before resumption of such rule. There was the potential for serious disagreement in this.[38]

While the war was going well for Japan, the prevailing notion was that it should retain full control of the conquests in substance if not always in form. The metaphor of childhood was employed, including the concept that the conquests were destined permanently to be dependent children, rather than offspring that would grow up and leave the parental Japanese home. As late as June 1943 the politician and propagandist Tsurumi Yuseke could write that: 'Without understanding this new concept, and the popular enthusiasm for this new concept, it is impossible to understand the basis of the Greater East Asia War. That is the sublime war aim which the Japanese people can display to the world.' The prominent businessman Ayukawa Gisuke had given this more concrete form when he stated at a conference in March 1942: 'As to Japanese war aims, generally they lie in the establishment of the GEACPS, but if we ask what is most basic, then Japan's rights and interests must be the primary object.'[39] It was in line with this that the Ministry of Greater East Asia was set up in November 1942 in disregard of warnings from Japanese moderates, who feared that it would alienate east Asians by separating them from the rest of the world and make a compromise peace with the western powers more difficult.[40]

After its surrender, Singapore became the colony of Syonon with a mayor drawn from the small Japanese minority in its population. In December 1942 Japan proclaimed the colony of Malai in succession to the patchwork quilt of colonies, protectorates and protected states that had been Malaya under British rule, though much of northern Malaya was to be ceded to Thailand in October 1943. There was to be no offer of independence to Malay nationalists until May 1945 when they were invited to consider whether they wished to link with their ethnic cousins in Java and Sumatra or whether they preferred their mainland entity to remain separate.[41] At a liaison conference in January 1943 agreement was reached on conditional independence for some conquests and on the colonial annexation of territories of strategic importance and 'sparsely populated areas and regions lacking the capacity for independence'.[42] Singapore clearly fell under the former of these two headings, and North Borneo, formerly divided among three British protected states and Dutch territory and now united into a single Japanese colony, equally clearly under the latter. The transformation of Malaya into a colony and the political limbo into which the surely 'civilised' and populous islands of Java and

Sumatra had been cast could hardly be justified under either. Japan simply wanted to retain complete control of these valuable territories, whether they were 'backward' or not.

Even the proclamation of independence for Burma in August 1943 and for the Philippines in October would probably not have happened but for Japanese and German setbacks in the war. In any case, these produced states with little more real independence than Manchukuo, though the Japanese did allow the Philippines the right to style itself a republic. Burma became simply a 'state' with its institutional form undecided. Again, Japan resisted its instinctive inclination to insist on the restoration of the Burmese monarchy. The proclamations did usher in a new phase in Japanese war aims in which complete victory was perceived to be impossible. The new policy was outlined to the Diet by foreign minister Shigemitsu Mamoru in a speech in October 1943 in which he called for the genuine liberation of the east Asian peoples to create a reality that the western imperialists would not be able to reverse. On that basis Japan could exit from the war with honour and then build a postwar cooperative relationship with the grateful peoples whose recolonisation by the west it had prevented. 'The emphasis on our war aims and the limits we assign to them will provide the groundwork for the restoration of peace.' He further defined his foreign policy as one of 'proclaiming "war aims" that had never been very clearly explained to the people – the liberation and rebirth of east Asia, the emergence of its nations from "colonialism", all countries to be on an equal footing as a bulwark of world peace'.[43] The new policy envisaged an even broader programme of liberation than one confined to the existing territories under Japanese military control. The purpose of the Japanese campaign into north-east India in 1944, which the British defeated at battles like Imphal, was to occupy a piece of Indian territory to which the Free Indian government under Subhas Chandra Bose, which Japan had created in 1943, could move and pose as a credible pro-Japanese government for the whole of India.[44] Shigemitsu's policy was proclaimed with great fanfare at the Greater East Asia conference that Japan convened in Tokyo in November 1943, at which the star guests were those from Burma, the Philippines and 'Free' India.

The new policy showed a characteristic Japanese descent into unreality as international relations developed in a way with which the Japanese mindset could not cope. In 1942 the concept of a new order in east Asia had not been wholly unrealistic, provided Germany had been able to smash the Soviet Union and bring Britain to its knees. The Vatican had certainly thought so when in March of that year it had braved Anglo-American fury by establishing diplomatic relations with Japan out of concern to protect the Catholic majority in the Philippines and the Catholic minorities elsewhere in south-east Asia, especially Vietnam. It would hardly have taken such a step, so provocative to London and Washington, if it had anticipated that Japanese rule would endure for less than four years.[45] While events like the British surrender of Singapore did make the restoration of European colonialism problematical, Shigemitsu and those who thought like him ignored the enmity that Japan was building up against itself by its brutal economic exploitation of its southern conquests and the self-defeating viciousness with which the Japanese soldiery treated the southern Asian populations without regard to age or sex. They also ignored the hypocrisy of a policy that was not applied to territories, notably Malaya and the East Indies, in which Japan had a particularly strong economic or strategic interest. Indonesian (East Indian) representatives were not invited to the conference in Tokyo.

Early in 1944 a memorandum produced in the foreign ministry tentatively recommended the offer of independence to Java, where more than half the Indonesian population lived, while adding that the promise could be broken if the fortunes of war turned in Japan's favour!

In September Japan actually promised independence to Java in recognition of the gratitude that its people had shown in return for the benefits of Japanese rule (this at a time when a famine was looming on the island caused directly by Japanese policies). The military commander on Java noted that the entire purpose of the promise was to create 'a country that would cooperate with Japan to win the war'.[46] Not until the war situation had become grotesquely unfavourable in May 1945 were Indonesian nationalists allowed to hold formal discussions about the shape of an independent state which was to be proclaimed on 7 September, the anniversary of the promise of independence. At first, such independence would be confined to Java, though other islands in what had been the Netherlands East Indies might join later. The Japanese authorities were considering whether the new state should be required to declare war on Britain, the US and Holland at the time of the dropping of the atomic bombs.[47] If, by that time, Japan was showing signs of abandoning its grip on south-east Asia that was not only because of the fortunes of war – American forces had recovered the Philippiness – but also because of the domestic aspect of war aims. The ruling elite hoped that, by presenting the western allies with a fait accompli of colonial liberation in south-east Asia, the war could be made to seem, if not worthwhile, then not barren of achievement to the Japanese people.

AMERICAN AND BRITISH WAR AIMS IN THE FAR EAST

The historian of Japan Peter Duus has written that Japanese imperialist war aims were a classic instance of unsustainable over-extension, not least because they resulted in 'self-encirclement', the creation of an opposing alliance of forces vastly outnumbering Japan.[48] It is appropriate to examine the war aims that Japan's major enemies formulated in response to Japanese imperialism. The most important of these, the US, inched towards war with decidedly modest aims in view. In mid-1940 a revised US war plan against Japan stated that the aim in any such war would not be to create an American version of the new order that Japan had declared itself to favour in east Asia but, on the contrary, the preservation of the status quo. America's allies would have to understand that it did not seek 'the economic and military crushing of Japan or the exchange of the domination of the Far East by Japan for the domination of the Far East by the United States. The United States has no interest in becoming the dominating Far Eastern power, and enjoys an economic position in relation to Japan that it does not care to destroy completely.'[49] Underlying this formulation was the opposition of Cordell Hull and the head of the Far Eastern department in the State Department, Stanley Hornbeck, to closed economic spheres. They still believed in the Open Door.[50]

The Pearl Harbor attack and the consequent wave of anti-Japanese sentiment that swept across America and which the administration made almost no attempt to restrain inevitably led to a reassessment. That archetypal member of the American establishment, Herbert Hoover, called in February 1942 for a fight to the death until Japanese power was completely overthrown, even if it took ten years and cost a million American lives.[51] What Hoover's successor as president thought about Japan at this time is uncertain. It can be inferred that Roosevelt was not far from Hoover because all his pronouncements dwelt on the need to build up China as the sole power of any importance, except for the Soviet Union and the US, in the postwar Far East. The US thought that it could, alone except for a little help from Australia, be dominant in the Pacific. This was reflected at the popular level in a key line of a wartime song: 'To be specific, it's our Pacific.' This popular ditty was exactly paraphrased in the words, spoken in 1943, of a member of a government committee on American territorial war aims in which he said that the Pacific was 'our lake'. This no doubt somewhat arrogant remark was made in the context of a consensus that this 'lake' needed to be studded with American island bases. At this point, a consciousness of America not being destined to be omnipotent came into play. The bases would be defensive to prevent renewed aggression from Asia against America. There was a surprising amount of concern that such aggression might emanate from China, not Japan.[52] Even if such fears were set aside, as they had to be in relation to China, the US did not foresee itself being able to exercise exclusive predominance in east Asia as well as in the Pacific. It could only do so with an ally, and from Pearl Harbor until at least early 1944 the ally of choice was China.

Winston Churchill could only sulk about this and was convinced, not wholly justifiably, that Roosevelt was only interested in China as a satellite or 'faggot vote' for the US. For him it was axiomatic that the preservation of Britain as a great power had to include the restoration of its position in east Asia. At dinner with Roosevelt and Stalin at Tehran in 1943 Churchill told them that 'England' would fight another war if necessary to keep Singapore and Hong Kong.[53] No doubt Britain's future position in China would have to be somewhat less than before the war, but, in compensation, Britain insisted on being accorded a role in the occupation of Japan and a significant voice in settling peace terms for that country as well as in the disposal of the Japanese colonial empire.[54] From 1943 Churchill worried about a strategy for the military defeat of Japan that advanced across the Pacific and into Japan, bypassing the Japanese in south-east Asia, a strategy in which the British contribution would inevitably have been small. He feared that if Japan was forced to relinquish Malaya and the Straits Settlements owing to defeat on the home islands, British prestige would not be restored in the minds of the native population, and the US would be placed in a strong position to demand that the colonies should be internationalised. By 1944 he was insistent that first Rangoon and then Singapore had to be retaken by force of arms for political, not military, reasons. Only the former of these cities was actually to fall to British arms, and the Labour government that took office in 1945 was to decide quickly against the restoration of colonial rule in Burma for more than a short interim period.[55]

However, while Churchill remained in office the restoration of old-style imperialism in south-east Asia was a British war aim. This included the restoration also of France in Indochina and of the Dutch in the East Indies, if only because that would buttress British power in its Asian colonies.[56] Nor did Churchill wish to stop at mere restoration. Roosevelt had not been wrong at his first Second World War meeting with him in August 1941 to form the view that he wanted to take advantage of the war to expand the empire.[57] In a frame of mind that harked back to a youth in which the British Empire had expanded massively, Churchill in May 1942 vetoed a proposed British–US–Chinese declaration guaranteeing the restoration of Thailand within its prewar borders because he wanted to leave the door open for the southern extension of that country, the Kra isthmus territory, to be annexed to the empire. This would have linked together Burma and Malaya and would have produced a continuous stretch of British imperial territory from Singapore to the borders of Afghanistan. Churchill was, it should be stressed, not alone in British wartime official circles in wanting to annex the Kra isthmus territories.[58]

Churchill came down to earth at the Cairo and Tehran conferences in the autumn of 1943. At the former he had to occupy himself as best he could while Roosevelt held four meetings with Chiang Kai-shek at which no records were kept but at which the President used all his charm to win over Chiang to agreeing that China should be one of the four policemen who would enforce security in the postwar world. The Cairo conference produced a declaration in favour of the restoration to China of all lands seized from it by Japan, going back to and including Taiwan and the Pescadores islands. There was no reference in the initial draft of this declaration to the expulsion of Japan from conquered British, French or Dutch territories. When Britain protested, the text was amended to state that Japan must lose all conquests, but there was no reference to British, French or Dutch colonial rule being restored. Churchill's next humiliation speedily followed at Tehran, where Roosevelt was at pains (successfully) to involve Russia in his deal with Chiang. Stalin agreed to recognise China as one of the Big Four and (with vehemence) to the restoration of all territory that it had lost to Japan in return for a privileged position for the Soviet Union in Manchuria. Churchill offered no protest. Although he was not to say it (to Anthony Eden) until the Yalta conference more than a year later, he now accepted that 'China is a United States concern'.[59] In the specific cases of Manchuria and Korea, the British could accept with little pain that it was unrealistic for them to assert that they should have a part to play in deciding their future. This contrasted with Stalin's detailed exposition at Tehran of the preparations that the Soviet Union was already making for a mighty onslaught into those territories and the northern islands of Japan within a few months of the war in Europe ending. He hardly needed to spell out that he would expect substantial political rewards in return.[60]

It is worth noting that Churchill's readiness for Britain to abdicate from the whole of China, a country for which he had never felt any enthusiasm, made him untypical of the British political establishment, which wanted a restored important role for Britain there, and which, during the last weeks of the war in Europe, suggested to the US that Britain would welcome the opportunity to be its junior partner in the reconstruction of China. The only response was that, for the first time, America officially urged Britain to return Hong Kong to China, taking advantage of Chiang's generous offer to turn it into a free port. The US wanted virtually to monopolise the postwar China market, with all that that would do for American jobs. It also suspected Britain of dark designs at this time. The American embassy in Chungking thought that Britain was seeking a deal with the Soviet Union under which Russian influence would predominate in north China and British in the south.[61]

The vision of China as any sort of actor in power politics faded after the high point of Roosevelt's wooing of Chiang at Cairo. From early 1944 the President found it increasingly difficult to ignore vitriolically anti-Chiang reports from the embassy in China, headed by Clarence Gauss, and from the head of the military mission, General Joseph Stilwell. The all too accurate picture painted by them, and in reports from China in the liberal media, was one of a corrupt regime steeped in brutality towards its own subjects and impotence towards the Japanese. However, Roosevelt could not actually turn against Chiang even if he had wished to do so. That would have alienated many on the political right in America, and might have caused Chiang to switch sides in the war, which would have transformed China from being still a minor asset into a major liability. He also saw this as involving big risks in the long term. In November 1944 he told the minister at the Australian legation in Washington that China had to be courted because 'in forty or fifty years' time' China might easily become a very powerful nation. Even so, by then he expected nothing from it for a long time. He remarked in early 1945 that, 'Three generations of education and training would be required before China could become a serious factor.'[62]

All this gave opportunities to a small 'Japan group' of diplomats like the former ambassador in Tokyo, Grew, and academics like Hugh Borton to work for a purged, in the proper dictionary sense of purified and cleared of undesirable elements, Japan to become the regional mainstay of an order dictated by America in the Far East. Japan would be democratised and disarmed, which could only be good for the Japanese people and for international security; it would be stripped of all its conquests, which could only be good for the numerous victims of Japanese imperialism; and it would serve as the Far Eastern hub of a global free-market economy that would ensure that America would never again be plunged into economic depression. The Emperor would be retained for as long as the people desired his services, though it would be no tragedy if they eventually decided to dispense with the Imperial House.[63] In British, as well as these specialised American, circles there was considerable faith in the 'malleability' of the Japanese to respond to defeat by adopting a democratic and peace-loving mindset of a kind that probably did not exist to any extent among the Germans.[64]

Roosevelt may, tentatively, be identified as being receptive to this view. In his public pronouncements, from after Pearl Harbor to the end of his life, he was harshly critical of the Japanese as a nation because most Americans would have been angered by anything else, but in March 1943 he did remark to Eden that, while Japan must lose all its conquests, including Taiwan and south Sakhalin, which would revert to China and Russia respectively, he favoured 'Japan for the Japanese'. This implied the early restoration of independence. Roosevelt believed that nothing was more important than untrammelled national independence; the 'pooling' of sovereignty would not have been for him. He was prepared to set it aside for a long period in the case of the first victim of Japanese aggression, Korea, in the belief that the Koreans were politically so immature that if their country was given early independence, 'it might become a real danger to world peace'.[65] He seems to have been ready to take a more favourable view of what a defeated Japan might do with restored independence.

With the President giving little guidance, US war aims towards Japan during the last two years of the war developed in ways that were influenced by the thinking of the Grew-Borton group. The State Department took the lead. In July 1943 Hull disbanded the war aims planning machinery in the department on the grounds that it had done the theoretical work that had been required of it and that the next stage was to negotiate with the allies and, in effect, with the rest of official Washington. By this time he was ready to dilute his universalism by conceding that the US could and should lead in the Pacific. He continued to pay lip service to the notion that China, and not Japan, had to be 'at the centre' of 'Oriental' affairs. Third countries were also entitled to a say in peacemaking for Japan, including in the matter of reparations for territories that had suffered under Japanese occupation. Britain was entitled to be listened to in relation to economic peace terms, including its desire for some protection against Japanese commercial competition. (In the actual negotiations that preceded the San Francisco peace treaty in 1951, the Americans were to be, at least in their own view, indulgent towards British economic desiderata that they regarded as petty or eccentric. The US was also to invite Britain to be the co-sponsor of the conference.)[66]

After returning from the Moscow conference of foreign ministers in October 1943, Hull set up a new war aims planning machinery in the State Department, including two general committees and several committees with a country or area remit. The one on the Far East was headed by the ubiquitous (in American Far East policy) Hornbeck. From these committees the model emerged of a three-stage occupation regime for Japan. In the first stage retribution, which was not clearly defined, would be exacted. In the second, occupation controls would be gradually relaxed. In the third, Japan would recover independence on terms that were such that it 'would properly discharge her responsibilities in a peaceful family of nations'. The package would include demilitarisation, democracy and economic arrangements that would allow Japan reasonable participation in world trade. In December 1944 the bureaucratic basis for the formulation of war aims was strengthened with the setting up of the famous State–War–Navy Coordinating Committee; the next month a sub-committee on Japan of this body was created to work out joint policies for the three departments that could then work their way up to the White House. A policy for Japan was worked out by July. It presupposed that Japan, like Germany, would at first have no government, though in the event it was to have one.

Some disagreements remained on the eve of the Japanese surrender. The army's demand that it should have not only permanent bases in Japan but also unimpeded free movement for its troops across the entire territory of the country was hard for the State Department to swallow. Early in 1945 the army and navy united to demand that the Ryukyu islands, including Okinawa, should cease to be part of Japan and should be administered by the US as a strategic trust territory of the United Nations, which would effectively have meant colonial status. (This was to become US policy in the later 1940s, but, in the peace treaty, America relented to the extent of vesting 'residual sovereignty' in Japan, with the UN playing no part. The Ryukyus were to be returned to Japan in 1972.) Much has been written about American agonising over the position of the Emperor. Japan's surrender without further bloodshed was made possible when, on 11 August, the US informed Japan that he could be retained, at least for an interim period, and permanently if that was the people's decision.[67]

SOVIET AIMS IN THE FAR EAST

This examination of Japanese war aims and of others' war aims towards Japan will conclude with the Soviet Union. Conclusion is, however, not the right word in the sense that, uniquely, a war aim achieved by one of the victorious powers remains unacceptable to the wartime loser. The visitor to modern-day Japan can hardly fail to notice, at any of the country's international airports, a giant wall diagram of the nation's islands in which are featured a number of small islands to the north of the largest main island, Hokkaido. These are the two southernmost islands of the Kurile chain, Kunashiri and Etorofu in Japanese, and the small islands of Shikotan and the Habomai islets which lie to the east and are not part of the chain. Japan is resigned to the loss of the northern Kurile islands that Russia ceded to Japan in 1875 but not to that of the southern islands, which had been Japan's without resort to war or even diplomacy.

The acquisition of the Kuriles was strongly advocated by Ivan Maisky in his recommendations in January 1944 to foreign minister Molotov on Soviet war aims: 'the Kurile island chain, which cuts the USSR off from the Pacific Ocean, must be ours'.[68] Equally or more important to Stalin was the acquisition of Karafuto, the southern half of the large island of Sakhalin, which had been Japanese since its victory in 1905 in the war with Russia, and the recovery of the Russian position in Manchuria, which had also been lost in 1905. The most glittering prize there was the naval base at Port Arthur (now Lushun) at the southern tip of the Liaotung peninsula, which had briefly been Russian on a lease from 1898 to 1905. During that time tsarist Russia had had aspirations to gain full control of Manchuria. These were not revived. As Molotov recalled in 1981: 'We couldn't take Manchuria. It was impossible. It contradicted our policy. We took a lot. But that's another matter.'[69] The 'policy' was one of supporting a China whose territorial integrity would be largely restored and which, or so Stalin told his western counterparts, would be under the rule of the anti-communist Chiang Kai-shek, who was exempted from all personal criticism in the Soviet media and who was lavishly praised by Stalin to Harry Truman's special envoy, Harry Hopkins, in June 1945. Stalin 'said he saw no other possible leader and that, for example, he did not believe that the Chinese Communist leaders were as good or would be able to bring about the unification of China'.[70] In return, China would have to restore to Russia what it had had in Manchuria up to 1904 – the leased territory and the Chinese Eastern and the South Manchurian railways – with modern trappings. The outright Russian control of the tsarist period was in fact replaced by 'joint' formulae that paid lip service to a supposedly post-imperialist age: nominal joint Sino-Soviet ownership of the railways, Port Arthur to be a joint naval base, and the twin port of Dairen (now Dalian) to be a free port, though with many of the port facilities specially allocated to the Soviet Union, which had the right to take them over on a thirty-year lease if it so wished. The harbour master at Dairen had to be a Soviet. The port passed under complete de facto Russian control, and the Soviets used it to funnel supplies to the communist forces in the Chinese civil war that ended in 1949. China did at least recover full formal sovereignty over the whole of Manchuria, now officially always referred to as the 'Three Eastern Provinces of China' to banish all memory of Manchukuo. More painfully, it had to accept the permanent and total loss of its former province of Outer Mongolia, which became the nominally fully independent Mongolian People's Republic. Actually under Russian control since the last tsarist years, it was effectively a Soviet colony. The necessity of this was explained by Stalin to Chinese foreign minister T. V. Soong in talks in the summer of 1945: 'Outer Mongolia has a geographical position from where one can overthrow the Soviet Union's position in the Far East,' he stated. Chiang agreed to this loss of Chinese sovereignty with utmost reluctance in return for what he took to be the promise that the Chinese communists would receive no help or support from the Soviet Union. A thirty-year Sino-Soviet treaty was then signed on 14 August.[71]

Mongolian 'independence' ended a one-year interregnum in which there had been no communist state in Asia on the Soviet model. Soviet rulers had long regarded such a state as valuable for their political aim of expanding communism, and had created one before the war in the People's Republic of Tuva, which straddled part of the Soviet– Mongolian border and which was known to some 1930s British schoolchildren from its exotic postage stamps. In 1944, in complete secrecy, this republic, with an area double that of Scotland, was annexed to the main Russian republic of the USSR. With the impending 'independence' of Mongolia as a more conspicuous communist state, the People's Republic of Tuva ceased to serve any useful purpose and was removed.[72]

Stalin's demands on China were considerable, but he had no desire to repeat Japan's folly by making ones that were impossible, and, even more important, he accepted American primacy in east Asia except in areas of particular Soviet concern, or pretended to do so. As noted above, the Tehran conference witnessed the makings of a Soviet–American deal on the Far East. The matter was further refined in talks between Stalin and ambassador Harriman on 14 December 1944, in which the former made his usual 'need for a warm water port' ploy, this time in relation not to the Baltic but to the Pacific.[73] The way became clear for the Soviet–American agreement at the Yalta conference on Soviet war aims in the Far East and on its entry into the war with Japan, the two issues being inextricably linked.

However, what Stalin revealed to the American and Chinese governments were really only his minimum aims in China. What he hoped for and, with reason, regarded as possible, though not inevitable, was a communist China under the rule of Mao Tse-tung (Mao Zedong). What he said to Hopkins about the Chinese communists was pure deception. Stalin and Mao had been working hard on their personal relationship since the 1930s and, from 1943, Stalin had granted Mao the unique privilege for a foreign communist of direct access to him via radio link. Stalin favoured the greatest possible success for Mao, providing that Russia was not drawn into conflict with the US. The deception had some success, though American policymakers were not influenced by it even if they half believed it. In 1945–6 it was to provide a useful smokescreen behind which the Red Army handed over large areas of Manchuria to Mao's army at the same time as President Truman's special envoy, George Marshall, was in China with public instructions to mediate a fair compromise between Chiang's Kuomintang and the communists, and secret instructions to do everything possible to weaken the latter because, otherwise, 'there would follow the tragic consequences of a divided China and of a probable resumption of Russian power in Manchuria, the combined effect of this resulting in the defeat or loss of the major purpose of our war in the Pacific'.[74]

Stalin seems not to have had any clear aims during the war in relation to Korea. He probably remembered tsarist overextension in that peninsular country and somewhat excluded it from his mind. He was evasive when Roosevelt tried to engage him in a discussion about the future of Korea at Yalta. Among the three great leaders, the American was left to do the thinking about it. As already noted, he took a very adverse view of the Koreans' ability to avoid becoming what would now be called a 'failed state'. He wanted Japanese rule to be succeeded by a lengthy trusteeship of the US, Russia, China and possibly Britain. An additional thought that he expressed in 1943 was that the US would need staging points in Korea for the increasing volume of trans-Pacific air traffic between North America and Asia. Not bound by any undertaking, Stalin, in mid-August 1945, accepted an unnecessarily generous American proposal by which more than half the territory of Korea, though only a third of the population, would pass under Soviet occupation north of the thirty-eighth parallel of latitude.[75]

A Korean might well have thought that if there was any justice then Japan, and not his or her country, should be partitioned. For a short time there was a possibility that that might happen. In the summer of 1945 Stalin ordered the Red Army command in the Far East to prepare military plans for the occupation not only of south Sakhalin and the Kuriles, as provided for at Yalta, but also the northern half of the Japanese large island of Hokkaido. He explained to Truman in a letter of 16 August that 'Russian public opinion' would not accept anything less than the occupation of some part of Japanese territory, by which he meant Japanese territory that he did not plan to annex. He cancelled the planned Hokkaido operation exactly a week later in response to a stern warning from Truman, and Russian publications intended for western audiences were to make no reference to it to the end of the Soviet period.[76]

As if to compensate for its Hokkaido disappointment, Russia, as a nation, has exalted in its gain of the Kuriles. There is a line of continuity from 21 July 1945 when Stalin, in rejecting a request from Truman to establish an air base on the islands to attack Japan, treated them as if they were already part of Soviet territory; to the late Soviet period when the capture of the islands was still being celebrated because: 'On August 31 the hostilities on the islands ceased entirely. Since then the Kuriles never again were an instrument of aggression and a bridgehead for the Japanese: they became a defence base for the Soviet Union, a gateway to the Pacific from the Sea of Okhotsk'; and on to post-communist Russia's determination to retain them, despite occasional Russo-Japanese agreements that the issue must be resolved.[77] Unfortunately for Japan in its desire to recover what it calls 'the Northern Territories', the US has been unable to give it support owing to the unqualified nature of Roosevelt's commitment to their acquisition by the Soviet Union at Yalta.[78] It can only offer a measure of support over the tiny Shikotan and Habomai islands, which are not part of the Kurile chain and which perhaps only Stalin would have had the nerve to occupy in a final land grab of the Second World War.

Notes

1. G. R. Storry, 'Rumours of a Japanese-German understanding on the eve of the armistice of 1918', in G. F. Hudson (ed.), *St Antony's Papers. Number 20: Far Eastern Affairs Number Four* (Oxford: Oxford University Press, 1967), pp. 23–36. See also Frank W. Iklé, 'Japanese-German peace negotiations during World War I', in *American Historical Review*, vol. LXXI, 1965, pp. 62–76.
2. Frederick R. Dickinson, *War and National Reinvention: Japan in the Great War, 1914–1919* (Cambridge, MA: Harvard University Press, 1999), pp. 45, 50, 56, 118–19, 140, 138–51, 174, 180, 195.
3. On the futile effort to secure Japanese military assistance in Europe during the war see V. H. Rothwell, 'The British government and Japanese assistance 1914–18', *History*, vol. 56, February 1971, pp. 35–45.
4. Christopher Thorne, *The Far Eastern War: States and Societies, 1941–45* (London: Unwin Paperbacks, 1986), p. 19.
5. W. G. Beasley, *The Rise of Modern Japan*, rev. edn (London: Phoenix, 2000), pp. 98–9.
6. Dickinson, *War*, pp. 197, 211.
7. Yoshika Tak Matsusaka, *The Making of Japanese Manchuria, 1904–1932* (Cambridge, MA: Harvard University Press, 2001), p. 402.
8. Nicholas Tarling, *A Sudden Rampage: The Japanese Occupation of Southeast Asia, 1941–1945* (London: Hurst, 2001), p. 77.
9. On the Washington conference see the articles in the special edition of *Diplomacy and Statecraft*, vol. 4, no. 3, 1993, edited by Erik Goldstein and John Mauer.
10. Walter LaFeber, *The Clash: A History of US–Japan Relations* (New York: Norton, 1997), p. 155.
11. LaFeber, *Clash*, p. 161; Mary L. Hanneman, *Japan Faces the World, 1925–1952* (Harlow: Longman, 2001), p. 38; William Henry Chamberlin, *Japan over Asia* (London: Duckworth, 1938), pp. 18–24, 172–7, 181–2, 187–92; Mark R. Peattie '"Nanshin": the "Southward advance", in 1931–1941, as a prelude to the Japanese occupation of southeast Asia', in Peter Duus, Ramon H. Myers and Mark R. Peattie (eds), *The Japanese Wartime Empire, 1931–1945* (Princeton: Princeton University Press, 1996), pp. 202–6.
12. W. G. Beasley, *Japanese Imperialism, 1894–1945* (Oxford: Clarendon, 1987), pp. 251, 254; see also Louise Young, *Japan's Total Empire: Manchuria and the Culture of Wartime Imperialism* (Berkeley: University of California Press, 1998), p. 435.
13. Chamberlin, *Japan over Asia*, p. 27.
14. Christopher Thorne, *Allies of a Kind: The United States, Britain and the War against Japan, 1941–1945* (Oxford: Oxford University Press, 1979), p. 37.
15. Ian Nish, *Japanese Foreign Policy in the Interwar Period* (Westport: Praeger, 2002), p. 126.

16. Shinichi Kitaoka, 'Diplomacy and the Military in Showa Japan', in Carol Gluck and Stephen R. Graubard (eds), *Showa: The Japan of Hirohito* (New York: Norton, 1992), p. 166.

17. Tarling, *Rampage*, p. 48; Robert Smith Thompson, *Empires on the Pacific: World War II and the Struggle for the Mastery of Asia* (Oxford: The Perseus Press, 2001), p. 88.

18. Barbara J. Brooks, *Japan's Imperial Diplomacy: Consuls, Treaty Ports, and War in China, 1895–1938* (Honolulu: University of Hawai'i Press, 2000), pp. 167–75.

19. See National Heritage Board: National Archives of Singapore, *The Japanese Occupation, 1942–1945* (Singapore, 1996), ch. 8, 'Battle for the hearts and minds'.

20. A jealously guarded place. Westerners who were shipwrecked on these islands were, if they were lucky, whisked away to somewhere else within days. If they were unlucky, they were never seen again. Between the wars Japan informed the relatives of several stranded westerners that they had died in 'accidents' on or after their landfall. Willard Price, *Japan's Islands of Mystery* (London: The British Publishers' Guild, 1944), p. 23. This evokes a longstanding Japanese policy, which was last reaffirmed in 1825, that foreign ships seeking humanitarian assistance were to be forced back to sea with cannon fire and left to their fate.

21. Kitaoka, 'Diplomacy and the Military in Showa Japan', in Gluck and Graubard (eds), *Showa*, p. 162.

22. Young, *Total Empire*, pp. 419–20; Chamberlin, *Japan over Asia*, p. 51.

23. Brooks, *Imperial Diplomacy*, pp. 201–2; see also Nish, *Interwar*, p. 127; William O. Walker III, *Opium and Foreign Policy: The Anglo-American Search for Order in Asia, 1912–1954* (Chapel Hill: University of North Carolina Press, 1991), p. 130.

24. This account of economic policy is based on the chapters by Timothy Brook and Parks M. Coble in David P. Barrett and Larry N. Shyu (eds), *Chinese Collaboration with Japan, 1932–1945: The Limits of Accommodation* (Stanford: Stanford University Press, 2001); and on the articles by Ramon H. Myers and Takafusa Nakamura in Duus et al. (eds), *Wartime Empire*.

25. Thompson, *Empires*, pp. 65–6.

26. David P. Barrett, 'Introduction', in Barrett and Shyu (eds), *Collaboration*, pp. 3–4; Joyce C. Lebra (ed.), *Japan's Greater East Asia Co-Prosperity Sphere in World War II: Selected Readings and Documents* (Kuala Lumpur: Oxford University Press, 1975), pp. 80–1.

27. Ch. 5 by David P. Barrett and ch. 3 by Huang Meizhen and Yang Hanqing, especially pp. 64–6, 69–76, in Barrett and Shyu (eds), *Collaboration*; editor's introduction by Duus in Duus et al. (eds), *Wartime Empire*, pp. xii-xiv.

28. Ikeda Kiyoshi, 'The road to Singapore: Japan's view of Britain, 1922–41', in T. G. Fraser and Peter Lowe (eds), *Conflict and Amity in East Asia* (Basingstoke: Macmillan, 1992), pp. 36–7. On Japan's limited stake in south-east Asia before 1940 see Beasley, *Imperialism*, pp. 223–4, and Peattie in Duus et al. (eds) *Wartime Empire*, pp. 207–9.

29. Peattie, 'Nanshin', in Duus et al. (eds) *Wartime Empire*, pp. 213–19.

30. Lebra, *Co-Prosperity Sphere*, pp. 68–70.

31. Tarling, *Rampage*, pp. 58–9.

32. Michael A. Barnhart, *Japan and the World since 1868* (London: Arnold, 1995), pp. 126–7; LaFeber, *Clash*, pp. 192–3.

33. David Reynolds, *The Creation of the Anglo-American Alliance, 1937–1941: A Study in Competitive Cooperation* (London: Europa Publications, 1981), pp. 240–50.

34. Tarling, *Rampage*, pp. 131–2; James L. McClain, *Japan: A Modern History* (New York: Norton, 2002), p. 494; Ken'ichi Goto in Duus et al. (eds), *Wartime Empire*, pp. 275–6.

35. On mosques, see Mark R. Peattie in Duus et al. (eds), *Wartime Empire*, pp. 230–1.

36. Peter Duus, 'Imperialism without colonies: the vision of a Greater East Asia Co-Prosperity Sphere', *Diplomacy and Statecraft*, vol. 7, March 1996, pp. 54–72; see also Duus in *Wartime Empire*, pp. xxiii–xxvii.

37. Duus in Duus et al. (eds), *Wartime Empire*, p. xiv; Tarling, *Rampage*, p. 132.

38. Bernd Martin, 'The German–Japanese alliance in the Second World War', in Saki Dockrill (ed.), *From Pearl Harbor to Hiroshima: The Second World War in Asia and the Pacific, 1941–45* (Basingstoke: Macmillan, 1994), p. 159; Nish, *Interwar*, pp. 140–1; Norman Rich, *Hitler's War Aims: The Establishment of the New Order* (London: Deutsch, 1974), vol. II, pp. 414–15; Goto in Duus et al. (eds), *Wartime Empire*, pp. 274–5; Robert Edwin Herzstein, *When Nazi Dreams Come True: The Third Reich's Internal Struggle over the Future of Europe after a German Victory* (London: Abacus, 1982), p. 195; Zhores A. Medvedev and Roy A. Medvedev, *The Unknown Stalin* (London: Tauris, 2003), p. 245. For more on Japanese territorial war aims, see also Chapter 7 'Conclusion' below.

39. Louis Allen, 'Wartime Japanese planning: a note on Akira Iriye', in Fraser and Lowe (eds), *Conflict and Amity*, pp. 84–5; Duus in *Diplomacy and Statecraft*, p. 72n.

40. Tarling, *Rampage*, p. 134.

41. Ibid. pp. 197–204.

42. Ibid. p. 135.

43. Ibid. p. 136; Nish, *Interwar*, p. 171.

44. Tarling, *Rampage*, pp. 111, 123.

45. Anthony Rhodes, *The Vatican in the Age of the Dictators, 1922–1945* (London: Hodder, 1973), pp. 307–9.

46. John Keay, *Last Post: The End of Empire in the Far East* (London; Murray, 1997), p. 208.

47. Tarling, *Rampage*, pp. 189–92, 251.

48. Duus in Duus et al. (eds), *Wartime Empire*, pp. xiii–xiv. This is a more realistic conclusion than that of a team of German historians who postulate a basic difference between 'grandiose' German and 'limited' Japanese war aims. Horst Boog et al., *Germany and the Second World War: Vol. VI, The Global War* (Oxford: Clarendon, 2001), p. 1220.

49. Ian Cowman, *Dominion or Decline: Anglo-American Naval Relations in the Pacific, 1937–1941* (Oxford: Berg, 1996), pp. 178–9.

50. LaFeber, *Clash*, p. 206; Frederick S. Dunn, *Peace-Making and the Settlement with Japan* (Princeton: Princeton University Press, 1963), pp. 6–7.

51. LaFeber, *Clash*, p. 217.

52. Wm Roger Louis, *Imperialism at Bay: The United States and the Decolonization of the British Empire* (Oxford: Clarendon, 1977), pp. 71–7.

53. Ibid. p. 285.

54. Keith Sainsbury, *Churchill and Roosevelt at War* (London: Macmillan, 1994), pp. 164–7; Thorne, *Allies*, pp. 655–6.

55. Tarling, *Rampage*, pp. 112–15.

56. Nicholas Tarling, *Britain, Southeast Asia and the Onset of the Cold War, 1945–1950* (Cambridge: Cambridge University Press, 1998), p. 39.

57. Theodore A. Wilson, *The First Summit: Roosevelt and Churchill at Placentia Bay, 1941* (London: Macdonald, 1970), p. 123.

58. Richard J. Aldrich, *The Key to the South: Britain, the United States, and Thailand during the Approach of the Pacific War, 1929–1942* (Kuala Lumpur: Oxford University Press, 1993), pp. 366, 370–3. In 1953 Churchill, again prime minister, was to return to the evidently congenial theme of bringing the Kra isthmus territories under British rule. James Cable, *The Geneva Conference of 1954 on Indochina* (Basingstoke: Macmillan, 1986), pp. 16–19.

59. T. G. Fraser, 'Roosevelt and the making of America's east Asian policy, 1941–45', in Fraser and Lowe (eds), *Conflict and Amity*, pp. 101–2; Sainsbury, *Churchill and Roosevelt*, pp. 172–4, 177.

60. Thorne, *Allies*, p. 660; John Erickson, *The Road to Berlin: Vol. 2 of Stalin's War with Germany* (London: Weidenfeld, 1983), p. 156.

61. Lenxin Xiang, *Recasting the Imperial Far East: Britain and America in China, 1945–1950* (London: M. E. Sharpe, 1995), pp. 13–33; Louis, *Imperialism*, pp. 437–8.

62. Fraser in Fraser and Lowe (eds), *Conflict and Amity*, pp. 102–7; Thorne, *Allies*, pp. 181–2; Louis, *Imperialism*, p. 424; LaFeber, *Clash*, p. 239.

63. LaFeber, *Clash*, pp. 237–8, 243.

64. Thorne, *Allies*, pp. 373–4, 492–3.

65. Louis, *Imperialism*, pp. 227, 235–6, 486–7; Steven Casey, *Cautious Crusade: Franklin D. Roosevelt, American Public Opinion and the War against Nazi Germany* (Oxford: Oxford University Press, 2001), pp. 66–9, 166, 173.

66. Dunn, *Peace-Making*, pp. 22–5, 29, 53, 137–41, 158–62; Cordell Hull, *The Memoirs of Cordell Hull: Volume Two* (London: Hodder, 1948), pp. 1582–1601.

67. Dunn, *Peace-Making*, pp. 31–41, 56–7.

68. Aleksei M. Filitov in Francesca Gori and Silvio Pons (eds), *The Soviet Union and Europe in the Cold War, 1945–53* (Basingstoke: Macmillan, 1996), p. 7.

69. Albert Resis (ed.), *Molotov Remembers: Inside Kremlin Politics: Conversations with Felix Chuev* (Chicago: Dee, 1993), p. 72.

70. W. Averell Harriman and Elie Abel, *Special Envoy to Churchill and Stalin, 1941–1946* (New York: Random House, 1975), pp. 472–3; Max Beloff, *Soviet Policy in the Far East, 1944–1951* (London: Oxford University Press, 1953), p. 28.

71. J. A. S. Grenville, *The Major International Treaties, 1914–1973: A History and Guide with Texts* (London: Methuen, 1974), pp. 237–40; Michael M. Sheng, *Battling Western Imperialism: Mao, Stalin, and the United States* (Princeton: Princeton University Press, 1997), p. 155; Bruce A. Elleman, *Diplomacy and Deception: The Secret History of Sino-Soviet Diplomatic Relations, 1917–1927* (London: M. E. Sharpe, 1997), pp. 233–6; Beloff, *Soviet Policy*, pp. 35–7.

72. For a recent treatment of the Soviet annexation of Tuva see Sharad K. Soni, *Mongolia–Russia Relations: Kiakhta to Vladivostok* (Delhi: Shipra, 2002), pp. 77–80.

73. Harriman and Abel, *Special Envoy*, pp. 379–80.

74. Sheng, *Battling*, pp. 54, 56, 75–85, 105–15, 121, 131–6, 148. According to Sheng (p. 105), Stalin regarded Chiang as 'an Anglo-American lackey'. See also Alexei Babin, 'The USSR's liberation mission in the Far East', in The USSR Academy of Sciences, *The Liberating Mission of the Soviet Union in the Second World War* (Moscow: Nauka, 1985), pp. 115–16, for the Soviet role as midwife for the 'Manchurian revolutionary base'.

75. William Stueck, *Rethinking the Korean War: A New Diplomatic and Strategic History* (Princeton: Princeton University Press, 2002), pp. 17–19; Bruce Cumings, *Korea's Place in the Sun: A Modern History* (New York: Norton, 1997), pp. 185–90; Louis, *Imperialism*, pp. 79–80, 228.

76. See e.g. V. Larionov et al., *World War II: Decisive Battles of the Soviet Army* (Moscow: Progress Publishers, 1984), which finds no space for it in a sixty-four-

page chapter on 'Far Eastern campaign: last battle of World War II'. For a scholarly treatment see John Erickson, 'Stalin, Soviet strategy and the grand alliance', in Ann Lane and Howard Temperley (eds), *The Rise and Fall of the Grand Alliance, 1941–45* (Basingstoke: Macmillan, 1995), pp. 164–7.

77. Andrei Ledovsky, *The USSR, the USA and the People's Revolution in China* (Moscow: Progress Publishers, 1982), p. 45; Larionov et al., *Decisive Battles*, p. 486; 'Russia and Japan sign accord to seek end to dispute over islands', *New York Times*, 11 January 2003.

78. Haruki Wada, 'The San Francisco peace treaty and the definition of the Kurile islands', in Gilbert Rozman (ed.), *Japan and Russia: The Tortuous Path to Normalization, 1949–1999* (Basingstoke: Macmillan, 2000), pp. 15–31.

7

Conclusion

What stands out from this study of the war aims of great and major powers during the Second World War is their frequent remoteness from the world as it was to be after 1945. There was a spectrum from a desire to maintain virtually everything in the prewar international status quo to ambitions to upset it completely. Both the latter desire and its modern-day remoteness are most evident in the transition of Germany and Japan from violent power politics to peaceful liberal democracies. In both there was a cult of perpetual struggle to achieve ever-expanding conquests. Hitler remarked in 1928 that, 'Wherever our success may end that will always be only the starting point of a new fight.'[1] It was not very different in Japan. In December 1941, at the very time of the Pearl Harbor attack, the Research Section of the War Ministry and the prestigious and official National Policy Investigation Society drew up a plan for a wider Japanese empire that was to be secured by another war to be launched about twenty years after the one on which Japan was just embarking had been concluded. If Australia, New Zealand and Sri Lanka (then called Ceylon) were not conquered in the first war, then they would be in the second, and each would be ruled by a Japanese governor-general. Definitely reserved for creation out of the second war were the future governments-general of Alaska and Central America. The former would include western Canada and Washington state in the USA as well as Alaska, the latter all of Central America, Colombia, Ecuador, part of Venezuela and most West Indian islands, including Cuba. Mexico, Peru and Chile would be punished by losing some of their territory to Japan if they declared war on it.[2] Prewar Japan had valid concerns not about its security, which was not threatened by anything other than the consequences of its own aggression, but rather in relation to the precarious economic circumstances in which it found itself after 1929. However, it embraced visions, as preposterous as they were reprehensible, of a Japanese super-empire, based on racial superiority and pitiless economic exploitation of non-Japanese, that could only lead to disaster.

In the case of Germany, it is even more difficult to write with any moderation. The least offensive aspect of German war aims was their hypocrisy. Hitler could rail in a speech in January 1941 that, 'What Britain called the Balance of Power was nothing but the disintegration and disorganisation of the continent.'[3] He, and the wider Nazi regime, aimed at replacing this putative British design with forms of 'integration' and 'organisation' in which, on the basis of racial-biological criteria, the non-German peoples of Europe and some other parts of the world would have been the servants or slaves of their German superiors. At one extreme of the racial hierarchy, some Nazis like Himmler wanted to include kindred Germanic peoples in the German racial community. At the other extreme of their racial spectrum, all Nazis were agreed that there were many peoples, besides the Jews, for whom there could only be death, who were so inferior that, if they were not needed for economic purposes, they were to be killed by starvation, shooting or other means. The defeat of these ghastly aims was brought about primarily by the ability of two European countries, the United Kingdom and the Soviet Union, to offer effective resistance to them, and by Hitler's paranoia, which facilitated the entry of the United States into the war against him at an earlier date than would otherwise have been possible. No supreme war aim against such gigantic and immeasurable vileness was possible except the complete destruction of German power. Roosevelt's decision and then announcement in January 1943 that Germany and the other Axis states must surrender unconditionally was a public statement of what most in American and British political circles already thought, though it was appropriate that it should have come from FDR in that he was out on a limb from most opinion in the English-speaking nations in believing that the Germans as a people were thoroughly, and probably incurably, infected with evil.

In Italy the war telescoped the country's involvement in large-scale empire into the space of considerably less than a decade. On 9 May 1936 Mussolini proclaimed that 'Italy has at last her Empire' after the conclusion of the campaign to conquer Ethiopia. He went on to assert that it was a victory that recalled the glories of the Roman Empire.[4] This book has traced how such vainglorious claims led Italy to ruin and temporary disintegration in a situation in which the loss of all of its colonies was the least of its problems.

In Britain and France the war accelerated their inevitable progression, given that they were already liberal democracies, to a post-imperial future. This remains true even when account is taken of ambitions to *expand* slightly the empire in wartime and immediate postwar British political circles. Interest in annexing the Kra isthmus from Thailand has been noted, and the postwar foreign secretary, Ernest Bevin, though not prime minister Attlee, wanted eastern Libya (Cyrenaica), already under military occupation, to be brought under British rule for a considerable period of time as a United Nations trusteeship territory, so that its harbours and sites for potential air bases could be utilised.[5] More realistically, however, the war forced Britain, partly and only partly in response to American pressure, to recognise that the full maintenance of the colonial empire was an impossible aim. Dependencies in addition to India, which was already on the road to self-government, would have to be conceded self-rule and ultimately independence. (France, reacting in part to the bitterness of defeat in 1940, was tragically slower to learn the same lesson, and was to fight wars to resist colonial liberation in Indochina and Algeria.)

On an even greater matter, the war left Britain with unresolved questions in relation to its supreme aim of ensuring future security. Roosevelt's Four Policemen idea within a greatly modified revival under a new name of the League of Nations held out some promise, and the Foreign Office drew up a variant in its Four Power Plan. Also seriously considered were a relatively lenient peace settlement with Germany, continuation of the wartime Anglo-Soviet alliance even at the price of imposing crushing terms on Germany that would have left it permanently resentful and a grouping of west European democracies consisting of Britain, France, the Benelux countries and western Scandinavia. The one alternative that was almost wholly lacking in attractions was a bilateral Anglo-American relationship as the key to Britain's postwar security. Not only did it seem unlikely that the US would offer it, except perhaps on unacceptable terms, but also the many slights and worse that Britain had to endure from America during the war eroded even Churchill's resilience as a proponent of a US–British special relationship. The slights included the petty insults that he suffered at the Tehran conference and later from Roosevelt as he tried to ingratiate himself with Stalin. The worse included the Prime Minister's discovery in 1943 that the US had prevailed upon Canada to sign a secret agreement under which it would sell all its uranium output to America, leaving none for Britain, which, according to his biographer, reduced Churchill to one of his blackest moods of despair during the entire war.[6]

Turning directly to the United States, its wartime journey was away from an 'isolationism' that was based on the belief that America needed only to mind its own business to guarantee its security, to a degree of involvement and frequent outside interventions that few in pre-1941 USA expected or desired. The US was forced by the war to face up to what should perhaps have been evident to it since at least 1917, which was that it could not avoid being the most important external influence in the power relationships of Europe and east Asia. It formulated policies for national security that involved dominance in the Pacific (with Australia as a very junior partner), near dominance in the north Atlantic area (with Britain as both junior partner and strategic outpost), and for a cordon of insular bases off the east Asian mainland. In relation to the latter, it is interesting to note how Washington policymakers differentiated between Okinawa and the other Ryukyu islands that were acknowledged to be legitimately owned by Japan, and Taiwan just to their south. The former were to be unceremoniously detached from a Japan whose cruelty and treachery left it without claim to the rights normally to be accorded to any country. Taiwan was to be returned to China, and any American military facilities there could only be established with the consent of the Republic of China. That state was to be yet another junior partner with the US in mutually beneficial security arrangements, though this vision was complicated by growing and paradoxical concerns that China would be too weak in the short and medium terms to be of much use to America and yet in the long term might become so powerful as to constitute a threat.

President Roosevelt tried deviously to manoeuvre his country into pursuing, as its supreme war aim, the creation of a new global order in which power politics, even in the relatively civilised form of spheres of influence which had been indisputably benign in certain places at certain times, gave way to non-intervention by strong or ambitious states in the affairs of others except with international approval. In a sense, this was a continuation of traditional American foreign policy even in the 1930s. 'Isolationism' is a misnomer; interwar America was non-interventionist but not truly isolationist. The difference was now that the country became ready to exert itself if other states would not also practise non-interventionism. The chosen instrument was to be a United Nations organisation in which the effective part was to consist of the Four (ultimately Five) Policemen with permanent seats in the governing body, the Security Council. The flaw was that the UN could not, by reason of its constitution, work in the event of aggression by one of the policemen himself. The power of veto entitled any rogue policeman to block action against him. So it was that, for example, spheres of influence, if not bonds of a tighter nature, were being developed by Britain in Greece and by the Soviet Union in Poland, Romania and Bulgaria even before the war ended. The most blatant, specific example of ruthless power politics, the annexation of Sub-Carpathian Ruthenia (renamed the Carpatho Ukraine) from a victim of Nazi aggression, Czechoslovakia, by the Soviet Union between October 1944 and June 1945 attracted minimal attention in the west; it was simply too small and too remote.

This brings the discussion to the enigmas of Soviet aims. In the revolution of 1917 and in the subsequent civil war the Bolsheviks had seized power in Russia imbued with a messianic ideology that aimed at achieving a world socialist state, to be followed by the ultimate withering away of that state. The question arises whether its costly victory in the war with Germany provided an opportunity to return to this original aspiration or whether the war facilitated a tendency in the rulers of the Soviet state to pursue more limited ambitions based on age-old concepts of national security, including a craving for recognition of their state's legitimacy. The evidence now available suggests that it did, with the qualification from Russian historian Vladimir O. Pechatnov that, 'It also enhance[d] the Soviet Union's appetite and created a sort of entitlement complex.' Stalin thought that that complex could be satisfied within Roosevelt's Four Police-men concept, which, for the Soviet Union, served the purposes of 'keeping it in the council of world powers, legitimising its postwar borders and spheres of influence, and keeping Germany and Japan down'. With an eye on the Leninist theory which postulated that the leading imperialist nations would turn on the Soviet Union unless they were manipulated in a contrary direction, the cooperation policy would also serve to prevent the formation of an Anglo-American bloc hostile to Russia. Finally, it would be a spur to the US not to renege on its proclaimed intention to withdraw all its troops from western Europe within two years of the end of the war. Then, as Ivan Maisky reflected in his report on war aims, the situation would be one 'in our best interest' in which 'postwar Europe [would] have only one great land power – the USSR – and only one great sea power – England'. Not till late 1945, a period outside the scope of this book, did Stalin begin to regard the US as a rival for hegemony in Europe.[7] The aims of the two superpowers of the postwar world became convergent during the Second World War to an extent that made the breakdown in relations between them that occurred soon afterwards all the more bitter.

Notes

1. Peter Mangold, *From Tirpitz to Gorbachev: Power Politics in the Twentieth Century* (Basingstoke: Macmillan, 1998), p. 75.
2. Richard Storry, *The Double Patriots: A Study of Japanese Nationalism* (London: Chatto and Windus, 1957), pp. 276–7, 317–19.
3. Peter Matthews, *European Balance* (London: Chatto and Windus, 1945), p. 101.
4. Report in *The Times*, 11 May 1936.
5. Scott L. Bills, *Empire and Cold War: The Roots of US–Third World Antagonism, 1945–47* (Basingstoke: Macmillan, 1990), pp. 95–9; Scott L. Bills, *The Libyan Arena: The United States, Britain, and the Council of Foreign Ministers, 1945–1948* (Kent: Kent State University Press, 1995), pp. 34–9; William Roger Louis, *The British Empire in the Middle East, 1945–1951: Arab Nationalism, The United States and Postwar Imperialism* (Oxford: Clarendon, 1984), pp. 268–71; Kenneth O. Morgan, *Labour in Power, 1945–1951* (Oxford: Clarendon, 1984), p. 241.
6. For references to Roosevelt's slights see n. 98 to Chapter 5 above. Martin Gilbert, *Road to Victory: Winston S. Churchill, 1941–1945* (London: Heinemann, 1986), pp. 418–19. In this book Gilbert states only that Churchill found out about the US–Canadian uranium deal and is silent on his emotional response. However, after a public lecture given in the University of Edinburgh on 12 May 2004 Martin Gilbert volunteered the information about Churchill's despair during questions and answers.
7. Vladimir O. Pechatnov in Ralph B. Levering et al., *Debating the Origins of the Cold War: American and Russian Perspectives* (Lanham: Rowman and Littlefield, 2002), pp. 96, 100, 109; see also Fraser J. Harbutt, *The Iron Curtain: Churchill, America, and the Origins of the Cold War* (New York: Oxford University Press, 1986), pp. 43–5, 107–20.

Bibliography

Abrash, Merritt, 'War aims toward Austria-Hungary: the Czech pivot', in Alexander Dallin et al., *Russian Diplomacy and Eastern Europe, 1914–1917* (New York: King's Crown Press, 1963).

Aga-Rossi, Elena and Victor Zaslavsky, 'The Soviet Union and the Italian Communist Party, 1944–8', in Francesca Gori and Silvio Pons (eds), *The Soviet Union and Europe in the Cold War, 1945–53* (Basingstoke: Macmillan, 1996).

Albrecht-Carrié, René, *A Diplomatic History of Europe since the Congress of Vienna* (London: Methuen, 1958).

Alcock, Antony Evelyn, *The History of the South Tyrol Question* (London: Joseph, 1970).

Aldrich, Richard J., *The Key to the South: Britain, the United States, and Thailand during the Approach of the Pacific War, 1929–1942* (Kuala Lumpur: Oxford University Press, 1993).

Alexander, G. M., *The Prelude to the Truman Doctrine: British Policy in Greece, 1944–1947* (Oxford: Clarendon, 1982).

Alfieri, Dino, *Dictators Face to Face* (London: Elek, 1954).

Allen, Louis, 'Wartime Japanese planning: a note on Akira Iriye', in T. G. Fraser and Peter Lowe (eds), *Conflict and Amity in East Asia* (Basingstoke: Macmillan, 1992).

Aly, Götz and Susanne Heim, *Architects of Annihilation: Auschwitz and the Logic of Destruction* (London: Weidenfeld, 2002).

Andrew, Christopher M. and A. S. Kanya-Forstner, *France Overseas: The Great War and the Climax of French Imperial Expansion* (London: Thames and Hudson, 1981).

'Anglo-Soviet political conversations at Moscow, October 9-October 17 1944', record of meetings on 9 and 17 October, copy in Ismay papers (King's College, London University), VI/10.

Armistice and Post-War Committee minutes, 17 May 1945, CAB 87/69.

Armistice and Post-War Committee minutes, 20 July 1944, CAB 87/66.

Armistice and Post-War Committee minutes, 23 August 1944, CAB 87/66.

Armistice and Post-War Committee minutes, 23 November 1944, CAB 87/66.

Armistice and Post-War Committee minutes, 27 July 1944, CAB 87/66.

Armistice and Post-War Committee minutes, 31 August 1944, CAB 87/66.

Armistice and Post-War Committee, minutes 20 July 1944, CAB 87/66.

Aronsen, Lawrence and Martin Kitchen, *The Origins of the Cold War in Comparative Perspective* (Basingstoke: Macmillan, 1988).

Babin, Alexei, 'The USSR's liberation mission in the Far East', in The USSR Academy of Sciences, *The Liberating Mission of the Soviet Union in the Second World War* (Moscow: Nauka, 1985).

Balfour, Michael, 'Re-education in retrospect', in Nicholas Pronay and Keith Wilson (eds), *The Political Re-education of Germany and Her Allies after World War II* (London: Croom Helm, 1985).

Balfour, Michael and John Mair, *Four-Power Control in Germany and Austria, 1945–1946* (London: Oxford University Press, 1956).

Banac, Ivo (ed.), *The Diary of Georgi Dimitrov, 1933–1949* (New Haven: Yale University Press, 2003).

Barker, Elisabeth, *British Policy in South-East Europe in the Second World War* (London: Macmillan, 1976).

Barker, Elisabeth, *Churchill and Eden at War* (London: Macmillan, 1978).

Barnhart, Michael A., *Japan and the World since 1868* (London: Arnold, 1995).

Barrett, David P. and Larry N. Shyu (eds), *Chinese Collaboration with Japan, 1932–1945: The Limits of Accommodation* (Stanford: Stanford University Press, 2001)

Beasley, W. G., *Japanese Imperialism, 1894–1945* (Oxford: Clarendon, 1987).

Beasley, W. G., *The Rise of Modern Japan*, rev. edn (London: Phoenix, 2000).

Beaumont, Joan, *Comrades in Arms: British Aid to Russia, 1941–1945* (London: Davis-Poynter, 1980).

Beloff, Max, *Soviet Policy in the Far East, 1944–1951* (London: Oxford University Press, 1953).

Ben-Israel, Hedva, 'Cross purposes: British reactions to the German anti-Nazi opposition', *Journal of Contemporary History*, vol. 20, 1985.

Berezhkov, Valentin, *History in the Making: Memoirs of World War II Diplomacy* (Moscow: Progress Publishers, 1983).

Berghahn, V. R., *Militarism: The History of an International Debate, 1861–1979* (Leamington Spa: Berg, 1981).

Beria, Sergo, *Beria, My Father: Inside Stalin's Kremlin* (London: Duckworth, 2001).

Bethell, Nicholas, *Gomulka, His Poland and His Communism* (London: Longmans, 1969).

Bills, Scott L., *Empire and Cold War: The Roots of US–Third World Antagonism, 1945–47* (Basingstoke: Macmillan, 1990).

Bills, Scott L., *The Libyan Arena: The United States, Britain, and the Council of Foreign Ministers, 1945–1948* (Kent: Kent State University Press, 1995).

Black, Cyril E., 'The pattern of Russian objectives', in Ivo J. Lederer (ed.), *Russian Foreign Policy: Essays in Historical Perspective* (New Haven: Yale University Press, 1962).

Bloet, Brian W., *Geopolitics and Globalization in the Twentieth Century* (London: Reaktion Books, 2001).

Bohlen, Charles E., *Witness to History, 1929–1969* (New York: Norton, 1973.

Bolsover, G. H., 'Aspects of Russian foreign policy, 1815–1914', in Richard Pares and A. J. P. Taylor (eds), *Essays Presented to Sir Lewis Namier* (London: Macmillan, 1956).

Boog, Horst et al., *Germany and the Second World War: Vol. VI, The Global War* (Oxford: Clarendon, 2001).

Bosworth, R. J. B., *Italy and the Wider World, 1860–1960* (London: Routledge, 1996).

Bower, Tom, *The Times*, 16 March 1985.

Brands, H. W., *Inside the Cold War: Loy Henderson and the Rise of the American Empire, 1918–1961* (New York: Oxford University Press, 1991).

Braunthal, Julius, *History of the International: Volume 2, 1914–1943* (London: Nelson, 1967).

Breitman, Richard, *Official Secrets: What the Nazis Planned, What the British and Americans Knew* (London: Penguin Books, 2000).

Breslow, Marvin Arthur, *A Mirror of England: English Puritan Views of Foreign Nations, 1618–1640* (Cambridge, MA: Harvard University Press, 1970).

Brewer, John, *The Sinews of Power: War, Money and the English State, 1688–1783* (London: Unwin Hyman, 1989).

Bridge, F. R. and Roger Bullen, *The Great Powers and the European States System, 1815–1914* (London: Longman, 1980).

Brockman, Roman, *The Secret File of Joseph Stalin: A Hidden Life* (London: Cass, 2001).

Brooks, Barbara J., *Japan's Imperial Diplomacy: Consuls, Treaty ports, and War in China, 1895–1938* (Honolulu: University of Hawai'i Press, 2000).

Buchanan, Sir George, *My Mission to Russia and Other Diplomatic Memories* (London: Cassell, 1923), vol. I.

Bullard, Julian and Margaret Bullard (eds), *Inside Stalin's Russia: The Diaries of Reader Bullard, 1930–1934* (Charlbury: Day Books, 2000).

Bullitt, Orville H. (ed.), *For the President: Personal and Secret* (London: Deutsch, 1973).

Burk, Kathleen, 'American foreign economic policy and Lend-Lease', in Ann Lane and Howard Temperley (eds), *The Rise and Fall of the Grand Alliance, 1941–45* (Basingstoke: Macmillan, 1995).

Burleigh, Michael, *Germany Turns Eastwards: A Study of Ostforschung in the Third Reich* (London: Pan, 2002).

Burridge, T. D., *British Labour and Hitler's War* (London: Deutsch, 1976).

Burrin, Philippe, *Hitler and the Jews: The Genesis of the Holocaust* (London: Arnold, 1994).

Butler, Rohan D'O., *The Roots of National Socialism, 1783–1933* (London: Faber, 1941).

Cable, James, *The Geneva Conference of 1954 on Indochina* (Basingstoke: Macmillan, 1986).

Carlton, David, *Anthony Eden; A Biography* (London: Allen Lane, 1981).

Caroe, Olaf, *Wells of Power: The Oilfields of South-Western Asia* (London: Macmillan, 1951).

Casey, Steven, *Cautious Crusade: Franklin D. Roosevelt, American Public Opinion, and the War against Nazi Germany* (Oxford: Oxford University Press, 2001).

Chamberlin, William Henry, *Japan over Asia* (London: Duckworth, 1938).

Child, Clifton J., 'The concept of the New Order' in Arnold and Veronica Toynbee (eds), *Hitler's Europe* (London: Oxford University Press, 1954).

Churchill, Winston S., *The Second World War Volume Three: The Grand Alliance* (London: Reprint Society edn, 1952).

Clarke, John, *British Diplomacy and Foreign Policy, 1782–1865: The National Interest* (London: Unwin Hyman, 1989).

Clemens, Diane Shaver, *Yalta* (London: Oxford University Press, 1970).

Cole, Margaret I. (ed.), *Beatrice Webb's Diaries, 1912–1924* (London: Longmans, 1952).

Cole, Tim, *Images of the Holocaust: The Myth of the 'Shoah' Business* (London: Duckworth, 1999).

Colville, John, *The Fringes of Power: Downing Street Diaries, 1939–1955* (London: Hodder, 1985).

Commentary by Grigg on the Non-Fraternisation Order, March 1945, Grigg papers, 9/9/20.

Committee on Post-War Settlement, 11 August 1943, FO 371/34461 no. 12172.

Corson, W. R. and R. T. Crawley, *The New KGB: Engine of Soviet Power* (Brighton: Harvester, 1986).

Corvaja, Santi, *Hitler and Mussolini: The Secret Meetings* (New York: Enigma Books, 2001).

Coutouvidis, John and Jaime Reynolds, *Poland, 1939–1947* (Leicester: Leicester University Press, 1986).

Cowman, Ian, *Dominion or Decline: Anglo-American Naval Relations on the Pacific, 1937–1941* (Oxford: Berg, 1996).

Cull, Nicholas J., 'Selling peace: the origins, promotion and fate of the Anglo-American new order during the Second World War', *Diplomacy and Statecraft*, vol. 7, 1996.

Cumings, Bruce, *Korea's Place in the Sun: A Modern History* (New York: Norton, 1997).

Dallek, Robert, 'Roosevelt and De Gaulle', in Robert O. Paxton and Nicholas Wahl (eds), *De Gaulle and the United States: A Centennial Reappraisal* (Oxford: Berg, 1994).

Dallek, Robert, *Franklin D. Roosevelt and American Foreign Policy, 1932–1945* (New York: Oxford University Press, 1979).

Dallin, Alexander, 'Stalin and the prospects for post-war Europe', in Francesca Gori and Silvio Pons (eds), *The Soviet Union and Europe in the Cold War, 1943–53* (Basingstoke: Macmillan, 1996).

Dallin, Alexander, 'The future of Poland', in Alexander Dallin et al., *Russian Diplomacy and Eastern Europe, 1914–1917* (New York: King's Crown Press, 1963).

Dallin, Alexander, *German Rule in Russia, 1941–1945: A Study in Occupation Policies*, 2nd edn (Basingstoke: Macmillan, 1981).

Dallin, David J., *The Big Three: The United States, Britain, Russia* (New Haven: Yale University Press, 1945).

Dau, Mary, 'The Soviet Union and the liberation of Denmark', *Survey: A Journal of Soviet and East European Studies*, no. 76, summer 1970.

Davenport, E. H. and S. R. Cooke, *The Oil Trusts and Anglo-American Relations* (London: Macmillan, 1923).

de Grand'Combe, Felix, *The Three Years of Fighting France, June 1940–June 1943* (London: Wells Gardner, Darton, 1943).

de Zayas, Alfred M., *Nemesis at Potsdam: The Anglo-Americans and the Expulsion of the Germans* (London: Routledge, 1977).

Deborin, Grigory, *Thirty Years of Victory* (Moscow: Progress Publishers, 1975).

Dehio, Ludwig, *Germany and World Politics in the Twentieth Century* (London: Chatto, 1959).

DePorte, A. W., *De Gaulle's Foreign Policy, 1944–1946* (Cambridge, MA: Harvard University Press, 1968).

Diamond, William, *The Economic Thought of Woodrow Wilson* (Baltimore: Johns Hopkins Press, 1943).

Dickinson, Frederick R., *War and National Reinvention: Japan in the Great War, 1914–1919* (Cambridge, MA: Harvard University Press, 1999).

Dilks, David (ed.), *The Diaries of Sir Alexander Cadogan O.M., 1938–1945*, (London: Cassell, 1971).

Divine, Robert A., *Second Chance: The Triumph of Internationalism in America during World War II* (New York: Atheneum, 1967).

Djilas, Milovan, *Conversations with Stalin* (Harmondsworth: Penguin, 1962).

Dommen, Arthur J., *Conflict in Laos: The Politics of Neutralization* (New York: Praeger, 1971).

Doran, Susan, *England and Europe, 1485–1603* (Harlow: Longman, 1986).

Douglas, Roy, *From War to Cold War, 1942–1948* (Basingstoke: Macmillan, 1981).

Dunn, Frederick S., *Peace-Making and the Settlement with Japan* (Princeton: Princeton University Press, 1963).

Duus, Peter, 'Imperialism without colonies: the vision of a Greater East Asia Co-Prosperity Sphere', *Diplomacy and Statecraft*, vol. 7, March 1996.

Earl of Avon, *The Eden Memoirs: The Reckoning* (London: Cassell, 1965).

Eden, Anthony, *Freedom and Order: Selected Speeches, 1939–1946* (London: Faber, 1947).

Eden, Anthony, *The Memoirs of Sir Anthony Eden: Full Circle* (London: Cassell, 1960).

Ekstein-Frankl, Michael G., 'The Development of British War Aims, August 1914–March 1915' (unpublished University of London Ph.D. thesis, 1969).

Elleman, Bruce A., *Diplomacy and Deception: The Secret History of Sino-Soviet Diplomatic Relations, 1917–1927* (London: M. E. Sharpe, 1997).

Ellwood, David W., *Italy, 1943–1945* (Leicester: Leicester University Press, 1985).

Epstein, Klaus, 'Gerhard Ritter and the First World War', in *Journal of Contemporary History*, vol. 1, no. 3, 1966.

Erickson, John, 'Stalin, Soviet strategy and the grand alliance', in Ann Lane and Howard Temperley (eds), *The Rise and Fall of the Grand Alliance, 1941–45* (Basingstoke: Macmillan, 1995).

Erickson, John, *The Road to Berlin* (London: Weidenfeld, 1983).

Feis, Herbert, *Between War and Peace: The Potsdam Conference* (Princeton: Princeton University Press, 1960).

Feis, Herbert, *Churchill, Roosevelt, Stalin: The War They Waged and the Peace They Sought* (Princeton: Princeton University Press, 1957).

Filitov, Aleksei M., 'Problems of post-war construction in Soviet foreign policy conceptions during World War II', in Francesca Gori and Silvio Pons (eds), *The Soviet Union and Europe in the Cold War, 1945–53* (Basingstoke: Macmillan, 1996).

Firsov, Fridrikh, 'Stalin and the Comintern', *New Times*, no. 18, 2–8 May 1989.

Fischer, Fritz, *Germany's Aims in the First World War* (London: Chatto, 1967).

Fischer-Galati, Stephen, 'The communist takeover of Rumania: a function of Soviet power', in Thomas T. Hammond (ed.), *The Anatomy of Communist Takeovers* (New Haven: Yale University Press, 1975).

Folly, Martin H., *Churchill, Whitehall and the Soviet Union, 1940–45* (Basingstoke: Macmillan, 2000).

Foreign Office memorandum, 27 December 1944, CAB 87/68 no. 127.

Foreign Office memorandum, November 1944, CAB 87/68 no. 118.

Foreign Relations of the United States. *The Conference of Berlin, 1945*, Vol. I (Washington: The State Department, 1960).

Fox, William T. R., *The Super-Powers* (New York: Harcourt, Brace, 1944).

Franks, Sir Oliver, *Central Planning and Control in War and Peace* (London: Longman, 1947).

Fraser, T. G., 'Roosevelt and the making of America's east Asian policy, 1941–45', in T. G. Fraser and Peter Lowe (eds), *Conflict and Amity in East Asia* (Basingstoke: Macmillan, 1992).

Gafencu, Grigore, *Prelude to the Russian Campaign* (London: Muller, 1945).

Galitsky, 'Vladimir, Uncovering previously unknown statistics', *New Times*, no. 24, 12–18 June 1990.

Gardner, Lloyd C. 'How we lost⌀ Vietnam, 1940–1954', in David Ryan and Victor Pungong (eds), *The United States and Decolonization* (Basingstoke: Macmillan, 2000).

Gardner, Lloyd C., 'The Atlantic Charter: idea and reality', in Douglas Brinkley and David R. Facey-Crowther (eds), *The Atlantic Charter* (Basingstoke: Macmillan, 1994).

Gardner, Lloyd C., *Spheres of Influence: The Partition of Europe, from Munich to Yalta* (London: Murray, 1993).

Gardner, Richard N., *Sterling-Dollar Diplomacy: Anglo-American Collaboration in the Reconstruction of Multilateral Trade* (Oxford: Clarendon, 1956).

Gatzke, Hans W., *Germany's Drive to the West: A Study of Germany's Western War Aims during the First World War* (Baltimore: Johns Hopkins Press, 1950).

Gelber, Lionel M., *The Rise of Anglo-American Friendship: A Study in World Politics 1898–1906* (London: Oxford University Press, 1938).

Gelfand, Lawrence E., *The Inquiry: American Preparations for Peace, 1917–1919* (New Haven: Yale University Press, 1963).

Gilbert, Martin, *Finest Hour: Winston S. Churchill, 1939–1941* (London: Heinemann, 1983).

Gilbert, Martin, *Road to Victory: Winston S. Churchill, 1941–1945* (London: Heinemann, 1986).

Gillies, Donald, *Radical Diplomat: The Life of Archibald Clark Kerr, Lord Inverchapel, 1882–1951* (London: Tauris, 1999).

Gladwyn, Hubert, *The Memoirs of Lord Gladwyn* (London: Weidenfeld, 1972).

Glees, Anthony, *Exile Politics during the Second World War: The German Social Democrats in Britain* (Oxford: Clarendon, 1982).

Goda, Norman J. W., *Tomorrow the World: Hitler, Northwest Africa, and the Path toward America* (College Station: Texas A. & M. University Press, 1998).

Goldman, Aaron, 'Germans and Nazis: the controversy over Vansittartism⌀ in Britain during the Second World War', *Journal of Contemporary History*, vol. 14, 1979.

Goldstein, Erik and John Mauer (eds), *Diplomacy and Statecraft* (special edition), vol. 4, no. 3, 1993.

Gooch, John, *Armies in Europe* (London: Routledge, 1980).

Goodman, Elliott R., *The Soviet Design for a World State* (New York: Columbia University Press, 1960).

Gordon, Leonard, 'American planning for Taiwan, 1942–1945', *Pacific Historical Review*, vol. XXXVI, 1968.

Gori, Francesca and Silvio Pons (eds), *The Soviet Union and Europe in the Cold War, 1943–53* (Basingstoke: Macmillan, 1996).

Gorodetsky, Gabriel, *Grand Delusion: Stalin and the German Invasion of Russia* (New Haven: Yale University Press, 1999).

Grenville, J. A. S., *The Major International Treaties, 1914–1973: A History and Guide with Texts* (London: Methuen, 1974).

Grigg to his father, 9 September 1943 and 30 July 1944, and Grigg to Field Marshal Montgomery, 25 July and 6 December 1944, Grigg papers (Churchill College, Cambridge), 9/6 and 8.

Hanneman, Mary L., *Japan Faces the World, 1925–1952* (Harlow: Longman, 2001).

Harbutt, Fraser J., *The Iron Curtain: Churchill, America, and the Origins of the Cold War* (New York: Oxford University Press, 1986).

Harriman, W. Averell and Elie Abel, *Special Envoy to Churchill and Stalin, 1941–1946* (New York: Random House, 1975).

Harris, Kenneth, *Attlee* (London: Weidenfeld, 1982).

Harvey, John (ed.), *The War Diaries of Oliver Harvey, 1941–1945* (London: Collins, 1978).

Haslam, Jonathan, 'Soviet war-aims', in Ann Lane and Howard Temperley (eds), *The Rise and Fall of the Grand Alliance* (Basingstoke: Macmillan, 1995).

Helmreich, J. E., 'Belgian concern over neutrality and British intentions, 1906–1914', in *Journal of Modern History*, vol. 36, 1964.

Herring, George C., Jr, *Aid to Russia, 1941–1946: Strategy, Diplomacy and the Origins of the Cold War* (New York: Columbia University Press, 1973).

Herzstein, Robert Edwin, *When Nazi Dreams Come True: The Third Reich's Internal Struggle over the Future of Europe after a German Victory* (London: Abacus, 1982).

Hinsley, F. H., *Power and the Pursuit of Peace: Theory and Practice in the Relations between States* (Cambridge: Cambridge University Press, 1963).

Hirszowicz, Lukasz, *The Third Reich and the Arab East* (London: Routledge, 1966).

Holtsmark, Sven G., 'The limits to Soviet influence: Soviet diplomats and the pursuit of strategic interests in Norway and Denmark, 1944–7', in Francesca Gori and Silvio Pons (eds), *The Soviet Union and Europe in the Cold War, 1945–53* (Basingstoke: Macmillan, 1996).

Hull, Cordell, *The Memoirs of Cordell Hull: Volume Two* (London: Hodder, 1948).

Iklé, Frank W., 'Japanese-German peace negotiations during World War I', in *American Historical Review*, vol. LXXI, 1965.

Irving, David, *Goebbels: Mastermind of the Third Reich* (London: Focal Point, 1996).

Jeffreys-Jones, Rhodri, *Changing Differences: Women and the Shaping of American Foreign Policy, 1917–1994* (New Brunswick: Rutgers University Press, 1995).

Jones, J. R., *Britain and Europe in the Seventeenth Century* (London: Arnold, 1966).

Kacewicz, George V., *Great Britain, the Soviet Union and the Polish Government in Exile (1939–1945)* (The Hague: Martinus Nijhoff, 1979).

Kajima, Morinosuke, *The Emergence of Japan as a World Power, 1895–1925* (Rutland: Tuttle, 1968).

Karski, Jan, *The Great Powers and Poland, 1919–1945: From Versailles to Yalta* (Lanham: University Press of America, 1985).

Keay, John, *Last Post: The End of empire in the Far East* (London; Murray, 1997).

Keiger, J. F. V., *France and the World since 1870* (London: Arnold, 2001).

Keiger, John F. V., *France and the Origins of the First World War* (Basingstoke: Macmillan, 1983).

Kennan, George F., *Memoirs, 1925–1950* (London: Hutchinson, 1968).

Kennan, George F., *The Fateful Alliance: France, Russia, and the Coming of the First World War* (Manchester: Manchester University Press, 1984).

Kennedy-Pipe, Caroline, *Stalin's Cold War: Soviet Strategies in Europe, 1943 to 1956* (Manchester: Manchester University Press, 1995).

Kenney, Rowland, *The Northern Tangle: Scandinavia and the Post-War World* (London: Dent, 1946).

Kernek, Sterling J., *Distractions of Peace during War: The Lloyd George Government's Reactions to Woodrow Wilson, Dec. 1916–Nov. 1918* (Philadelphia Transactions of the American Philosophical Society), new series, vol. 65, pt 2, 1975.

Kersaudy, Franois, *Churchill and De Gaulle* (London: Collins, 1981).

Kimball, Warren F., 'The two-sided octagon: Roosevelt and Churchill at Quebec, September 1944', in David B. Woolner (ed.), *The Second Quebec Conference Revisited* (Basingstoke: Macmillan, 1998).

Kimball, Warren F., *Forged in War: Churchill, Roosevelt and the Second World War* (London: HarperCollins, 1997).

Kimball, Warren F., *The Juggler: Franklin Roosevelt as Wartime Statesman* (Princeton: Princeton University Press, 1991).

King, Frank, 'Allied negotiations and the dismemberment of Germany', in Walter Laqueur (ed.), *The Second World War* (London: Sage, 1982).

Kissinger, Henry A., *A World Restored: The Politics of Conservatism in a Revolutionary Age* (New York: Grosset, 1964).

Kissinger, Henry, *Diplomacy* (New York: Simon and Schuster, 1994).

Kitaoka, Shinichi, 'Diplomacy and the Military in Showa Japan', in Carol Gluck and Stephen R. Gaubard (eds), *Showa: The Japan of Hirohito* (New York: Norton, 1992).

Kitchen, Martin, *British Policy towards the Soviet Union during the Second World War* (Basingstoke: Macmillan, 1986).

Kiyoshi, Ikeda, 'The road to Singapore: Japan's view of Britain, 1922–41', in T. G. Fraser and Peter Lowe (eds), *Conflict and Amity in East Asia* (Basingstoke: Macmillan, 1992).

Knox, MacGregor, 'The fascist regime, its foreign policy and its wars: an anti-fascist☒ orthodoxy?', in Patrick Finney (ed.), *The Origins of the Second World War* (London: Arnold, 1997).

Knox, MacGregor, *Common Destiny: Dictatorship, Foreign Policy, and War in Fascist Italy and Nazi Germany* (Cambridge: Cambridge University Press, 2000).

Knox, MacGregor, *Mussolini Unleashed, 1939–1941: Politics and Strategy in Fascist Italy's Last War* (Cambridge: Cambridge University Press, 1982).

Knox, MacGregor, reviewing one of De Felice's volumes, in *Times Literary Supplement*, 26 February 1999.

Kolarz, Walter, *Myths and Realities in Eastern Europe* (London: Lindsay Drummond, 1946).

Kolko, Gabriel, *The Politics of War: The World and United States Foreign Policy, 1943–1945* (New York: Vintage, 1968).

Koszyk, Kurt, 'The press in the British zone of Germany', in Nicholas Pronay and Keith Wilson (eds), *The Political Re-education of Germany and Her Allies after World War II* (London: Croom Helm, 1985).

Kot, Stanislaw, *Conversations with the Kremlin and Dispatches from Russia* (London: Oxford University Press, 1963).

Kulikov, Marshal V., 'Internationalist assistance to peoples of Europe', in USSR Academy of Sciences, *The Liberating Mission of the Soviet Union in the Second World War* (Moscow: Nauka, 1985).

Kuniholm, Bruce Robellet, *The Origins of the Cold War in the Near East* (Princeton: Princeton University Press, 1980).

Kusin, Vladimir V., 'Czechoslovakia', in Martin McCauley (ed.), *Communist Power in Europe, 1944–1949* (London: Macmillan, 1977).

LaFeber, Walter, *The Clash: A History of US–Japan Relations* (New York: Norton, 1997).

Lamb, Richard, *Mussolini and the British* (London: Murray, 1997).

Lamb, Richard, *The Ghosts of Peace, 1935–1945* (Salisbury: Michael Russell, 1987).

Langford, Paul, *Modern British Foreign Policy: The Eighteenth Century, 1688–1815* (London: Black, 1976).

Laqueur, Walter, *Russia and Germany: A Century of Conflict* (London: Weidenfeld, 1965).

Larionov, V. et al., *World War II: Decisive Battles of the Soviet Army* (Moscow: Progress Publishers, 1984).

Laughland, John, *The Tainted Source: The Undemocratic Origins of the European Idea* (London: Warner, 1998).

Lebra, Joyce C. (ed.), *Japan's Greater East Asia Co-Prosperity Sphere in World War II: Selected Readings and Documents* (Kuala Lumpur: Oxford University Press, 1975).

LeDonne, John P., *The Russian Empire and the World, 1700–1917* (New York: Oxford University Press, 1997).

Ledovsky, Andrei, *The USSR, the USA and the People's Revolution in China* (Moscow: Progress Publishers, 1982).

Leffler, Melvyn P., 'The American conception of national security and the beginnings of the Cold War, 1945–48', *The American Historical Review*, vol. 89, 1984.

Leonhard, Wolfgang, *Child of the Revolution* (London: Ink Links, 1979).

Levering, Ralph B. et al., *Debating the Origins of the Cold War: American and Russian Perspectives* (Lanham: Rowman and Littlefield, 2002).

Lieven, Dominic, *Empire: The Russian Empire and Its Rivals* (London: Murray, 2000).

Link, Arthur S., *Wilson: Campaigns for Progressivism and Peace, 1916–17* (Princeton: Princeton University Press, 1965).

Loth, Wilfried, 'Stalin's plans for post-war Germany', in Francesca Gori and Silvio Pons (eds), *The Soviet Union and Europe in the Cold War, 1945–53* (Basingstoke: Macmillan, 1996).

Louis, William Roger, *Great Britain and Germany's Lost Colonies, 1914–1919* (Oxford: Clarendon, 1967).

Louis, William Roger, *The British Empire in the Middle East, 1945–1951: Arab Nationalism, The United States and Postwar Imperialism* (Oxford: Clarendon, 1984).

Louis, Wm Roger, *Imperialism at Bay: The United States and the Decolonization of the British Empire, 1941–1945* (Oxford: Clarendon, 1977).

Lyons, Graham (ed.), *The Russian Version of the Second World War: The History of the War as Taught to Soviet Schoolchildren* (London: Leo Cooper, 1976).

Macartney, Maxwell H. H. and Paul Cremona, *Italy's Foreign and Colonial Policy, 1914–1937* (London: Oxford University Press, 1938).

Maisky, Ivan, *Memoirs of a Soviet Ambassador: The War 1939–43* (London: Hutchinson, 1967).

Malone, Gifford D., 'War aims towards Germany', in Alexander Dallin et al., *Russian Diplomacy and Eastern Europe, 1914–1917* (New York: King's Crown Press, 1963).

Mangold, Peter, *From Tirpitz to Gorbachev: Power Politics in the Twentieth Century* (Basingstoke: Macmillan, 1998).

Martin, Bernd, 'The German–Japanese alliance in the Second World War', in Saki Dockrill (ed.), *From Pearl Harbor to Hiroshima: The Second World War in Asia and the Pacific, 1941–45* (Basingstoke: Macmillan, 1994)

Martin, Lawrence W., *Peace without Victory: Woodrow Wilson and the British Liberals* (New Haven: Yale University Press, 1958).

Mastny, Vojtech, 'Soviet war aims at the Moscow and Teheran Conferences of 1943', in *Journal of Modern History*, vol. 47, 1975.

Mastny, Vojtech, 'Stalin and the prospects of a separate peace in World War II', *American Historical Review*, vol. 77, 1972.

Mastny, Vojtech, *Russia's Road to the Cold War: Diplomacy, Warfare, and the Politics of Communism, 1941–1945* (New York: Columbia University Press, 1979).

Matsusaka, Yoshika Tak, *The Making of Japanese Manchuria, 1904–1932* (Cambridge, MA: Harvard University Press, 2001).

Matthews, Peter, *European Balance* (London: Chatto and Windus, 1945).

May, Ernest R., *The World War and American Isolation, 1914–1917* (Cambridge, MA: Harvard University Press, 1959).

Mayer, Arno J., *Political Origins of the New Diplomacy, 1917–1918* (New Haven: Yale University Press, 1959).

Mayers, David, *The Ambassadors and America's Soviet Policy* (New York: Oxford University Press, 1995).

Mayers, David, *Wars and Peace: The Future Americans Envisioned, 1861–1991* (Basingstoke: Macmillan, 1998).

Mazower, Mark, 'Hitler's New Order, 1939–45', *Diplomacy and Statecraft*, vol. 7, no. 1, 1996.

McCagg, William O., Jr, *Stalin Embattled, 1943–1948* (Detroit: Wayne State University Press, 1978).

McClain, James L., *Japan: A Modern History* (New York: Norton, 2002).

McDermott, Kevin and Jeremy Agnew, *The Comintern: A History of International Communism from Lenin to Stalin* (Basingstoke: Macmillan, 1996).

McElligott, Anthony, 'Reforging Mitteleuropa in the crucible of war', in Peter Stirk (ed.), *Mitteleuropa: History and Prospects* (Edinburgh: Edinburgh University Press, 1994).

Medvedev, Zhores A. and Roy A. Medvedev, *The Unknown Stalin* (London: Tauris, 2003).

Memoranda by Attlee and Eden, 11 and 19 July 1944, CAB 87/67 nos. 43 and 47.

Memorandum by Chiefs of Staff, 12 December 1943, CAB 87/83 no. 20.

Memorandum by Law, 14 April 1944, CAB 87/84 no. 23.

Memorandum by Orme Sargent, 5 February 1942, in Graham Ross (ed.), *The Foreign Office and the Kremlin: British Documents on Anglo-Soviet Relations, 1941–45* (Cambridge: Cambridge University Press, 1984), document 687.

Memorandum by Sargent, 'Stocktaking after VE Day', FO 371/50912 no. 5471.

Memorandum for committee by Eden, 19 March 1945, CAB 87/69 no. 40.
Memorandum from German Department of Foreign Office, 15 July 1944, FO 371/39116 no. 9330.
Mikolajczyk, Stanislaw, The Pattern of Soviet Domination (London: Sampson Low, Marston, 1948).
Ministerial committee on Armistice Terms and Civil Administration, minutes 3 April 1944, CAB 87/84
Minute by Con O'Neill, November 1944, FO 371/26559 no. 16074.
Minute by Harrison, 9 December 1944, FO 371/39226 no. 16074.
Minute by Jebb, 1 May 1943, FO 371/34458 no. 4611.
Minute by Roberts, 1 December 1942, FO 371/31519 no. 1464.
Minute by Roberts, 20 September 1944, FO 371/39116 no. 12405.
Minute by Roberts, 28 July 1944, FO 371/39079 no. 9626.
Minute by Roberts, 6 August 1941, FO 371/26559 no. 7108.
Minute by Strang, October 1939, National Archives (London), FO 371/23058 no. 17104.
Minute by Troutbeck, February 1944, FO 371/39091 no. 2261.
Minutes of Armistice and Post-War Committee, 21 September 1944, CAB 87/66.
Minutes of Committee, 11 August 1943, FO 371/34461 no. 12405.
Minutes of Armistice and Post-War Committee, 4 January 1945, CAB 87/69.
Mlechin, Leonid, 'Vlasov and Vlasovites', New Times, 44, 30 October–5 November 1990.
Mommsen, Wolfgang J., 'The debate on German war aims', in Journal of Contemporary History, vol. 1, no. 3, 1966.
Monroe, Elizabeth, The Mediterranean in Politics (Oxford: Oxford University Press, 1938).
Montefiore, Simon Sebag, Stalin: The Court of the Red Tsar (London: Weidenfeld, 2003).
Morgan, Kenneth O., Labour in Power, 1945–1951 (Oxford: Clarendon, 1984).
Moseley, Ray, Mussolin's Shadow: The Double Life of Count Galeazzo Ciano (New Haven: Yale University Press, 1999).
Mosse, W. E., The Rise and Fall of the Crimean System, 1855–71 (London: Macmillan, 1963).
Mulligan, Timothy Patrick, The Politics of Illusion and Empire: German Occupation Policy in the Soviet Union, 1942–1943 (New York: Praeger, 1988).
Myant, M. R., Socialism and Democracy in Czechoslovakia, 1945–1948 (Cambridge: Cambridge University Press, 1981).
Naimark, Norman M., The Russians in Germany: A History of the Soviet Zone of Occupation, 1945–1949 (Cambridge, MA: Harvard University Press, 1995).
Nation, R. Craig, Black Earth, Red Star: A History of Soviet Security Policy, 1917–1991 (Ithaca: Cornell University Press, 1992).
National Heritage Board: National Archives of Singapore, The Japanese Occupation, 1942–1945 (Singapore, 1996).
Neilson, Keith, Britain and the Last Tsar: British Policy and Russia, 1894–1917 (Oxford: Clarendon, 1995).
Nevakivi, Jukka, 'The Soviet Union and Finland after the war, 1944–53', in Francesca Gori and Silvio Pons (eds), The Soviet Union and Europe in the Cold War, 1945–53 (Basingstoke: Macmillan, 1996).
Ninkovich, Frank, The United States and Imperialism (Oxford: Blackwell, 2001).
Nish, Ian, Japanese Foreign Policy in the Interwar Period (Westport: Praeger, 2002).
Novak, Bogdan C., Trieste, 1941–1954: The Ethnic, Political, and Ideological Struggle (Chicago: Chicago University Press, 1970).
Oman, Sir Charles, A History of the Art of War in the Sixteenth Century (London: Methuen, 1937).
Oman, Sir Charles, Things I Have Seen (London: Methuen, 1933).
Orders, Paul, 'Adjusting to a new period in world history⊠: Franklin Roosevelt and European colonialism', in David Ryan and Victor Pungong (eds), The United States and Decolonization (Basingstoke: Macmillan, 2000).
Oren, Nissan, Revolution Administered: Agrarianism and Communism in Bulgaria (Baltimore: Johns Hopkins University Press, 1973).
Ovendale, Ritchie, Britain, the United States and the End of the Palestine Mandate, 1942–1948 (Woodbridge: Royal Historical Society/The Boydell Press, 1989).
Overy, Richard, Interrogations: The Nazi Elite in Allied Hands, 1945 (London: Allen Lane/Penguin, 2001)
Owen, Richard, summarising a book by Fabio Andriola on Mussolini: Hitler's Secret Enemy, Daily Telegraph, 29 August 1997.
Padfield, Peter, Himmler: Reichsführer SS (London: Cassell reprint, 2001).
Pauwels, Jacques R., The Myth of the Good War: America in the Second World War (Toronto: Lorimer, 2002).
Peattie, Mark R., 'Nanshin⊠: the Southward advance⊠, in 1931–1941, as a prelude to the Japanese occupation of southeast Asia', in Peter Duus, Ramon H. Myers and Mark R. Peattie (eds), The Japanese Wartime Empire, 1931–1945 (Princeton: Princeton University Press, 1996).
Pechatnov, Vladimir O., in Ralph B. Levering et al., Debating the Origins of the Cold War: American and Russian Perspectives (Lanham: Rowman and Littlefield, 2002).
'Pentad', The Remaking of Italy (Harmondsworth: Penguin, 1941).
Perlmutter, Amos, FDR & Stalin: A Not So Grand Alliance, 1943–1945 (Columbia: University of Missouri Press, 1993).
Peterson, Sir Maurice, Both Sides of the Curtain (London: Constable, 1950).
Pollard, Robert A., Economic Security and the Origins of the Cold War, 1945–1950 (New York: Columbia University Press, 1985).

Polonsky, Antony and Boleslaw Drukier, *The Beginnings of Communist Rule in Poland, December 1943-June 1945* (London: Routledge, 1980).

Polvinen, Tuomo, *Between East and West: Finland in International Politics, 1944–1947* (Minneapolis: University of Minnesota Press, 1986).

Preti, Luigi, 'Fascist imperialism and racism', in Roland Sarti (ed.), *The Ax Within: Italian Fascism in Action* (New York: New Viewpoints, 1974).

Price, Willard, *Japan's Islands of Mystery* (London: The British Publishers' Guild, 1944).

Pronay, Nicholas and Keith Wilson (eds), *The Political Re-education of Germany and Her Allies after World War II* (London: Croom Helm, 1985).

Raack, R. C., *Stalin's Drive to the West, 1938–1945: The Origins of the Cold War* (Stanford: Stanford University Press, 1995).

Reitlinger, Gerald, *The House Built on Sand: The Conflicts of German Policy in Russia, 1939–45* (London: Weidenfeld, 1960).

Renouvin, Pierre, 'Le gouvernement français et les tentatives de paix en 1917', in *La Revue des Deux Mondes*, 15 October 1964.

Renouvin, Pierre, 'Les buts de guerre du gouvernement français 1914–1918', in *Revue Historique*, Tome CCXXV, January–March 1966.

Report by Joint-Intelligence Sub-Committee, September 1944, CAB 87/68 no. 80.

Research Institute for Military History (various contributors), *Germany and the Second World War: Volume I, The Build-up of German Aggression* (Oxford: Clarendon, 1990).

Resis, Albert (ed.), *Molotov Remembers: Inside Kremlin Politics: Conversations with Felix Chuev* (Chicago: Dee, 1993).

Reynolds, David, *The Creation of the Anglo-American Alliance, 1937–1941: A Study in Competitive Co-operation* (London: Europa Publications, 1981).

Reynolds, David, *From Munich to Pearl Harbor: Roosevelt's America and the Origins of the Second World War* (Chicago: Dee, 2001).

Rhodes, Anthony, *The Vatican in the Age of the Dictators, 1922–1945* (London: Hodder, 1973).

Rice, Condoleezza, 'The evolution of Soviet grand strategy', in Paul Kennedy (ed.), *Grand Strategies in War and Peace* (New Haven: Yale University Press, 1991).

Rich, Norman, *Hitler's War Aims: The Establishment of the New Order* (London: Deutsch, 1974).

Riste, Olav, 'Free ports in north Norway: a contribution to the study of FDR's wartime policy towards the USSR', *Journal of Contemporary History*, vol. 5, no. 4, 1970.

Robertson, Esmonde M., *Mussolini as Empire-Builder: Europe and Africa, 1932–36* (London: Macmillan, 1977).

Rothwell, V. H., 'The British government and Japanese assistance 1914–18', *History*, vol. 56, February 1971.

Rothwell, V. H., *British War Aims and Peace Diplomacy, 1914–1918* (Oxford: Clarendon, 1971).

Rothwell, Victor, 'British policy on the South Slav question during World War I', in *Yugoslav–British Relations: papers delivered at Kragujevac, 23–25 September 1987* (Belgrade: ISI, 1988).

Rothwell, Victor, *Britain and the Cold War, 1941–1947* (London: Cape, 1982).

Rothwell, Victor, *The Origins of the Second World War* (Manchester: Manchester University Press, 2001).

Rozanov, Herman, *Behind the Scenes of Third Reich Diplomacy* (Moscow: Progress Publishers, 1984).

'Russia and Japan sign accord to seek end to dispute over islands', *New York Times*, 11 January 2003.

Rzheshevsky, Oleg A., *War and Diplomacy: The Making of the Grand Alliance, Documents from Stalin's Archives* (Amsterdam: Harwood Academic, 1996).

Rzheshevsky, Oleg, *World War II: Myths and the Realities* (Moscow: Progress Publishers, 1984).

Sainsbury, Keith, 'British policy and German unity at the end of the Second World War', *English Historical Review*, vol. 94, 1979.

Sainsbury, Keith, *Churchill and Roosevelt at War* (Basingstoke: Macmillan, 1994).

Sainsbury, Keith, *The Turning Point* (Oxford: Oxford University Press, 1985).

Sallager, Frederick M., *The Road to Total War* (New York: Van Nostrand Reinhold, 1969).

Santis, Hugh De, *The Diplomacy of Silence* (Chicago: University of Chicago Press, 1980).

Schechtman, Joseph B., *The United States and the Jewish State Movement, The Crucial Decade: 1939–1949* (New York: The Herzl Press/Thomas Yoseloff, 1966).

Schwendemann, Heinrich, 'Drastic measures to defend the Reich at the Oder and the Rhine ...': a forgotten memorandum of Albert Speer of 18 March 1945', *Journal of Contemporary History*, vol. 38, 2003.

Sharp, Tony, *The Wartime Alliance and the Zonal Division of Germany* (Oxford: Clarendon, 1975).

Sheng, Michael M., *Battling Western Imperialism: Mao, Stalin, and the United States* (Princeton: Princeton University Press, 1997).

Shennan, Andrew, *Rethinking France: Plans for Renewal, 1940–1946* (Oxford: Clarendon, 1989).

Sherwin, Martin J., *A World Destroyed: The Atomic Bomb and the Grand Alliance* (New York: Knopf, 1975).

Sherwood, Robert E., *The White House Papers of Harry L. Hopkins: Volume II, January 1942–July 1945* (London: Eyre, 1949)

Sivachev, Nikolai V. and Nikolai N. Yakovlev, *Russia and the United States: US – Soviet Relations from the Soviet Point of View* (Chicago: University of Chicago Press, 1979).

Skidelsky, Robert, *John Maynard Keynes: Fighting for Britain, 1937–1946* (Basingstoke: Macmillan, 2000).

Skorzeny, Otto, *Special Mission* (London: Futura, 1974).

Slusser, Robert M., 'Soviet policy and the division of Germany, 1941–1945', in Susan J. Linz (ed.), *The Impact of World War II on the Soviet Union* (Totowa: Rowman, 1985).

Smith, C. Jay, 'Great Britain and the 1914–15 Straits agreement with Russia and the British promise of November 1914', in *American Historical Review*, vol. LXX, 1965.

Smith, C. Jay, Jr, *The Russian Struggle for Power, 1914–17: A Study of Russian Foreign Policy during the First World War* (New York: Philosophical Library, 1956).

Smith, Denis Mack, *Italy and Its Monarchy* (New Haven: Yale University Press, 1989).

Smyser, W. R., *From Yalta to Berlin: The Cold War Struggle over Germany* (Basingstoke: Macmillan, 1999).

Soni, Sharad K., *Mongolia–Russia Relations: Kiakhta to Vladivostok* (Delhi: Shipra, 2002).

Sorge, Martin K., *The Other Price of Hitler's War: German Military and Civilian Losses from World War II* (Westport: Greenwood Press, 1986).

Soutou, Georges-Henri, 'General de Gaulle and the Soviet Union, 1943–5', in Francesca Gori and Silvio Pons (eds), *The Soviet Union and Europe in the Cold War, 1943–53* (Basingstoke: Macmillan, 1996).

Spriano, Paolo, *Stalin and The European Communists* (London: Verso, 1985).

Stern, Fritz, *The Failure of Illiberalism* (New York: Columbia University Press, 1992).

Stevenson, David, *French War Aims against Germany, 1914–1919* (Oxford: Clarendon, 1982).

Stirk, Peter M. R., 'The Idea of Mitteleuropa', in Stirk (ed.), *Mitteleuropa: History and Prospects* (Edinburgh: Edinburgh University Press, 1994).

Stoakes, Geoffrey, *Hitler and the Quest for World Dominion: Nazi Ideology and Foreign Policy in the 1920s* (Leamington Spa: Berg, 1986).

Stoler, Mark A., *The Politics of the Second Front: American Military Planning and Diplomacy in Coalition Warfare, 1941–1943* (Westport: Greenwood Press, 1977).

Storry, G. R., 'Rumours of a Japanese-German understanding on the eve of the armistice of 1918', in G. F. Hudson (ed.), *St Antony's Papers. Number 20: Far Eastern Affairs Number Four* (Oxford: Oxford University Press, 1967).

Storry, Richard, *The Double Patriots: A Study of Japanese Nationalism* (London: Chatto and Windus, 1957).

Strachan, Hew, *The First World War: Volume I, To Arms* (Oxford: Oxford University Press, 2001).

Strang, Lord, 'Prelude to Potsdam: reflections on war and foreign policy', *International Affairs*, vol. 46, 1970441–54.

Streit, Christian, 'The German Army and the policies of genocide', in Gerhard Hirschfeld (ed.), *The Policies of Genocide: Jews and Soviet Prisoners of War in Nazi Germany* (London: Allen and Unwin, 1986).

Strik-Strikfeldt, Wilfried, *Against Stalin and Hitler: Memoirs of the Russian Liberation Movement, 1941–1945* (London: Macmillan, 1970).

Strobl, Gerwin, *The Germanic Isle: Nazi Perceptions of Britain* (Cambridge; Cambridge University Press, 2000).

Stueck, William, *Rethinking the Korean War: A New Diplomatic and Strategic History* (Princeton: Princeton University Press, 2002).

Sudoplatov, Pavel and Anatoli Sudoplatov, *Special Tasks: The Memoirs of an Unwanted Witness – A Soviet Spymaster* (London: Warner, 1995).

Sullivan, Brian R., 'More than meets the eye: the Ethiopian War and the origins of the Second World War', in Gordon Martel (ed.), *The Origins of the Second World War Reconsidered*, 2nd edn (London: Routledge, 1999).

Swain, Geoffrey, 'Stalin's wartime vision of the postwar world', *Diplomacy and Statecraft*, vol. 7, no. 1, March 1996.

Tarling, Nicholas, *A Sudden Rampage: The Japanese Occupation of Southeast Asia, 1941–1945* (London: Hurst, 2001).

Tarling, Nicholas, *Britain, Southeast Asia and the Onset of the Cold War, 1945–1950* (Cambridge: Cambridge University Press, 1998).

Taubman, William, *Stalin's American Policy* (New York: Norton, 1982).

Taylor, A. J. P. (ed.), *W. P. Crozier: Off the Record: Political Interviews, 1933–1943* (London: Hutchinson, 1973).

Taylor, A. J. P., *The Troublemakers: Dissent over Foreign Policy, 1792–1939* (London: Hamish Hamilton, 1957).

Terry, Sarah Meiklejohn, *Poland's Place in Europe: General Sikorski and the Origin of the Oder–Neisse Line, 1939–1943* (Princeton: Princeton University Press, 1983).

Thomas, R. T., *Britain and Vichy: The Dilemma of Anglo-French Relations, 1940–42* (London: Macmillan, 1979).

Thompson, Robert Smith, *Empires on the Pacific: World War II and the Struggle for the Mastery of Asia* (Oxford: The Perseus Press, 2001).

Thorne, Christopher, *Allies of a Kind: The United States, Britain and the War against Japan, 1941–1945* (Oxford: Oxford University Press, 1978).

Thorne, Christopher, *The Far Eastern War: States and Societies, 1941–45* (London: Unwin Paperbacks, 1986).

Trukhanovsky, V., *British Foreign Policy during World War II, 1939–1945* (Moscow: Progress Publishers, 1970).

Ulam, Adam B., *Expansion and Coexistence: The History of Soviet Foreign Policy, 1917–67* (London: Secker, 1968).

Uldricks, Teddy J., *Diplomacy and Ideology: The Origins of Soviet Foreign Relations* (London: Sage, 1979).

Urban, G. R. (ed.), *Stalinism: Its Impact on Russia and the World* (London: Wildwood House, 1985).

Urban, Joan Barth, *Moscow and the Italian Communist Party: From Togliatti to Berlinguer* (London: Tauris, 1986).

Vago, Bela, 'Romania', in Martin McCauley (ed.), Communist Power in Europe, 1944–1949 (London: Macmillan, 1977).

Vagts, Alfred, A History of Militarism Civilian and Military (London: Hollis, 1959).

van der Pijl, Kees, The Making of an Atlantic Ruling Class (London: Verso, 1984).

Vehviläinen, Oppi, Finland in the Second World War: Between Germany and Russia (Basingstoke: Palgrave, 2002).

Villari, Luigi, Italian Foreign Policy under Mussolini (New York: Devin-Adair, 1956).

'Voinov', The Autobiography of a Soviet Waif (London: Harvill, 1955).

von Below, Nicolaus, At Hitler's Side: The Memoirs of Hitler's Luftwaffe Adjutant, 1937–1945 (London: Greenhill Books, 2001).

Wada, Haruki, 'The San Francisco peace treaty and the definition of the Kurile islands', in Gilbert Rozman (ed.), Japan and Russia: The Tortuous Path to Normalization, 1949–1999 (Basingstoke: Macmillan, 2000).

Wagner, Wolfgang, The Partitioning of Europe: A History of the Soviet Expansion up to the Cleavage of Germany, 1918–1945 (Stuttgart: Deutsche Verlags Anstalt, 1959).

Walker, William O., III, Opium and Foreign Policy: The Anglo-American Search for Order in Asia, 1912–1954 (Chapel Hill: University of North Carolina Press, 1991).

War Cabinet minutes, 5 October 1943, CAB 65/40.

Ward, Patricia Dawson, The Threat of Peace: James F. Byrnes and the Conference of Foreign Ministers, 1945–1946 (Kent: Kent State University Press, 1979).

Watt, D. Cameron, Succeeding John Bull: America in Britain's Place, 1900–1975 (Cambridge: Cambridge University Press, 1984).

Watt, Donald C., 'The European civil war', in Wolfgang J. Mommsen and Lothar Kettenacker (eds), The Fascist Challenge and the Policy of Appeasement (London: Allen and Unwin, 1983).

Webster, C. K., The Congress of Vienna, 1814–1815 (London: Bell, 1945).

Weeks, Albert L., Stalin's Other War: Soviet Grand Strategy, 1939–1941 (Lanham: Rowman, 2002).

Weinberg, Gerhard L., 'German plans for victory, 1944–1945', in his Germany, Hitler and World War II: Essays in Modern German and World History (Cambridge: Cambridge University Press, 1995)274–86.

Weiss, Steve, Allies in Conflict: Anglo-American Strategic Negotiations, 1938–44 (Basingstoke: Macmillan, 1996).

Weston, Rubin Francis, Racism in US Imperialism, 1893–1946 (Columbia: University of South Carolina Press, 1972).

Wheeler-Bennett, John W. and Anthony Nicholls, The Semblance of Peace: The Political Settlement after the Second World War (London: Macmillan, 1972).

Wilson, Theodore A., The First Summit: Roosevelt and Churchill at Placentia Bay, 1941 (London: Macdonald, 1970).

Winant, John G., A Letter from Grosvenor Square (London: Hodder, 1947).

Winkler, Henry R., The League of Nations Movement in Great Britain, 1914–1919 (New Brunswick: Rutgers University Press, 1952).

Winterbotham, F. W., Secret and Personal (London: Kimber, 1969).

Wiskemann, Elizabeth, The Rome-Berlin Axis (London: Collins/Fontana, 1966).

Wistrich, Robert S., Hitler and the Holocaust: How and Why the Holocaust Happened (London: Phoenix, 2001).

Woods, Randall Bennett, A Changing of the Guard: Anglo-American Relations, 1941–1946 (Chapel Hill: University of North Carolina Press, 1990).

Woodward, E. L., War and Peace in Europe 1815–1870 and Other Essays (London: Cass, 1963).

Woodward, Sir Llewellyn, 'Some reflections on British policy, 1939–45', International Affairs, vol. 31, 1955.

Woodward, Sir Llewellyn, British Foreign Policy in the Second World War, single vol. edn (London: Stationery Office, 1962).

Woodward, Sir Llewellyn, British Foreign Policy in the Second World War: Volume V (London: Stationery Office, 1976).

Woodward, Sir Llewellyn, British Foreign Policy in the Second World War: Volume II (London: Stationery Office, 1971).

Woolner, David B., 'Coming to grips with the German Problem□: Roosevelt, Churchill, and the Morgenthau Plan at the Second Quebec conference', in David B. Woolner (ed.), The Second Quebec Conference Revisited (Basingstoke: Macmillan, 1998).

Xiang, Lenxin, Recasting the Imperial Far East: Britain and America in China, 1945–1950 (London: M. E. Sharpe, 1995).

Yerusalimsky, Arkady, German Imperialism: Its Past and Present (Moscow: Progress Publishers, 1969).

Young, Louise, Japan's Total Empire: Manchuria and the Culture of Wartime Imperialism (Berkeley: University of California Press, 1998).

Zeman, Z. A. B., Pursued by a Bear: The Making of Eastern Europe (London: Chatto, 1989).

Zinoviev, Alexander, The Reality of Communism (London: Paladin Books, 1985).

Zubok, Vladislav and Constantine Pleshakov, Inside the Kremlin's Cold War: From Stalin to Khrushchev (Cambridge, MA: Harvard University Press, 1996).

Index